MONSIEUR X

MONSIEUR X

THE INCREDIBLE STORY OF THE MOST AUDACIOUS GAMBLER IN HISTORY

JAMIE REID

BLOOMSBURY

LONDON · OXFORD · NEW YORK · NEW DELHI · SYDNEY

BLOOMSBURY SPORT
Bloomsbury Publishing Plc
50 Bedford Square, London, WC1B 3DP, UK

BLOOMSBURY, BLOOMSBURY SPORT and the Diana logo are trademarks
of Bloomsbury Publishing Plc

First published in Great Britain 2018

A catalogue record for this book is available from the British Library.

Library of Congress Cataloguing-in-Publication data has been applied for.

ISBN: HB: 978-1-4729-4229-6
TPB: 978-1-4729-4228-9
eBook: 978-1-4729-4231-9

2 4 6 8 10 9 7 5 3 1

Typeset in Minion by Deanta Global Publishing Services, Chennai, India
Printed and bound in Great Britain by CPI Group (UK) Ltd, Croydon CR0 4YY

To find out more about our authors and books visit www.bloomsbury.com.
and sign up for our newsletters.

For VC and the stories yet to come.

'There are two kinds of gambler. The good and the bad. They have one thing in common. In the end . . . they all lose.'

– Patrice des Moutis

'When the French take revenge, it ravages the innocent along with the guilty. They do it principally through the murderous inefficiency with which they operate their pari-mutuel system of betting.'

– Hugh McIlvanney

Prologue

1974

It was cold in Paris in the Parc de Saint-Cloud at twilight on a winter's day. In summer the gardens of the former royal château on a hillside overlooking the Seine were a favourite setting for picnics, games and family outings. But by half-past four on a December afternoon the children's play area by the northwestern entrance was deserted. The smart mothers and nannies had all swept up their charges and set off back to their *haute bourgeois* homes in the suburbs. Other than a gardener making a bonfire of old leaves there were just a few solitary dog-walkers and a middle-aged man in an old rugby shirt and a pair of tracksuit bottoms.

The 54-year-old had been coming to the park for years, running miles along the manicured pathways and over the forested hillside that covered more than a thousand acres between Saint-Cloud and Garches. He was proud of his fitness and routine. It reassured him of his readiness for the battle and his ability to live 'like an English milord', smoking five Havana cigars a day yet retaining the energy of a much younger man. He wasn't about to stop now, he'd assured friends, despite all the rumours and the stories in the press. But on his own in the fading light, with the smell of bonfire smoke hanging on the frosty air, he found it harder to dispel the tension and the mounting fear of arrest or worse.

The man slowed down as he reached the crossroads by the ornamental fountain and the little café that was closed and boarded up now until the spring. After satisfying himself that he was alone and not being followed, he turned left down a gravelled path that led to a viewpoint beside some wooden benches and a green painted wicket fence. The city lay stretched out before him with the Bois de Boulogne and the Eiffel Tower in the foreground and Sacré-Cœur on the far horizon. This was his home. This was where he had grown up and been educated, married and had children. He knew its offices and boardrooms, its bedrooms and salons, cafés, restaurants and bars. He knew all the racetracks too and all the leading owners, trainers and jockeys.

He'd made the running in his time. He'd set the pace and maintained it for almost fifteen years. Taunting and outwitting a massive bureaucratic monolith and leaving it chasing his shadow. At the highpoint of his success they had called him the 'Prince of Gamblers' and a 'modern-day Robin Hood'. But he had ended up becoming the reluctant leading man in an increasingly dangerous *roman noir* from which there seemed to be no escape. And if the tip-offs he'd been given were correct, he was starting to believe that he might have run his race.

There had already been two deaths – one a jockey, the other a gangster in Marseille – and now the French champion jockey was in the Santé prison, with more arrests expected soon. People were asking, who was the mastermind? And when would he be unmasked? The story was all over that morning's papers, the sensational news of the police swoop on the 'Mafia du Tiercé' sharing top billing with reports of President Valéry Giscard d'Estaing's forthcoming trip to Guadeloupe and the Sûreté Nationale being on the lookout for Lord Lucan. When would they come for him? he wondered . . . and who would come first?

Down below he could see lights coming on in the houseboats on the Seine, and a barge heading downstream towards Sèvres. The noise of the rush-hour traffic drifted back up the hillside. Commuters hurrying home to the comfort and warmth of wives, husbands, lovers, family and friends. Good food, sex and untroubled sleep. Pleasures he could no longer count on.

He took one last, long lingering look at the city lights. Then he turned away and began to run back down the empty path towards the dark places beneath the trees.

Chapter 1

1950

It was the last weekend of August and Deauville was packed with well-to-do families and gambling high rollers in town for the climax of the summer season. The weather, as so often on the Normandy coast, was variable, but early each morning strings of superbly bred racehorses came down into the town from the racecourse stables to enjoy a canter by the water's edge. Later on, children cavorted happily on the sandy beach and ran screeching in and out of the waves indifferent to the temperature and the Channel breeze. Adults posed elegantly behind windbreaks or stayed lounging around the swimming pools at the Normandy and Royal hotels, interrupting hands of bridge and gin rummy for cocktails at the pool bar or a round of golf on the slopes of Mont Canisy.

As was the case every year at Deauville, people-watching was a major pastime. The composer Vincent Scotto, who had written the music for the films of Marcel Pagnol, caused a sensation by strolling up and down the wooden boardwalk, accompanied by a pet lion cub with whom he later shared a drink at an outdoor table at the Bar du Soleil.

Another to make a big impression was King Farouk of Egypt, who arrived in a red Bentley and was staying at the Hôtel du Golf. The moustachioed overweight monarch was a compulsive gambler who spent his afternoons at the races and his nights at the casino. On the evening of Saturday 26 August Farouk and his entourage turned up late for the Grand Prix de la Chanson in the casino ballroom. Other guests, all attired in evening dress, looked on in astonishment as the gluttonous potentate proceeded to devour an entire *gigot d'agneau* and a couple of lobsters which were served to him on a special table at the front of the room. The occasion culminated in a concert by Maurice Chevalier, but the King was more interested in cards than chansonneurs and left for the gaming tables halfway through.

Farouk and the exiled King Peter of Yugoslavia were two of the biggest players, and losers, at the casino. But out at the racecourse, La Touques, on Avenue Hocquart de Turtot, it was Prince Aly Khan, one of the richest and most successful racehorse owners in the world, who made the headlines. The Aly, who was the eldest son and heir of the 'old' Aga Khan, or Aga Khan III, was a debonair playboy as renowned for his gambling as he was for his pursuit of beautiful women. In Deauville that August he was accompanied by his second wife, the Hollywood actress Rita Hayworth, who he had married the previous year.

The Aly had bought Hayworth a few racehorses as a present and on Sunday 27 August one of them, a colt called Skylarking, won the Prix de Saint-Arnoult, while her filly Double Rose finished second in the Grand Prix de Deauville, the climactic race of the meeting. The sun refused to shine but a huge crowd still came out to the racecourse to watch. It was the usual mix of *comtes* and concierges, chancers and gigolos. The serious owner–breeders were there in their hats and suits with their well-worn binocular cases. Their wives and mistresses were there too, in black cat-eye sunglasses by Lanvin and Dior, and then there were the curious once-a-year racegoers tempted away from the beach by the prospect of celebrity. Double Rose did her best, leading the field for much of the race until she was unable to match Baron Guy de Rothschild's three-year-old colt Alizier in the home straight.

The Aly Khan and Rita Hayworth were waiting for Double Rose in the unsaddling enclosure in front of the old half-timbered Norman weighing room. The Aly, hatless but dapper in a lightweight jacket and cravat, was debriefed by the filly's trainer Alec Head while *La Belle* Rita, wearing one of her New Look cartwheel hats, stroked Double Rose's ears and patted her svelte and shimmering coat.

After the racing was over, Hayworth returned to her father-in-law's villa outside Trouville while the Aly Khan joined a small group of fellow *turfistes* in the Normandy hotel's ground-floor bar. The intimate, club-like room with its oak panelling and comfortable leather chairs was the ideal setting in which to enjoy a post-race *whisky sur les rocks* and a smoke and to conduct a review of the day's action and make a tally of who owed what to who.

Aly Khan may have been the only royalty present but the others were all members of *le monde* and the French moneyed upper class. There was the *Comte* de Kerouara, an aristocratic Breton racehorse owner and breeder who owned a half-share in the jewellers Van Cleef and Arpels. There was the textile tycoon Roger Saint, a prominent owner and gambler and a partner in Établissements Saint Frères, which was the biggest jute manufacturer in France. There was Saint's and the *comte's* trainer Georges Pelat, a rumbustious character originally from the southwest whose passions included rugby and bull-fighting and who ran horses both on the flat and over jumps. And then there was the man doing the accounting albeit discreetly and with a light touch.

Patrice Jean Henry des Moutis shared the same background and social circle as the rest of them. The 29-year-old had been born in Paris in 1921 and grew up in the smart surburb of Neuilly-sur-Seine. Patrice's father, Henry des Moutis, was a wealthy insurance broker with offices in the capital. But the family roots were partly in Normandy, where they owned a summer house near Sées in the valley of the Orne, and partly in Brittany. Earlier generations of the Des Moutis clan included imperial grandees, generals, diplomats and admirals of the fleet.

Patrice was one of six children – three boys and three girls – and the boys all attended the prestigious Paris day school, the Lycée Janson de Sailly on the Rue de la Pompe. But in 1939, as war with Germany looked increasingly inevitable, Patrice and his younger brother Gilbert were sent away to a boarding school, the Lycée Montesquieu, near Le Mans. It was not a happy experience. Patrice was extremely bright but he railed against the petty rules and close confinement of boarding-school life. A report in March 1940 warned that his work was 'superficial' and that a 'big effort' would be necessary if he was to improve.

Patrice's older brother François had been called up and was an officer serving with the 104th French infantry regiment when the Germans invaded in May. On 13 June 1940 François des Moutis died a hero's death in a rearguard action at Luzancy, a village in the department of Seine-et-Marne 63 kilometres north of Paris. He was 27 years old.

After the French surrender and the establishment of Marshal Pétain's puppet government, Patrice returned to Paris and in 1941 he was admitted to the École Centrale, which was one of the Grandes Écoles, or elite universities, that were at the summit of the nation's hierarchical education system. In peacetime or war, the Grandes Écoles were designed to groom high flyers to become the civil servants who would run the country, intellectuals who would pronounce on its spiritual wellbeing, or industrialists who would drive its economy.

The École Centrale was an engineering school founded in the nineteenth century and situated next to the Conservatoire des Arts et Métiers on the Rue Montgolfier. Along with Patrice's father, former students included Gustave Eiffel, André Michelin, Armand Peugeot and Louis Blériot, who was the first man to fly the Channel.

Patrice, who became Pat to his friends, studied mathematics and engineering, graduating with honours in the wartime class of 1943. It may have been the lowest point of the Occupation, with the French economy on its uppers but, then as now, a Grande École diploma was seen as a certain passport to future success. Other notable Grandes Écoles graduates that year were a future Prime Minister of France, Jacques Chaban-Delmas, a future Finance Minister, Félix Gaillard – who would also serve briefly as PM – and the future founder of *L'Express* magazine, Jean-Jacques Servan-Schreiber. All three of them would remember Patrice des Moutis.

After the Liberation Patrice worked as a risk assessor in his father's firm, taking over the reins of the business in 1948. By then he had proposed to Marie-Thérèse Queret, an attractive, self-possessed blonde debutante from the same Breton and Norman nobility as himself. Marie-Thérèse was assured that she had made the perfect marriage dreamed of by every girl of her class in that era. Patrice had money, brains and social cachet. He was six feet tall with dark brown hair, blue eyes, a firm jaw and an aquiline nose. He wore tailormade suits from Sulka on the Rue de Rivoli, white or blue Charvet shirts with a Charvet tie, and black, handmade brogues. He was an inveterate smoker who always had a Gauloise or Dunhill in his hand but he kept himself fit too: running, cycling, riding, skiing in winter and playing rugby and tennis. In private he was loving and tender. In company he could be funny and seductive and always seemed to be at the centre of every conversation, radiating energy and charm.

But all of these personal and financial skills only described one half of Patrice des Moutis. He was also a passionate devotee of horse racing, having first learned about it at his father's knee at the family house in Normandy, and he was a consummate gambler. Patrice didn't believe in luck or chance. He liked playing bridge, and was happy to spend a sociable evening at the tables, but generally he disdained casino games in favour of the horses. He based his wagering on his knowledge of people and form and on his mathematical grasp of odds and percentages. No matter how many respectable business meetings and working lunches he attended as an insurance broker in Paris, he was always yearning to get back to his first love: Longchamp in the spring; Auteuil and Chantilly in June – along with trips across the Channel to Epsom and Royal Ascot; Longchamp again in the autumn; and, before that, the sacrosanct summer pilgrimage to Deauville.

When the gentlemen in the Normandy Bar had settled their accounts that August Sunday evening in 1950 the meeting broke up. Not that anything as vulgar as money changed hands there and then. That would come later after *la rentrée* when everyone had returned to Paris at the end of the holidays. For now some of them agreed to reconvene that night for drinks and dinner, cards or baccarat in the casino. Patrice des Moutis was eager to get back to the villa he and Marie-Thérèse were sharing with her parents fifteen minutes outside town. He hurried down the Normandy's front steps and crossed the little square to where his car was parked in front of the restaurant Chez Miocque. But just as he was about to open the door three men got out of an adjacent black Citroën Traction Avant and blocked his path.

A quick glance told Des Moutis that the men were unlikely to be guests at the Normandy hotel. Their suits, hats and shoes looked too old and worn – evidence of the grinding austerity that, outside of the gilded world of horse racing, still held the French in its grip five years after the war had ended. One of the men held out a warrant card which proclaimed that he was *Commissaire* Roger Taupin of the French gambling police, the Police des Courses et Jeux.

'Can I help you?' Patrice asked politely. Taupin, who had a tight mouth and hair *en brosse*, replied that the police would like to ask him a few questions. Patrice asked if it could wait, explaining that his wife would be expecting him and he really should be going. But Taupin was insistent. They needed to talk now, he said, holding open the back door of the Traction Avant.

Patrice des Moutis was cornered. 'Very well,' he said. But he couldn't think how he could possibly be of assistance. Glancing over his shoulder to make sure that none of his racing friends were watching, he climbed reluctantly into the back seat of the Citroën.

Deauville's office of the Police Judiciaire was about a ten-minute drive away, in a half-timbered building in a side road not far from the roundabout that led up to the racetrack. Patrice was shown into a small bare interview room at the back. There was just one high window, which didn't look as if it was opened very often, and the air was close and smelled of stale cigarette smoke and sweat. Less than half an hour ago, Patrice reflected, he'd been in Deauville's best hotel drinking pre-war Scotch with the Aly Khan.

Commissaire Taupin sat down at a table. Patrice took the chair on the other side, while the other two men remained standing. Des Moutis lit up a Gauloise, sat back in his chair and crossed his legs. 'Now then,' he began. What was this all about?

'You know what it's about,' replied Taupin primly. Patrice said he hadn't the faintest idea. The *commissaire* said he wanted to know about the men Des Moutis had just been talking to in the Normandy hotel. 'Friends,' explained Patrice. 'Fellow racing lovers. Very distinguished men, some of them. Men who appreciate discretion.' As he was sure the *commissaire* and his colleagues would understand.

Taupin wasn't impressed. He dared Patrice to deny that his 'friends' were all high-stakes gamblers on the horses. 'I confess,' said Des Moutis with a smile. They were in Deauville, after all. Was betting on racing now a crime? 'Maybe not,' said Taupin. As long as their betting was conducted through the proper channels. 'Ah, yes,' said Patrice. 'The Pari-Mutuel.' 'Of course,' said Taupin. 'The PMU. The correct way.' Patrice des Moutis shrugged his shoulders and nodded. 'The French way,' he agreed.

'But you and your friends,' continued Taupin, leaning closer, 'I think you prefer another way?' Patrice admitted that some of the gentlemen in question might have bookmaking accounts in England which, as free citizens, was their right. 'What about the accounts they have with you?' asked Taupin. The *commissaire* had got up out of his chair now to come round and perch on the edge of the table, and his two colleagues moved in closer too. 'I beg your pardon,' said Patrice, looking confused. 'Don't treat us like fools, Monsieur,' said Taupin. 'We know all about you. You're one of the biggest bookmakers in France.'

Patrice laughed, made a face and threw up his hands as if the accusation was absurd. It was ridiculous, he said. The *commissaire* and his superiors had been misinformed. Whatever they'd been told, it was a complete fantasy, an invention. Of course gossip and rumour were widespread in racing, but he wouldn't have expected the police force to be taken in.

It was a good act. The lines had been well rehearsed and, to the untutored eye, it was a flawless performance. But it was a lie.

Patrice des Moutis wasn't just a punter. For the last few years the former Grande École student with the brilliant future had seen a way to make betting as much of a sure thing financially as insurance: by acting as a private bookmaker to racing swells like the Aly Khan, Roger Saint, the *Comte* de Kerouara, and his other companions in the Normandy Bar. This would have been considered louche enough for someone of Patrice's background in England, where it was at least within the law, but in France there was another problem altogether. Ever since its inception, the French had modelled their racing industry as closely as possible on the pattern long established across the Channel. With one exception: in France bookmaking was illegal.

Whereas the first official race meeting at Newmarket took place in 1671, and the first Derby was run at Epsom in 1779, there was no organised programme of horse racing in France until the early nineteenth century. It owed its birth to a group of Francophile Englishmen led by Lord Henry Seymour, who was the second son of the Marquis of Hertford and lived all his life in France. In company with assorted French aristocrats they formed the Jockey-Club de Paris, valuing (like their counterparts in Newmarket) breeding, wealth and good form – in the social sense as well as knowledge of the Turf – as the most important qualities in aspiring members.

A governing body called the Société d'Encouragement pour l'Amélioration des Races de Chevaux en France was set up and, in 1836, they presided over the first running of the Prix du Jockey Club, or French Derby, at Chantilly. More big races followed, and at the outset the training centres at Chantilly and Maisons-Laffitte resounded with English voices as trainers, jockeys and stable lads were lured across the Channel by the prospect of employment. They were accompanied by English bookmakers, alive to new business, who opened premises on the grand boulevards in Paris. The bookies, who soon had local rivals to contend with, set up brightly painted betting booths in caravans on race days at places like the Champ de Mars, the future site of the Eiffel Tower, and trade boomed.

But skulduggery was never far away in nineteenth-century racing, and most of it emanated from plots and conspiracies involving betting. French church and civic leaders held the bookmakers responsible – they were mostly Englishmen, after all – and accused them of having a vested interest in seeing that horses they had laid large amounts of money on didn't win.

To counter the criticisms, an enterprising Catalan *émigré* called Joseph Oller proposed an alternative pool-based system that he termed the Pari-Mutuel – *pari* being the French word for a bet or a wager.

Oller, who had run an English-style fixed-odds bookmaking business on horse racing and cock fighting in his native Spain, suggested replacing the bookies with an operator acting as a stakeholder with no individual interest in the outcome. The more bets there were on a race the larger the pool would be and, after the operator had taken out a percentage to cover their profit and expenses, winning punters would share the rest in proportion to their stakes. When the favourite won, the payout would be lower; but if a rank outsider won and relatively few punters had backed it, the payout could be huge.

Informed gamblers were unimpressed, pointing out that they couldn't be sure what odds they'd get paid out at when they placed a bet, and that the odds on a fancied horse might get shorter and shorter because there would be no competition from bookmakers willing to take it on. They also objected that the Pari-Mutuel operator's take might comfortably exceed a traditional bookie's profit margin or 'over-round'.

But while bookmakers continued to lay the odds on the racecourses in Britain – and were permitted to offer credit-account, though not cash, betting facilities off it – in France the authorities preferred Oller's system. Not that the inventor was able to profit from it for very long. The French racecourses, run by various *sociétés*, or local management committees, decided that betting rights at the tracks belonged to them, and in 1874 they had Oller committed to prison for fifteen days for 'illegal bookmaking'.

Oller suffered a further blow in 1887 when his partner, the Frenchman Albert Chauvin, set up a Pari-Mutuel business of his own, offering an improved system for calculating odds and paying dividends. That same year the National Assembly, going through one of its periodic spasms of moral rectitude, decided to impose a wholesale ban on racecourse gambling. But when attendances plummeted and the racetrack managements and their aristocratic patrons protested, parliament backed down, to Albert Chauvin's advantage. In 1891 the government outlawed all fixed-odds bookmaking and awarded Chauvin's company the monopoly right to run Pari-Mutuel pool betting in France.

With Chauvin having put him out of the bookmaking business, Joseph Oller devoted the rest of his life to becoming an impresario in partnership with the entrepreneur Charles Zidler. In 1889 they opened the Moulin Rouge in Pigalle, which soon became the most famous cabaret in the world, and four years later they opened the Olympia, the first Parisian music hall. Oller, who described the Moulin Rouge as 'a temple dedicated to women and dance', died in 1922 and was posthumously immortalised by the great screen actor Jean Gabin in Jean Renoir's 1955 film *French Cancan*.

At the time of his death Oller was a wealthy man, but his estate was still only a fraction of the fortune that it could have been had his one-time partner not effectively hijacked the concept of pari-mutuel betting. From the late nineteenth to the early twentieth century Chauvin's family devoted themselves to turning their Compagnie du Pari-Mutuel into one of the biggest and most cash-rich businesses in France, one from which the government's tax collectors would profit handsomely. In 1930 the company was reborn as the PMU, or Pari-Mutuel Urbain, after the legislators gave them the right to organise betting off-course in approved outlets in towns and cities, as well as on the course. By then the day-to-day running of Oller's and Chauvin's creation had passed into the hands of a dedicated administrator and civil servant who was as indifferent to the attractions of racing and gambling as a man like Patrice des Moutis was enamoured of them.

In the years to come the name of André Carrus would frequently be mentioned in the same breath as that of Des Moutis. But if one was a Robin Hood figure intent on taking on the system, the other was the sheriff and state's bookmaker determined to bring him down.

Chapter 2

By the time Patrice finally left Deauville police station the beach was deserted but the cafés were buzzing and the restaurants filling up with hungry Sunday evening diners. Driving back along the coast towards Villers-sur-Mer, the sun slipping low over the horizon, Des Moutis felt pretty sure that the police had no concrete evidence with which to charge him. Neither did he believe that any of his clients would have willingly incriminated him and, by implication, themselves in illegal betting. He suspected it was more of a warning shot ordered from higher up the chain of command.

Patrice always maintained that he was not a bookmaker in the British sense of the word; more a commission agent taking and placing bets for friends. The principal illegal bookmaker in France after World War II was François Spirito, a Marseille gangster and former business partner of the Corsican Godfather Paul Carbone, who was killed in a train crash in 1943. Spirito took over Carbone's book and related rackets in Paris and on the Côte d'Azur but, like many underworld figures, he had been a wartime collaborator with the French Gestapo, and well-to-do racehorse owners like the Aly Khan felt uncomfortable betting with him. The charming Des Moutis offered them an alternative, whether fielding their wagers himself or placing them, at the best available odds, with legitimate bookmakers in London. It was understood that Patrice charged a basic fee for these transactions as well as a commission when the horses won.

Des Moutis could see no reason why the French authorities needed to bother with his activities, which he regarded as little different to being a risk assessor, but unfortunately *Commissaire* Taupin thought otherwise. It had certainly been a tedious few hours in police custody going round and round the same accusations and denials like the children's carousel on the quayside in Trouville. Time and again Patrice suggested to his interrogators that they surely must have something better to do with their evening than to spend it with him. But then France was the only country in Europe to have its own specialist police unit dedicated to patrolling the worlds of horse racing and gambling. Des Moutis had met detectives from police headquarters at 36 Quai des Orfèvres in Paris, and most of them were traditional cops or *flics*: cynical, hard-bitten characters who enjoyed a drink and a chat and had no problem with betting. When they approached him on the street or at his office in Neuilly it usually meant they wanted money, and as long as a few favours arrived every now and then – be it in the shape of cash, tips or a good night out – they were happy to ignore what they regarded as a harmless social misdemeanour.

But the Police des Courses et Jeux were different. A branch of the Sûreté Nationale but reporting directly to the Ministry of the Interior, they weren't clubbable and they seemed to have been recruited specifically because of their resistance to temptation. Regular punters regarded them as joyless prigs, while some gambling racehorse owners looked down on them as social inferiors lacking the intelligence and connections to catch them out. Des Moutis wasn't about to fall for such snobbish delusions but neither was he inclined to curtail his activities on the basis of one uncomfortable interview.

It's not clear if Marie-Thérèse was fully aware in 1950 of the range and scale of her husband's gambling. She was a strong character who didn't welcome the disruption of established social patterns like family meal times and gatherings. But she understood that horse racing was Patrice's principal pleasure and seemingly just accepted his betting as a recreational pastime he liked to share with his friends. For his part, Patrice was unlikely to have disabused her and wouldn't have wanted her to know about the maximum seven-year sentence for illegal bookmaking that Taupin had told him was about to be introduced.

By the first week of September the French summer holidays were over and Patrice, Marie-Thérèse and all the other wealthy Parisian families had packed up and left the beaches and returned to the worlds of home, work, school and city life.

On the national stage the outlook was bleak. The fledgeling Fourth Republic, which had been inaugurated in 1946 after months of wrangling, had given birth to a whole series of weak and indecisive governments – there would be twenty-one of them before its abolition in 1958 – while an entrenched bureaucracy, attempting to preserve the status quo, inflicted stagnation and protectionism on the economy. In 1947 there had been a crippling five-month strike involving more than three million workers protesting at spiralling inflation and their own flat-lining wages. They shut down factories, mines and power stations. They stopped the buses. The rubbish went uncollected, the mail undelivered and newspapers ceased production. 'The life of the nation is paralysed by strife,' warned *Le Monde*.

Strikes were still commonplace three years later while the nation's coffers were being drained by ever more expensive colonial wars. Independence movements were flourishing in Algeria, Morocco and Tunisia, and in Indo-China more than a hundred thousand French troops were now deployed in Cambodia and Vietnam in a doomed attempt to defend the crumbling empire of Emperor Bao Dai against the insurgent Communist Viet Minh.

Displaying their customary mixture of rage and contempt towards their elected representatives, the public turned to frivolous pleasures for distraction. There was much excitement that American cigarettes were on sale officially again in Paris for the first time since the war. Alarmed commentators warned of the dangers of American cultural imperialism – or 'Coca-Colonisation' as it was dubbed – but their warnings had little effect on young smokers enjoying a Chesterfield or Camel in a jazz bar in Saint-Germain.

There was titillation of a more traditional kind in May 1951 when the Crazy Horse Saloon opened in a cellar on Avenue George V. The nightclub's setting was a kitsch Wild West saloon but the clientele were upmarket, many of the men in black tie, and one of the most popular attractions was a brunette dancer called Miss Candida who slowly undressed, bathed and then dressed again while the audience looked on. Miss Candida's wardrobe had been purchased from Christian Dior, whose New Look, first launched in 1947, had caused a fashion sensation. The designer spoke evocatively of bringing back 'the ripe bosom, wasp waist and soft shoulders' and moulding them to 'the natural curves of the feminine body'. The Communist newspaper *L'Humanité* raged about capitalists and their squandering of resources while 'poor children go hungry'. But Dior's customers were thrilled with what he described as 'a nostalgic voyage back to elegance' and, bankrolled by the textile manufacturer and racehorse owner Marcel Boussac, the designer branched out into lingerie, scarves and sunglasses.

Moral guardians, be they Communist or Catholic, didn't only object to *couture* dressmaking and Lucky Strikes. They didn't think much of racing and gambling either but the crowds continued to make their way out to Longchamp and Auteuil at weekends, and Des Moutis was usually there in the vicinity of the weighing room discussing form and odds with his friends.

There were regular 'faces' at French racetracks just as there were in Britain, and Patrice had a network of informants. Professional gamblers like the earthy Parisien Jules 'Julie' Carrax, who'd spent a lifetime backing horses, and good friends like the young publisher Alain Ayache, who was born in Algiers in 1936 and became a Des Moutis acolyte at an early age. Ayache was a compulsive punter but he was always positive and cheerful and as dismissive of the Pari-Mutuel bureaucracy as his hero. From time to time they encountered *Commissaire* Roger Taupin and his cohorts from the Police des Courses et Jeux and were careful to greet them politely, even ensuring they saw Patrice strolling up to the PMU windows to place a legal bet. But away from the public gaze Des Moutis continued to take instructions from his regular clients, including the Aly Khan, Roger Saint and the trainers Georges Pelat and Geoff Watson, an Anglo-Frenchman who was a heavy gambler.

It was a time when French horses were enjoying conspicuous success at prestigious meetings like Royal Ascot and in the big-betting events that were a recurring feature of the English flat-racing season. Patrice knew that he could always lay off bets he'd taken on English races with his bookmaking contacts in London like William Hill – who was known as 'the King of the Ring' – and the wily East Ender Max Parker, who would go on to buy Ladbrokes.

Some French owners had separate accounts with Parker and 'Bill' Hill. But the bookmakers' rough manners and inability to speak the language didn't endear them to Patrice's more discerning female clients like the Austro-Hungarian countess, Etti Plesch, and Suzy Volterra, who had been a dancer at the Folies Bergère until marrying the owner Leon Volterra just before his death in 1948. Madame Suzy inherited her late husband's horses as well as his money and enjoyed many successes in both England and France over the next thirty years. Vivacious and elegant, she was nicknamed *La Sourire de Longchamp*, or the 'Longchamp Smile', and her admirers included both Des Moutis and his good English friend, the legendary racing journalist and broadcaster Peter O'Sullevan.

In France this was the era of *cinq à sept*, when sexually sophisticated men and women were accustomed to enjoy a late-afternoon rendezvous before returning to the bosom of their family. There were days when Patrice would bring good news and cash winnings to the houses and apartments of smart racing women like Suzy Volterra; and there were maybe days when their appreciation for his tips and services went beyond just a kiss and a glass of wine, Patrice explaining the precise balance of their account as the grateful hostesses led him coolly to their bedrooms, kicking off a shoe, discarding an earring and slipping out of a Dior dress along the way.

But what went on so enjoyably between consenting adults behind closed doors in the 16th *arrondissement* couldn't hide the fact that illegal bookmaking was siphoning off money from the PMU, French racing and the French state. For more than two and a half years since their Deauville encounter, Des Moutis had joked with friends, including leading racehorse owners and trainers, that his relationship with the Police des Courses et Jeux was like a game of cat and mouse. In the spring of 1953 the Société d'Encouragement, torn between the gambling preferences of many of its members and pressure from the government, finally decided to support the cat.

Chapter 3

The beginning of the new season at Longchamp always took place on Easter Monday and was eagerly anticipated each year. In April 1953 a correspondent for the popular daily newspaper *L'Aurore* – which was part-owned by Marcel Boussac – described the excitement of greeting familiar faces once again at the races as 'one of the ten great sporting pleasures'. But unfortunately for Des Moutis, the Société d'Encouragement deemed that his face should be excluded not only from Longchamp's 1953 opening but from all French racecourses until further notice.

The first thing Patrice knew about it was when he arrived at the racecourse gates on the morning of 3 April. The weather in Paris had been wet and windy with temperatures more akin to winter than spring. But the prospect of reacquainting himself with the leading owners and trainers as well as with gambling jockeys like the Australian Rae Johnstone – who also marked Peter O'Sullevan's card – was too good to resist. A few choice thoroughbreds would be making their seasonal debuts and Patrice wanted to get the inside track on how riders like Johnstone thought their mounts were shaping up.

As Des Moutis approached a turnstile to show his owner's and member's badges that usually guaranteed him free entry, a sombre racecourse official appeared by his side. The official said he regretted it, of course. It was most unfortunate. But what could he do? 'Regret what?' asked Patrice. The official shrugged and pointed to where *Commissaire* Roger Taupin was advancing towards them in the company of two uniformed gendarmes in kepis and capes. For an awful moment Des Moutis thought he was about to be arrested but instead Taupin, wearing his sternly belted trenchcoat and a thin victor's smile, handed him a letter from the Police des Courses et Jeux headquarters in Clichy.

'Read it,' said Taupin. Patrice said he'd read it later. Taupin insisted that he read it now. When Patrice opened the envelope he saw that the letter was from the Minister of the Interior, Charles Brune, and had been countersigned by the Société d'Encouragement. A single typed page explained that due to his failure to respond to previous warnings about illegal bookmaking, the Société had 'agreed' with the recommendation of the Minister and the Police des Courses et Jeux that Monsieur des Moutis should be barred from all racecourses throughout France. With immediate effect.

With high-profile owners – and clients – arriving at the racetrack at that very moment Patrice knew that it was neither the time nor the place to make a scene. So, ignoring Taupin but nodding at the lugubrious official who looked enormously relieved that there'd be no further embarrassment, he turned on his heel and walked away.

In the days and weeks that followed, Patrice and his lawyers had numerous telephone conversations and confidential meetings with Société members and other influential racing figures. Just like the official at Longchamp, they said they regretted it, but what could they do? An odour of moral opprobrium was in the air once again. The short lived administration of the Radical Prime Minister René Mayer – who took office on 8 January 1953 but would be gone by 28 June – was under pressure from conservative rivals and was being urged to crack down on delinquency at home to boost its standing.

The brothels had been closed in 1946, driving women onto the streets, but prostitution had since moved into the so-called *hôtels de passe* which rented rooms by the hour, and the big-city police forces were suspected of taking a cut from the businesses.

Then there was the Norman aristocrat, the Marquis de Balleroy, who had been arrested for buying opium from a private detective called Louis Metra, a former head of the vice squad in Paris where he was known as 'Loulou *Le Beau Chasseur*' (the handsome hunter). If *les flics* were involved in illegal drug dealing and prostitution, moralists argued, they were probably mixed up in illegal gambling too. It was time for Mayer's government to make a stand and, while barring Des Moutis from entering Longchamp or any other racecourse was hardly confining him to the Bastille, it was seen as a blow for propriety and the rule of law.

Patrice was sad to be excluded from the unique atmosphere and camaraderie of the racetrack, and he was angry at being disqualified from ever riding again in amateur races in which he had sometimes competed against the Aly Khan. It was also going to be harder to offer odds on horses he hadn't been able to assess with his own eyes. When he wanted to watch the great Italian racehorse Ribot running in the 1955 Prix de l'Arc de

Triomphe he had to invest in a new television set, though racing coverage on TV in France in the early 1950s was in its infancy and nowhere near as extensive as in the UK.

But what really angered Des Moutis was his designation as some sort of criminal or moral outcast when he regarded the PMU monopoly itself as an outrage. What was not generally known about Patrice at the time was that in 1951 he'd gone to Morocco for nine months to run a Pari-Mutuel betting service in Casablanca. The colony had its own racing calendar, offering a mix of thoroughbred and pure-bred Arabian racing in a dusty imitation of the programme in mainland France. Both the French and Arab populations also enjoyed betting on events at Longchamp, Auteuil and Saint-Cloud.

The Moroccan PMU concession was permitted to set its own rates in response to local demand. In an attempt to boost turnover, Patrice cut the total take out from the pool from 15.5 per cent, the rate then in operation in France, to 14 per cent. It was not an altruistic move. Des Moutis calculated that – with minimal radio and television coverage – it was difficult for Moroccan punters to pick the winners of races taking place nearly 1,500 miles away in Paris. And so it proved. But the more generous odds and better terms Patrice was offering compared to his predecessors resulted in a boom in business and he was soon able to open twenty new PMU bureaux in Casablanca as well as outlets in Rabat, Meknes and Fez.

Des Moutis was flying back and forth to Paris several times a month and, while he was away on one of these breaks with Marie Thérèse, he was informed that one Casablanca PMU office was suddenly reporting a sharp increase in winning bets on French races. The phenomenon continued for several weeks and puzzled Patrice until he realised that one of the local PMU *fonctionnaires* was 'past posting', or fraudulently betting on races after the results had been declared.

The culprit was an elderly French aristocrat with a large house in Casablanca run by Moroccan servant boys who he was reputed to beat with a cane. One afternoon in March 1951 Patrice caught him placing a 20,000-franc bet on a race at Saint-Cloud, adding his ticket to 864 legitimate winning tickets ten minutes after the race had been run. Patrice told him that the matter need go no further but that there was no longer a job for him in the Casablanca office or any other PMU office in Morocco. The old colonialist reacted indignantly, telling Patrice that, as a fellow white man, he should have looked the other way as others had done before him. If the story got out, he said, his name would be disgraced and he'd have to join the French Foreign Legion. Patrice never saw him again but the experience contributed to his disillusion with the system. Within six months he was back in Paris, convinced that the PMU was a corrupt and inefficient service that in a properly free society ought to have to compete for custom with independent bookies.

Even though he couldn't actually go racing any more, Patrice's ban didn't stop him from continuing to take bets from his wealthy clients in the 16th *arrondissement*. He had to be extra careful, as he had no desire to go to prison, but *Commissaire* Taupin couldn't stop him flying over to England to go racing at Ascot and Sandown Park while hedging his liabilities with his London bookmaking friends.

Neither did the ban dissuade his well-heeled male and female punters from continuing to welcome him into their homes. Patrice and Marie Thérèse were both members of *le Gratin*, that self-selecting French upper crust of aristocrats, politicians and certain businessmen, actors, authors and artists. They shared the same kind of marriages, affairs, children, houses, clothes and codes of behaviour. The women met regularly at fashion shows, soirées and openings. The men went hunting together, shooting wild boar in the forests of Rambouillet and Versailles and duck in the Sologne. It was a world of pruned hedgerows and brushed gravel, old leather and English sports cars. It was lunch at the Polo Club de Paris in the Bois de Boulogne and husbands returning home from an assignation clutching beautifully wrapped and packaged pastries from Ladurée and bottles of Madame Rochas. It was skiing at Val-d'Isère in January and going to the beach in July and August and then returning to the clean Swiss prosperity of Neuilly, Saint-Cloud and the Hauts-de-Seine. Discretion was a byword in this company and Patrice's illegal bookmaking an enjoyable secret to be gossiped over and no more shocking than reports of a friend's latest affair.

The impenetrable confidence and *savoir-vivre* of *le Gratin* was being severely tested in the France of the mid-1950s. In January 1954 the Viet Minh launched a new assault on the perimeter of Dien Bien Phu, the French military stronghold deep in the highlands of northwest Vietnam. Four months later, at daybreak on 7 May, and after six months of fierce fighting, the French garrison – many of them Legionnaires and members of the Foreign Colonial Parachute regiments, the cream of the regular army – was overrun. It was a crushing defeat that spelled the end of French influence in Indo-China and was perceived to be as much of a national humiliation as the rapid defeat by the Germans in June 1940.

Then in November 1954 the Front de Libération Nationale, or FLN, began carrying out acts of terrorism in Algeria, and by spring the following year the whole of the country was caught up in a savage civil war. The Muslim forces of resistance were ranged against the French settlers or *pieds noirs* (so called because of the black shoes they supposedly wore when first moving to Algeria from Italy, Corsica and the south of France) who feared the loss of their lives, homes and businesses.

In 1956 another weak Prime Minister, Guy Mollet, sent the acclaimed World War II veteran General Jacques Massu to Algiers with the 10th Parachute Division. What followed was a bloody struggle for control of the city in which the FLN planted *plastique* (plastic explosive) bombs indiscriminately in civilian cafés, buildings and squares, and the French paratroopers responded with systematic acts of torture.

Meanwhile in mainland France a shopkeeper from the southwest called Pierre Poujade started a mini peasants' revolt nicknamed 'Poujadism' and directed at the supposed perfidy and haughtiness of Paris political life in general and tax collectors in particular. But there was one revenue-raising measure that escaped the Poujadists' wrath, and that was the subtle redistribution of wealth – from small-change, working-class punters to rich racehorse owners and the Finance Ministry's coffers – practised by the Pari-Mutuel.

Chapter 4

Unsurprisingly in the closed world of French public life, the future rivals Patrice des Moutis and the PMU director general André Carrus were both graduates of the Grandes Écoles. The director general's Alma Mater was the École Polytechnique, which was another of the great French educational institutes. A school of science and engineering like the École Centrale, it used to be situated in a similarly grand nineteenth-century building not far from the Pantheon in the Latin Quarter. And just as Patrice had achieved high marks as a 'Centralien' in 1943, his future adversary was an equally distinguished 'Polytechnicien' albeit from an earlier era.

André Raoul Abraham Carrus, who was born in Algiers in 1898, was the son of a college faculty head and grandson of a rabbi. He graduated from the École Polytechnique in 1918 in time to see action with the French army before the end of World War I. Returning to peacetime life, he was appointed Chief Engineer of Public Works in the city of Paris. It was a slightly Pooterish description for an eagerly sought-after position as a well-paid civil servant or *fonctionnaire* who, in France in the twentieth century, could expect to be in the job for life.

The chief's new duties included supervising and maintaining the railway bridges and clearing leaves from the lines leading out of the Gare du Nord, repairing the metal grilles around the city's trees and attending to the upkeep of the paving stones. It was the sort of honest, diligent if boring work that could have led in time to an opening in politics and local government. But in 1922 everything changed for André Carrus when he married his long-time fiancée, Madeleine Chauvin.

Madeleine's father thought highly of the Polytechnique graduate and, when Albert Chauvin died in 1927, his son-in-law was persuaded to change jobs and take the helm of the PMU Chauvin which was renamed PMU Carrus. Then when the government relaxed its restrictions on off-course betting in 1930, the company combined with the various racecourse associations to form the Pari-Mutuel Urbain, with Monsieur Carrus as director general.

It was André Carrus who presided over the opening of new PMU bureaux and betting facilities in bistros and *café-tabacs* nationwide, and the move was a huge success. In 1931 the French gambled some 240 million *ancien* francs on horse racing but by 1938, with the opportunity to enjoy a bet along with a glass of wine and some convivial company in a local café, that sum had risen to over a billion. As business grew, new and improved machines that were able to process bets faster and increase turnover were installed both in the cafés and on the racecourses.

The French government was delighted. The PMU operated under the umbrella of the state and Carrus reported to the ministers of Agriculture and Finance, who were in turn answerable to the Prime Minister's office in the Hôtel

Matignon. Between them the various government departments were taking 12 per cent out of the pool in tax. The princes, tycoons and blue-blooded nabobs of the Turf were delighted, as another 8 per cent of the PMU's revenues went to subsidise prize money and improve facilities at French racetracks. The PMU senior management were delighted too because they were able to award themselves a profit of 6 per cent on top of their expenses, even after the other deductions had been accounted for.

The French racecourses closed when World War II broke out in September 1939 but they reopened a year later, little more than three months after the capitulation to the Germans. Victorious Wehrmacht and Luftwaffe officers liked nothing better than an afternoon at Longchamp or Auteuil in the company of their mistresses and awarded themselves free entry and the best seats in the house. Off-course wagering was banned by the German Military Governor but the PMU continued to run a racecourse betting service and, despite his Jewish heritage, André Carrus remained in charge.

Not all Jewish French racing figures were so lucky. The Nazis had been quick to loot the stallions and horses in training belonging to the Rothschild family, including their principal sire Brantôme, who stood at their family-owned Haras de Meautry in Normandy. They stole the textile tycoon Marcel Boussac's top stallion Pharis too, although Boussac, who was the biggest racehorse owner in France, was not Jewish and enjoyed a close relationship – some would say disgracefully so – with the Vichy regime's Minister of Commerce, a plump-faced Polytechnicien called Jean Bichelone. As a result of Boussac's lobbying, his French factories were awarded a contract to supply the cloth for German army uniforms. Boussac later claimed that he was simply trying his best to maintain French jobs, just as he supported the continuation of the French racing programme lest French bloodstock and the assets of the nation's racehorse owners and breeders should be damaged irreparably by the conflict.

Despite the Occupation and the deprivations of rationing, sixty-five thousand spectators, more than forty thousand of them French, turned up at Longchamp on 28 June 1942 for the second wartime running of the Grand Prix de Paris. But fifteen days later the Germans stepped up their 'Aryanisation' programme and 13,152 Jews were rounded up in Paris and held at the Vélodrome d'Hiver cycle stadium near Bir-Hakeim. André Carrus belatedly realised it was high time to get out and he and his wife sought refuge with relatives in the department of Isère in the Auvergne, while their eldest son Pierre escaped over the Pyrenees to Spain and then to the US, and their youngest son Jacques was hidden by family in Algiers.

After the Liberation in 1944, Carrus returned to Paris having been summoned by Raoul Dautry, who had been appointed Minister for Reconstruction in General Charles de Gaulle's provisional government. Dautry, who had a small toothbrush moustache and bore an uncanny resemblance to Charlie Chaplin, was a former director of the French National Railways, SNCF. At his behest Carrus forsook betting and racing for two years to harness his former skills as Director of Public Works to the task of rebuilding war-damaged railway lines, roads and bridges. But political life in immediate post-war France was riven by internecine disputes between De Gaulle's coalition of supporters and the Communists. When the General resigned in 1946 Raoul Dautry resigned too, and shortly afterwards Carrus went back to his old job in the PMU head offices on the Rue la Boétie just off the Champs-Élysées.

French racing – so prosperous in the late 1930s and even during the first few years of the war – was in a bad way. Most of the racecourses had closed following the Allied invasion in 1944, and many PMU cafés and machines had been destroyed during the bombing. Restoration would not be easy, especially against a background of incessant industrial conflict at home and evermore expensive wars overseas. But recovery was essential not only for the sake of French racing but because of the contribution the PMU's finances could make to the nation's exchequer.

In September 1947 Carrus was summoned by the then Agriculture Minister Pierre Pflimlin whose ministry was directly responsible for betting and racing. Neither Pflimlin, a sober Catholic lawyer from Alsace, nor Carrus had much time for gambling. The PMU director general enjoyed an occasional game of bridge, like Des Moutis, but otherwise he still regarded punters as thriftless, immoral types whose behaviour should be deplored not encouraged. But as Pflimlin made clear, there was no room for that kind of sentiment in government circles. 'This is France, Carrus,' he reminded him. 'And in France vice must be organised.'

Together Carrus and Pflimlin presided over a gradual improvement in their estate. They methodically repaired racecourse buildings, recruited groundsmen to restore the damaged turf, and installed new betting machines and counters on course and off.

In an attempt to offer a more varied menu, Carrus introduced a new bet, the 'Couplé', which invited punters to pick the first two in any order in any race, and saw a modest increase in turnover and revenues. But the majority of the PMU's customers remained recreational small-change punters content to wager the minimum stake in their local café in between a game of dominos or cards. French racing's professionals, including most of the top owners and trainers, continued to regard the PMU as soulless and inflexible. They liked the payments to boost prize money, if not the hefty cut creamed off by the government. But the PMU gave them no chance to beat the market by taking the best price available about a horse when betting opened on a race. To enjoy that privilege they continued to wager by telephone or telegram with a credit bookmaker in England.

Alternatively, they could use the services of a charming, educated Frenchman and fellow member of *le Tout-Paris*.

Chapter 5

In the summer of 1953 – shortly after the racecourse ban was imposed on Patrice des Moutis – Marcel Boussac invited André Carrus to dinner at Maxim's. The tycoon, whose runners were dominating European racing at the time and who was now director general of the Société d'Encouragement, complained that PMU growth was not robust enough. French racing lacked the finance needed to maintain its prize-money levels and rebuilding plans, never mind the percentage going to the government. What was needed, Boussac said, was an exciting new bet to capture the public's imagination: a daily and weekly wager that would attract the high rollers *and* the small-change punters, and result in a massive pool with the potential to win a huge sum for a modest outlay. Carrus and his staff, urged Boussac, should start work on it without delay.

The sober *fonctionnaire* in Carrus – who now sported grey hair to go with his spectacles and moustache, making him look like a French schoolmaster from an earlier generation – was conflicted. He still had no time for racing or for gamblers and what he regarded as their improvident weaknesses. But he also knew that Boussac was right and that the future of the PMU, not

34

to mention the Carrus family stake in it, depended on attracting a new generation to gambling on a regular basis.

With the help of his sons – Pierre, who now had a degree from the Massachussets Institute of Technology; and Jacques, who had returned to France to join the family business – Carrus conducted surveys of racecourse and *café-tabac* punters across the land and sought the views of owners and trainers as to what kind of hook would be needed to pull in the crowds. He also drew on the experience of the young TV presenter Guy Lux, who had started off working as a salesman in a hardware store in the Paris suburbs. Bored by the monotony of shop life, Lux organised a promotion during the Tour de France offering 5,000 francs to any customer who predicted the first three home in the correct order in the Tour's daily stage, and 500 francs for predicting the first three finishers in any order. The idea was a big hit and throughout the neighbourhood people flocked to take part. Unfortunately hardware sales simultaneously declined, and after a few days the shop manager intervened and cancelled the promotion. But Carrus remembered the popularity of Lux's concept and adopted the principle as the basis of his new bet, the Tiercé.

Every day of the week, every week of the year – including Good Friday, Easter Sunday and Christmas Day – there would be a designated Tiercé race in which punters would be encouraged to try to predict the first three home in the correct order or any order. The biggest Tiercé of the week would always take place on a Sunday and feature at least fourteen runners. It wouldn't be a classic race like the Prix du Jockey Club or the Grand Prix de Paris, where all the runners carry the same weight. It would be a handicap in which the horses with the best form have to concede weight to the less distinguished contestants, the aim being to bring all the runners in the race as close together as possible and ensure a competitive spectacle with lots of hypothetical outcomes for punters to bet on.

The Sunday Tiercé, which would have enhanced prize money to encourage owners and trainers to target their horses at it, would have the biggest pool. And it would offer players the notional chance to win a lottery-scale payout for as little as a ten-franc stake (less than a shilling in English money).

The first ever Tiercé race was run on 14 January 1954 at Enghien-les-Bains, a spa town on the northwestern edges of Paris. The once-picturesque course was described by Ernest Hemingway in his posthumous memoir *A Moveable Feast* as a 'small, pretty and larcenous track that was the home of the outsider'. Unfortunately the debut of the Tiercé at Enghien was an underwhelming occasion. The Prix Uranie was a trotting race for fillies run over 2,700 metres, and the favourites finished in the first three places. But despite a big PMU advertising campaign in the sports pages, interest in the new bet was minimal and the Tiercé payout modest. Carrus and his sons were disappointed but they should perhaps have reflected that it was hardly a propitious moment to launch a new initiative. In Indo-China the battle for Dien Bien Phu was moving towards its climax, while Paris was in the grip of one of the coldest winters of the twentieth century, and the newspapers were less interested in horse racing than the efforts of the saintly campaigner Abbé Pierre to organise clothing and sanctuary for the homeless.

It was a similar story for the next few years. High-rolling gamblers continued to spurn the PMU – and not just the wealthy Paris clients of Patrice des Moutis but regular horse-racing devotees in cities like Marseille, Nice and Lyon who had always bet with illegal bookies in their home towns or relayed their custom to the credit offices in England.

The small-change punters, who Carrus needed to win over in large numbers, showed some interest but had plenty of other attractions to entertain them. They followed football and cycling, revering France's greatest player, Raymond Kopa, the 'Little Napoleon' who joined Real Madrid in 1956, and the three-times Tour de France winner Louison Bobet, who had been in the Resistance in World War II. They went to the cinema to laugh at the comic genius of Jacques Tati, as the accident-prone Monsieur Hulot on his holidays, and thrilled to the jewellery heist *Rififi* with its nailbiting thirty-minute section depicting the robbery with neither music nor dialogue. In the summer of 1956 they feasted on the blanket coverage of Grace Kelly's marriage to Prince Rainier of Monaco, the first celebrity wedding of the television age. And they lapped up lurid crime stories in the tabloids, especially murder trials where there was always the chilling possibility that the accused might lose their head.

But then, as 1956 gave way to 1957, newspaper stories began to circulate about Tiercé winners who, for a mere ten or 20 francs, had won 2,000,000 old francs on successive weekends. The drip-drip of positive publicity became a regular stream and turnover increased until it was generally agreed that the Tiercé was a success and that, thanks to its generous slice of the pool, French racing's fortunes were on the upgrade. Prize money for everything from the Prix du Jockey Club to quite moderate events at rural tracks was eclipsing levels for comparable events in England, and French breeders were getting subsidies to help them improve their stock. A delighted Marcel Boussac told Carrus that all the Tiercé needed now was a few really big winners to take its popularity to the next level. The textile magnate was about to get his wish.

It was in the summer of 1958 that the possibility of scooping the Tiercé jackpot first attracted the attention of the nation's shrewdest gambler. The holiday base for Patrice and Marie-Thérèse des Moutis during July and August was Brignogan, the Queret family château in Finistère on the northwestern coast of Brittany. The pristine, white sand beaches, rockpools and bracingly cold but clear waters were a paradise for small children, like the couple's son François, who was born in 1956, and his older sisters. The house was large enough to accommodate plenty of friends with young children of their own and Patrice loved presiding over big family meals and taking them all out sailing in his boat or fishing for crayfish by night.

But the annual six-week *vacances* weren't exclusively devoted to children and *haute bourgeois* family life. Even though Pat remained barred from entering Deauville racecourse, he and Marie-Thérèse still went up to Normandy for the last ten days of August. There was a valuable bridge tournament to play in at the Hôtel du Golf. There were old friends to catch up with in the hotels and restaurants, and there were punters, like the Aly Khan, to do business with discreetly and well out of sight of the Police des Courses et Jeux.

François André, whose family ran the Deauville casino as well as owning the Golf, Normandy and Royal hotels, had promised his 1958 visitors 'sun, celebrities and elegance agogo'. The sun may have been in short supply but the celebrities arrived as usual, led by the Maharanee de Rajpipla (whose husband had won the 1936 Derby with Windsor Lad), the Duke and Duchess of Windsor and the sultry Mexican actress María Félix, who was accompanied by her fourth husband, the French-Romanian banker and racehorse owner, Alexander Berger.

One of the biggest victors at the racetrack was the Parisian theatre producer Benoît Léon-Deutsch who was enjoying his eighth winner in a fortnight when his colt Tremens II won the Prix de Cabourg. By contrast Prince Aly Khan, who had been divorced by Rita Hayworth in 1953 and was now in the company of the Givenchy model and muse Bettina Graziani, was right out of luck. The Aly had two well-backed losers on Saturday 16 August but the following day his highly rated two-year-old Taboun, trained by Alec Head, was considered a certainty in one of the most prestigious juvenile races in France, the Prix Morny. To the horror of the favourite backers, who sent the colt off at PMU odds of 4-6 (meaning that if you wagered 6 francs you'd only win 4), Taboun was turned over by a 33-1 outsider called Oceanic trained by Patrice des Moutis' friend, Georges Pelat.

If the Aly Khan was betting on his usual scale it must have been a profitable few days for his illegal French bookmaker, though Patrice always said that the Khan, like King Farouk, was a big punter but 'an extremely bad payer'. But money won from one of his oldest and most charming clients was not Pat's only significant victory that weekend. He also won the Tiercé.

The featured Tiercé race on Sunday 17 August was the Grand Handicap de la Manche, which was a competitive event run over 2,400 metres, or one and a half miles. The first three home were Astre Brillant ridden by Jean Massard, Le Tremont and Magic North – and, using his judgement and knowledge of form, Patrice backed them in the correct order wagering a total of 50,000 old francs to win some 600,000 francs less stake money. The exchange rate at the time was 1,382 francs to £1 and Patrice's profit was approximately £443. An insignificant amount by the standards of the trading he was used to as a bookie, but Des Moutis was testing a system. And what was important about the Grand Handicap was that it left the gambler hungry for more. Much more.

For years Des Moutis had wanted nothing to do with Pari-Mutuel betting, by turns repelled by its rigidity and raging against its monopoly. But at some point that summer, bored perhaps by cards and frustrated by his continued exile from the track, he'd begun to study Tiercé races and results. Numerous small players were now treating the bet like the lottery and picking horses numbers because they corresponded to the dates of their wives' or children's birthdays or their identity card or social security number.

Des Moutis would adopt a very different and more cerebral approach, drawing on his mathematical skills honed as a young man at the École Centrale and his understanding of statistics and probability. But it wasn't all dry calculation. He said later that he kept thinking about the huge Tiercé pools and the moderate sums being paid out and the thousands of small punters who had no chance of winning, poor things . . . and he decided that it would be 'a crime not to enjoy it'.

Chapter 6

That year not only marked the beginning of the long duel between Des Moutis and the PMU; it was also a year of high political drama in France, in which the enfeebled Fourth Republic finally collapsed. From its birth in 1945 it had been continually torn this way and that by different interest groups – from farmers, coal miners and vintners, to North African colonists – and it was the escalating drama in Algeria that provoked the end.

After almost four years of civil war the death toll in the colony was mounting daily, whether it be Front de Libération Nationale members brutally tortured by the French army, or French-Algerian settlers, administrators and Harkis – local Arabs loyal to Paris – murdered by the FLN. Thousands more men and women in mainland France, repelled by the excesses perpetrated in their name, were calling for an end to French colonial rule.

In May there was a mutiny in Algiers led by a group of regular French army officers who suspected, correctly, that Guy Mollet's government in Paris were surreptitiously engaging in talks with the FLN. The President René Coty – described by

Time magazine's Paris correspondent Stanley Karnow as a 'good natured mediocrity' – feared that a mass insurrection was imminent. So he dismissed Mollet's administration and sent for the one man who he believed had the stature and strength of character to restore order – the hero of June 1940 when he'd refused to surrender to the Germans and had vowed to continue the Free French struggle overseas: Charles de Gaulle.

The General, whose unshakeable self-belief was matched by his faith in the glorious destiny of France, had warned all along that without a strong executive the Fourth Republic would be no more effective than its discredited predecessor that had collapsed so ignominiously in the face of the German advance. This time he was determined to fashion a France in which an elected head of state would enjoy greater powers than in any other Western country including the USA. He also realised that if not resolved, the war in Algeria had the potential to threaten not just the stability but the very survival of France itself. But, wily politician that he was, De Gaulle understood that he would have to move carefully and that initially his position depended on the support of the army and convincing them that he would defend the interests of the French colonists or *Algérie Française*.

The National Assembly in Paris confirmed De Gaulle as the new Prime Minister on 1 June. A few days later he flew to Algiers attired in his military uniform and addressed a huge crowd of French-Algerians gathered in the square outside the main administrative building. '*Je vous ai compris*,' he told them. 'I have understood you.' It was one of those masterful but ambiguous phrases that the General excelled in, and it convinced both the crowd and the hardline army leaders, like France's most decorated soldier General Raoul Salan, that he was on their side. Little did they know then that within three years he would have negotiated Algerian independence.

In December De Gaulle was elected the first President of the Fifth Republic, completing what critics described as a virtual *coup d'état*, and appointed Michel Debré – a pudgy-faced ex-cavalryman and founder of the École Nationale d'Administration – as his Prime Minister. The new constitution entitled the President to revoke the PM's appointment, and those of his cabinet, at any time if he saw fit and take whatever measures he deemed necessary, including dissolving parliament, if he believed France was under threat. Political opponents feared that concentrating so much sovereignty in the hands of one man was like going back to the era of absolute monarchy. An irony not lost on the various former royals who'd sought exile in France since the end of World War II. The Duke and Duchess of Windsor leased a château in the Bois de Boulogne and owned a millhouse in the country. Portly King Farouk of Egypt, who had been deposed in 1952, had been living in Paris but would shortly be moving on to Rome, while ex-Emperor Bao Dai of Indo-China had taken up residence on the Côte d'Azur. But while they may have retained their titles and a small retinue of supporters, the royal exiles were all insignificant nobodies compared to President Charles de Gaulle.

As the Republic moved towards a new era of strong central government and authoritarian rule, there was a symbolic reminder of the price paid by an earlier generation to maintain the glory of France: 11 November 1958 was the fortieth anniversary of the end of World War I and the signing of the armistice in a railway carriage at Compiègne 40 miles north of Paris. The occasion was marked by a public holiday, the Fête d'Armistice, which included a parade of veterans and a commemoration at the Arc de Triomphe where President René Coty, whose term in office wouldn't officially expire until January, laid a wreath at the tomb of the Unknown Soldier.

The Société d'Encouragement had decided to mark the day with a special Fête d'Armistice meeting at leafy Saint-Cloud racecourse in the prosperous suburb on the western edges of the city. A correspondent for *Le Figaro* pronounced it '*un très beau succès*'. The feature event was the day's Tiercé race, the Prix de l'Elevage, a seventeen-runner handicap for fillies run over 2,500 metres. The winner was the top weight and favourite, Messenia, sporting the 'popular colours of Monsieur Marcel Boussac' according to *Le Figaro*. There were some surprises – notably the 'fine effort' of the unfancied runner-up, Matines, who had previously put in a series of rather moderate displays. But with an outsider in second place, the Tiercé paid 25,525 *ancien* francs for a 30-franc stake to punters who had predicted the outcome in the correct order, and 5,105 francs for a ten-franc stake to punters who had gone correctly for the first three in the *désordre* (any order).

The big story was that for total stakes of just under 300,000 francs, one 'lucky unknown punter' as *L'Aurore* described him, had scooped a Tiercé of 21,441,000 francs, equivalent to roughly £15,500 sterling or more like £295,240 at today's rates. The gambler, who said he didn't want any publicity at the time, was Patrice des Moutis, and he would have disputed *L'Aurore*'s view that his big win, not a fortune but not bad for an opening shot, had much to do with luck.

Patrice had been waiting for weeks for a Tiercé race he could go to war on. Every morning he scrutinised the racing journal

Paris Turf which, as well as giving the runners and riders – and tips – for the meetings taking place that day and the next, also listed the entries for events up to five days ahead. On Saturday 8 November Des Moutis decided that the Prix de l'Elevage, taking place at his local course the following Tuesday, suited his purposes for a variety of reasons.

By 1958 there were approximately three thousand five hundred *café-tabacs* in France, and on weekdays around three hundred thousand punters went into one of them to place a bet on the Tiercé. But on Sundays and public holidays the number shot up to more like five million. In all Pari-Mutuel betting the winners shared what everybody else lost, minus the deductions, and Patrice reckoned that on a special holiday like the Fête d'Armistice the pool would be one of the biggest of the year. It was an important consideration for him. He didn't just want to prove he could win the Tiercé to satisfy his vanity – although some *amour propre* was involved. He was like a bank robber planning a heist on a day when he knows that there will have been a substantial deposit, and he wanted to win as much money as he could.

What was also attractive about the Prix de l'Elevage was that Patrice knew in advance from his contacts in Chantilly that Marcel Boussac's filly Messenia was a definite runner and that her gambling trainer Geoff Watson thought she was in a different class to the handicappers she'd be meeting at Saint-Cloud. So there was no question that Messenia would be Patrice's number-one selection. But he also believed that the likely second and third favourites were overrated and unlikely to win, whereas several of the less exposed runners had a better than expected chance of being placed.

Patrice's clients and connections could tell him that one of the dark horses, the filly Matines, who had underperformed in her last few races, had been successfully treated for a sinus problem and had been working like a different horse since. This was the kind of inside information, not readily available to the general public, which bookmakers and professional gamblers turned to their advantage all the time.

But Des Moutis didn't merely rely on inside information to help him place his bets. He approached the race systematically in an attempt to assess the probability of various outcomes. In particular he recalled Bayes' Theorem – which he had studied at the École Centrale – and which was formulated in the eighteenth century by the Reverend Thomas Bayes, an English theologian and mathematician. In Bayesian theory a level of probability can be assigned to any hypothesis, backing up the Reverend's view that subjective belief should rationally change to account for evidence.

Des Moutis calculated that in a twenty-runner Tiercé race there were 6,840 possible winning Tiercé combinations. But if you could eliminate eight runners in advance the number of combinations would fall to 1,320, and then a professional punter would be in business. He would apply the same mathematical analysis to the seventeen-runner Prix de l'Elevage. He had bought numerous books of tickets, or *bordereaux* – the special betting slips that were available in PMU outlets and *café-tabacs* and had to be filled out by hand when placing a Tiercé bet – and once his preliminary studies of the runners were complete he worked through the night of 10–11 November to finalise his selections. Sustaining himself with cigarettes, cigars and regular shots of black coffee, he systematically applied a level of probability to the chances of all the runners in the race. He assessed form, weight, preferences for soft or firm going, the skill and strike rate of the trainer and the reliability and expertise of the jockey. After a lengthy study he managed to rule out nine of the seventeen runners. He then proceeded to marry the banker Messenia with the other seven horses in a series of combinations – 1 to beat 15 and 11, 1 to beat 11 and 15, 1 to beat 8 and 12, and so on – in both the correct order and any order.

In total he had 42 permutations, each of them to a 200-franc stake and he was planning to back each of them thirty-five times in the belief that, providing any one of his permutations triumphed, he would win at least ten times more than he'd laid out in stake money.

Tuesday 11 November was cold and grey and there was talk of snow in Paris before the end of the week. It was 'the first offensive of the winter' said the weathermen. But conditions were good enough for racing to go ahead at what was one of the final flat-racing meetings of the season.

At half-past ten Patrice des Moutis left his Saint-Cloud home and got in to his black Mercedes 220 to drive down to the Café Lutétia on Avenue Jean Baptiste in Boulogne-Billancourt. The bustling PMU *café-tabac* was just south of the Bois and not far from Longchamp racecourse. As usual on Sundays and holidays, the café was packed with eager, animated punters, some standing at the bar, some sitting down, some nursing a coffee, some an *apéro* or a glass of wine. The air was thick with cigarette smoke and the café reverberated with the sound of conversation, as everyone exchanged tips and views while poring over the racing form in their copies of *Le Parisien* and *Paris Turf*.

The punters were mostly but not all male. There were a few single women too, including elderly cleaning ladies, or *femmes de ménage*, waiting patiently in line to place their three-franc minimum bets. These were the ordinary *parieurs*, thought Des Moutis – the little people supposedly so precious to the PMU and close to the heart of the French government. He wondered how many of them ever stopped to think about the 26 per cent taken out of the pool by that government. Did they not sometimes feel they deserved a better service and a broader choice of odds provided by some bookmaking competitors? Had anybody asked them? It was outrageous that they should effectively be prisoners of a state-supported monopoly. But what the ignorant captives lost today, Des Moutis planned to win.

Boulogne-Billancourt, like neighbouring Auteuil, was a prosperous *quartier* and by no means all the Tiercé punters were small-stakes players. Even so, when Patrice got to the front of the queue and handed over his 42 different tickets and his wad of francs he was pleasantly surprised that the bets were accepted and the tickets punched by the machine without query. Was it just a case of a bored or complacent cashier? he wondered. Or were really big Tiercé winners still such a rarity that they were dismissive of his chances of scooping the pot?

The Sunday Tiercé race had been televised on the state-run TV channel RTF 1 since June 1956. It occupied a ten-minute slot during the broadcaster's Sunday afternoon sports programme, and the journalist Georges de Caunes, father of Antoine, was the first commentator. But there was no coverage of the Prix de l'Elevage as it was on a Tuesday, albeit a bank holiday, and there were moral objections to two racing and gambling broadcasts going out in the same week.

Barred from actually being at Saint-Cloud racecourse, the closest Patrice could get was to sit in his Mercedes in the car park outside. Not that he was entirely alone. Des Moutis wasn't the only illegal odds-maker in Paris. There were others with varying degrees of probity and capital who regularly gathered across the road from the city's racetracks when there was an important meeting going on. They were rather like the well-dressed prostitutes strolling up and down the Avenue Foch. They didn't force themselves on anyone but if a member of the public, perhaps temporarily coming out of the racecourse, came up to enquire about a horse and a price they would take them over to their cars and do the business. *Commissaire* Roger Taupin and his fellow zealots with the Police des Courses et Jeux may have disapproved, but few of the other bookmakers were trading on Patrice's scale. And as long as the local cops received a few backhanders from time to time, and as long as the illegal betting didn't take place inside the racecourse itself, they tended to leave them alone.

The Prix de l'Elevage was due to start at 3 p.m. As the hour drew near, Des Moutis got out of his car to await the outcome. It was more than five years since he'd actually set foot inside a racetrack and he still felt the deprivation as keenly as he had in 1953. But if he was afflicted by nerves, his stomach churning at the thought of the race about to get under way and the stakes he was playing for, he didn't show it. He had faith in his system and it amused him to think that if Taupin had appeared at that moment, he could have assured him quite truthfully that he was waiting for the outcome of a perfectly legal Tiercé bet with the PMU.

Racecourse crowds in Paris in 1958 were much bigger than they are today, and the waxing and waning noise from the grandstand told Patrice when the leaders must have passed the winning post. Within a few minutes the burly 'Julie' Carrax and the equally excited Alain Ayache were running out of the racecourse towards him. The expressions on their faces left no doubt as to the result. Messenia, ridden by Boussac's stable jockey Jean Deforge, had won by three lengths from Matines, with another one of Patrice's choices, Val Olga, in third place. Numbers 1, 15 and 11. Patrice's friends and the other bookies and their customers all gathered round to slap him on the back and congratulate him on his smoothly executed success.

The full Tiercé return was announced on the radio at 8 p.m. that evening and, after breakfast the following day, Des Moutis drove back down to the Café Lutétia to collect his cheque for 21 million francs. The PMU had already put out an excited statement of their own, and all the papers were carrying the story. Patrice had taken the precaution of telephoning ahead to the café proprietor, André Calmels, to say that he preferred to remain anonymous and Monsieur Calmels contented himself with telling journalists that the big winner was 'an extremely charming and knowledgeable gentleman' who often dropped by.

Nobody cried foul and there was no reason to. Patrice may have had the benefit of a bit of inside information but he had made no attempt to influence the result and, for their part, the PMU management were delighted with the publicity which they hoped would encourage other, previously sceptical, punters to try their luck on the Tiercé next time around.

On the Wednesday night Patrice and Marie-Thérèse dressed up and went out to Pré Catelan, a favourite restaurant of the racing community situated in a pavilion in the Bois de Boulogne. Patrice cut a dashing figure in his evening clothes while Marie-Thérèse glowed like Romy Schneider, the film actress and lover of Alain Delon, in her new black Trapeze Line Dior dress designed by Yves Saint Laurent and recently modelled at a fashion show attended by Princess Margaret at Blenheim Palace. Good looks. High times. Wealth. Success.

Pré Catelan's *Belle Époque* dining room had been the setting for many a celebration, including the retirement party for the jockey Rae Johnstone the previous year. Patrice had been present then too, along with the Aly Khan, Suzy Volterra, Georges Pelat, Alec Head and Patrice's English friend Peter O'Sullevan. At the time Des Moutis was an insurance man from Neuilly who also happened to be an illegal bookie. Now he was the punter with the divine touch who had just won the Tiercé and shown that, potentially, it could be done on a much bigger scale than anyone had imagined before. Next time he'd play for much higher stakes.

At the end of a delicious candlelit dinner, accompanied by the finest wines, champagne and Calvados, Patrice and Marie-Thérèse went on to Le Grand Cercle at 12 Rue de Presbourg, little more than a hundred yards away from where President René Coty had laid his wreath at the Arc de Triomphe the previous morning. The handsome couple strolled in through the double doors, across the small courtyard, up the steps past the greeters in black tie and on into the tactile world of the gaming salons with their thick pile carpets, soft lighting, studiedly posed men and cool, bouffant women.

The Grand Cercle was one of the high-end gaming clubs in Paris run by the 'Unione Corse', or Corsican Mafia, supposedly as a reward for the support they gave De Gaulle and the Resistance in World War II. The Marseille Godfather Antoine Guérini and his family had taken care of Vichy sympathisers and kept Marseille and Toulon harbours open for the Allied landings in Provence in July 1944. After the war was over they had acted as strike breakers in the Marseille docks, curbing the powers of the Communist-backed trade unions and strengthening their hold on the city's prostitution, cigarette smuggling and other rackets. Nowadays the Guérini family owned the Grand Cercle, though they left the day-to-day running of the club to their fellow Corsican, Jean-Baptiste Andréani, who'd made his fortune in Indo-China, owning brothels in Saigon.

Aside from playing bridge and the old French card game Scarlet and Black, Patrice never bet in large sums in a casino. He liked the ambience and the sensuality, but the odds were stacked too heavily in favour of the house. But standing beside the roulette wheel with his proud wife that November night and waiting to see where the white ball would land, he must have sensed that he was at the beginning of a golden run and that, with the formula cracked, there would be more and bigger Tiercé wins to come, and more celebrations too.

The results seemingly pre-ordained by France's most audacious mathematician and gambler.

Chapter 7

As the 1950s drew to a close the conservatism and formality of traditional French bourgeois life began to be assailed by the youthful energy of a less deferential generation. Charles de Gaulle's Fifth Republic, underpinned by a deeply Catholic and nationalistic idea of the moral order, did its best to limit the distribution and influence of rock and roll music from the USA. But it was less successful at controlling the cinema.

Olympian intellectuals may have continued to deplore all things American as vulgar and debased, but to a handful of young French filmmakers the noirish themes of American movies and popular culture were the inspiration for a series of brilliantly innovative films that were collectively dubbed the 'Nouvelle Vague'.

Nineteen fifty-eight saw the release of *Ascenseur pour l'Échafaud*, or *Lift to the Scaffold*, a black and white thriller directed by the 27-year-old prodigy, Louis Malle. The story of doomed lovers and a perfect murder gone wrong featured Jeanne Moreau and a haunting trumpet score by Miles Davis. The lingering sadness of the music was the perfect match for Moreau's tortured beauty and the neon-lit images of Paris by night. It was passionate and sexy but also cerebral and cool and seemed a cultural lifetime away from the romantic stereotypes beloved of an earlier school of French filmmakers. Then in 1960 Jean-Luc Godard broke box-office records with *Au Bout de Souffle*, which was filmed entirely on location with a hand-held camera and starred Jean Seberg and Jean-Paul Belmondo in his breakthrough role as a cheeky young tough intent on living fast and dying young.

These tales of existential heroes riding their destiny all the way to the end of the line seemed to define the spirit of the age, and as Des Moutis kept working alone through his white nights, sustained only by cigarettes and coffee as he pursued more Tiercé coups at the expense of the PMU, his friends began to feel an increasingly noirish aura enveloping the gambler.

Regardless of his mounting profits from the Tiercé, Patrice was often playing cards late at night around Paris and he continued acting as a private bookmaker or commission agent for a few select clients and friends. In the autumn of 1959 he helped to place a series of wagers with the London bookies on behalf of the Aly Khan, whose colt Saint Crespin was running in the Prix de l'Arc de Triomphe at Longchamp. In one of the most exciting finishes ever recorded in the Arc, Saint Crespin dead-heated with a horse called Midnight Sun but, after a lengthy inquiry, Saint Crespin was awarded the race when his rival was found to have hampered him in the closing stages.

Patrice had to content himself with watching the event on television, but he joined in the post-race celebrations that night, where Saint Crespin's owner talked of the plans and gambles he was already envisioning for the following season. But Saint Crespin's Arc was the Aly Khan's last throw. In May 1960 he was killed in a car crash at a roundabout in Suresnes on the edges of the Bois de Boulogne. At the time he was on his way from Longchamp to his brother Prince Sadruddin's house near St Cloud golf course. The gambling prince, described by one friend as 'too alive to die', was 48 years old.

The death of the Khan came less than two years after the demise of King Farouk – who had expired, appropriately, over dinner in an Italian restaurant – and seemed to mark the passing of an age. All across Europe the old aristocratic plungers of the first half of the twentieth century were slowly succumbing to democratic change, mortality and taxes. In their place was a new breed of numerate self-made gamblers, and Des Moutis was at the forefront of them.

In November 1958 Patrice had wagered hundreds of thousands of old francs on his big Tiercé win. By 1959 he was betting in millions, and by the start of the 1960s his bets had gone up to as much as 80 million francs, or approximately £60,000 in UK currency. By then his name and background, which he had been at pains to keep private after the Messenia coup, had come to the attention of some of the highest people in the land. The Gaullist Prime Minister Michel Debré sometimes dropped in to the same smart 16th *arrondissement* salons as Patrice and Marie-Thérèse, and in the course of catching up on the latest gossip he was told of the exploits of the gentleman punter from Saint-Cloud. Debré, a cold fish not naturally sympathetic to betting and racing, mentioned the name to his Finance and Agriculture ministers, whose civil servants talked in turn to André Carrus. They wanted to know what the PMU knew about this elegant gambler and whether the extent of his wagering raised any issues they should be concerned about. Carrus admitted that the scale of the man's betting was unprecedented. He also agreed that it might be time for him to meet this Monsieur des Moutis in person.

On a wet Monday morning in January 1961 Patrice was in his office in Neuilly studying a particularly complex insurance portfolio. He had told his secretary that he didn't want to be disturbed and was annoyed when she buzzed him over the intercom. The secretary explained that she had the PMU director general on the line and that he wanted to talk to him. Patrice was confused but also suspicious. 'Do you mean André Carrus?' he asked. 'Yes, Monsieur.' 'What the devil does he want?' 'He wouldn't tell me, Monsieur,' replied the secretary. 'But he said it was very important.' 'All right,' said Patrice. 'Put him through.'

Carrus was soft spoken, formal and extremely polite. He wondered if it would be possible for the two of them to meet? He would be happy to come to Patrice's office if that would be convenient for him.

Des Moutis hesitated. He had never met Carrus but he knew that he was a former Grande École student like himself, and he also believed he was about twenty years older than him. French courtesy demanded that he should offer to call upon the director general rather than the other way around.

'Is it urgent?' he asked.

'We would like to talk to you as soon as possible, Monsieur,' replied Carrus.

'Very well,' said Patrice, who didn't believe in wasting time. 'I will come to your office in one hour.'

'Perfect, Monsieur,' replied Carrus. 'At whatever time suits you I'll be waiting.'

After he had put the phone down Patrice felt a mixture of excitement and relief. At least now he wouldn't have to spend the whole day going through a turgid insurance claim. But what exactly did the inventor of the Tiercé, the great game that had gripped France and enabled him personally to win millions, want to talk to him about? Then he laughed to himself. Perhaps Carrus just wanted a tip?

The PMU head office, number 83 Rue la Boétie, was in a narrow street connecting the Rue Faubourg St Honoré with the Champs-Élysées. Nowadays the top end is dominated by a tatty souvenir shop and a Burger King branch, while the shop nextdoor sells sex aids and cheap lingerie. But back between 1918 and 1940 the street was a place of pilgrimage for visitors to Pablo Picasso's home and studio at number 23, and Picasso's art dealer Paul Rosenberg had a gallery two doors down. In the 1950s and 1960s number 58 Rue la Boétie was the Paris office of the CIA. The PMU headquarters were further down on the opposite side of the street in a four-storey limestone building with a Haussmann-style façade. Black wrought iron gates concealed a central courtyard and entrance hall where a porter in *bleu de travail* – looking like one of the supporting characters in *Ascenseur pour l'Échafaud* – directed Patrice to take the rickety cage lift to the fourth floor.

Just like a Las Vegas casino manager researching his high rollers, Carrus had prepared for the meeting by studying Patrice's file with the Police des Courses et Jeux. It was a bulky dossier containing *Commissaire* Roger Taupin's assertion that Des Moutis was an illegal bookie and malign influence, and Patrice's counter claims of police harassment in the early 1950s.

But other than the warning off in 1953 there seemed much to approve of. The man was an aristocrat, well mannered and well spoken – Carrus had been impressed by his courtesy on the telephone – and his part-Norman part-Breton background included diplomats and admirals of the line. And had he not graduated among the top tier of students at the École Centrale in 1943? This was clearly someone who loved his racing. He was knowledgeable about bloodstock. He had ridden as an amateur rider and for a while he had owned horses in training in the southwest with Vladimir Hall, an enthusiastic and irreproachable trainer, as even *Commissaire* Taupin had been forced to agree. There were character references written to the Société d'Encouragement by Hall and other trainers like Geoff Watson, Georges Pelat and the inscrutable François Mathet who trained for the Hôtel Georges V owner, François Dupré. Yet at the same time this impeccably bred gentleman with the iron nerve was gambling more on the Tiercé on a Sunday than hundreds of thousands of other punters combined, and he was winning consistently. He was also the only PMU customer to be paid, at his insistence, by cheque.

When Patrice arrived, Carrus found himself face to face with a tall dark-haired man, his face tanned from a recent skiing trip, with a look at once direct and yet ironic, as if he found the whole situation faintly amusing.

For his part Patrice was taking in the director general's office with its *fonctionnaires'* rolltop desks, card indexes, exposed central-heating pipes and brown stains on the wainscotting. Patrice's office in Neuilly had comfortable modern furniture, abstract paintings on the walls, telex machines and a recently installed Espresso coffee machine. But the refreshments at number 83 Rue la Boétie were of a different order, and shortly after Patrice and Carrus had shaken hands an elderly female employee appeared pushing a trolley bearing cups, saucers and a gas bottle heating a percolator of scaldingly hot government-issue coffee.

Outside the office window the sky was dark and rain had begun to beat against the pane. Patrice took his silver cigarette case out of his inside pocket and offered a Gauloise to Carrus. The director general politely declined, pointing to the pipe in an ashtray on his desk.

'But you don't mind if I do?' asked Des Moutis, echoing that Sunday evening interview with Roger Taupin in Deauville in 1950.

'Of course not,' said Carrus. The two men lit up and soon the office was infused with the pleasantly complementary smells of coffee and tobacco smoke.

'Very well, Monsieur Director,' said Patrice. 'How can I help you?'

'Monsieur des Moutis,' began Carrus. 'You are our biggest winner—'

'I am also your best client,' interjected Patrice. 'And when I lose you keep all the money.'

'Indeed,' replied Carrus. 'But you are a client who poses us a serious technical problem. In the course of the last three Sundays you have wagered 70, 60 and 80 million francs in your usual PMU café in Boulogne-Billancourt. As you are no doubt aware, the motorcycle messengers we employ to bring the tickets and funds back here are not insured to carry more than two million francs. Yesterday, to cope with your bets, we had to send forty riders to the Café Lutétia in total. You must admit that it's complicated and becoming dangerous.'

Patrice nodded politely. 'Yes,' he said. 'I can understand that.'

The director general had taken off his spectacles for a moment and was holding them in his hand. Des Moutis was struck by how old and small Carrus looked, with his short grey hair and his miniscule moustache. He had the air of a kindly grandpapa. He'd heard that the elderly Polytechnicien had no time for racing or for punters. He wondered what he was like at bridge.

'What we are therefore proposing, Monsieur,' Carrus was saying, 'is an exceptional arrangement just for you. Instead of using a *café-tabac* like the Lutétia, we suggest that from now on you drop off your bets each Sunday morning at our main accounting office just around the corner from here in the Rue Penthièvre. That would simplify matters considerably. What do you say?'

'I think that's an excellent idea,' said Des Moutis. 'But you haven't said anything about my commission.'

'Your commission?' asked Carrus. 'I don't understand. What commission?'

'The one per cent you allow café owners to deduct from winning bets placed there,' said Patrice. 'If I am no longer betting in a café there is no longer any justification for the PMU to impose that extra charge.'

Carrus looked uncomfortable. 'I am not sure there is any justification for paying you a refund either,' he said. 'It wouldn't be ethical.'

'In those circumstances,' said Patrice with a smile, 'I am obliged to decline your offer. That said, Monsieur Carrus,

I feel fortunate to have made your acquaintance. It has been a pleasure.' He stood up and the two men shook hands again formally.

No sooner had Patrice turned on his heel and left the room than Carrus picked up the telephone to call his second-in-command. Maurice Alexandre, another former Polytechnicien, had been deputy director general since 1955, having been encouraged to join the business by his father-in-law who had been a PMU director in the 1930s. Alexandre was working on the installation of new totalisator machines at racecourses but, like Carrus, he had little personal interest in racing and gambling.

'I have seen Des Moutis,' said the director. 'It's a complete deadlock. He wants an extra one per cent. What a nerve. No question of giving in to him.' Alexandre concurred.

Half an hour later Patrice was on the phone to his friend Alain Ayache. After leaving the PMU offices the Centralien had gone to a café round the corner on the Rue d'Artois and ordered a double *tasse* that was considerably stronger than the PMU's blend, and a token for the telephone in the back. Ayache laughed out loud when Des Moutis recounted the conversation he'd just had with Carrus. 'Wait until you've hit them a few more times,' he said. 'Then they'll be desperate to pay you the one per cent.'

Ayache was right. The following Sunday Patrice was back in the Café Lutétia in Boulogne-Billancourt betting 60 million francs on a Tiercé race at Enghien and winning 90 million. When he got to work the next day there was a message from his secretary to please ring Monsieur André Carrus. When they were connected the director general explained that he and his colleagues had thought over the pros and cons of the situation and had decided to grant Monsieur des Moutis his wish. He added that if Patrice would like to come and see him in his office that morning he would outline the details of the new arrangement while also presenting him personally with a cheque, plus one per cent commission, for his latest win.

Later that day Patrice met up with Alain Ayache at his favourite café-restaurant, Le Flandrin on Avenue Henri-Martin in the heart of the 16th. Des Moutis told Ayache about the PMU's volte-face. 'Can you imagine Ladbrokes or Bill Hill giving in that easily?' he asked. The friends laughed and, for perhaps the only time in their lives, raised a glass to the Pari-Mutuel.

Chapter 8

Over the course of the next few months Patrice presented himself most Sunday mornings, as agreed, at the PMU office on Rue Penthièvre. Each time, his pockets were filled with hundreds of combination bets and bundles of cash.

After he had handed over the originals he took the countersigned *bordereaux* back home to Saint-Cloud, and more often than not he was back at Rue Penthièvre the next day to collect his winnings. But in an act of generosity towards the Boulogne-Billancourt café which had lost his custom, Patrice kept just two-thirds of his one per cent commission and gave the remaining third to the Café Lutétia owner, André Calmels.

Des Moutis could afford to look after his friends. His racecourse ban was now approaching seven years which ought to have been devastating for a man with such a passion for the sport. But he was enjoying ample compensation from his Tiercé coups which were the talk of Longchamp, Saint-Cloud and Auteuil, and he was flattered by the number of people – ranging from his former bookmaking clients Suzy Volterra, Roger Saint and the *Comte* de Kerouara to Marie Thérèse's eminently respectable father – who wanted tips and advice. As long as it wasn't a race where he was betting personally Patrice was happy to oblige.

Another old racing friend regularly placed his bets by cheque but then, one day, the cheque bounced and, although his selections were the correct ones, the PMU refused to pay out. Don't worry, said Des Moutis. I'll fix it. And he did.

It was a similar story when another associate failed to collect her winnings within the payment deadline and was told by the PMU that her bet had expired. 'Don't worry,' said Patrice again. 'I'll fix it.' And he did, each time finding that his status and reputation in the eyes of the PMU management guaranteed him a level of preferential service accorded to no other punter in France.

He still couldn't go racing in person but the wretched business with Roger Taupin and the Police des Courses et Jeux seemed to be in the past, and Patrice told friends that his bookmaking would soon be in the past too. He hardly needed it when every time he turned up at the Rue Penthièvre or the Rue la Boétie the PMU executives bowed, scraped and smiled as if they were old-school Côte d'Azur casino owners from Beaulieu or Menton welcoming Russian royalty in the *Belle Époque.*

The same executives were acutely aware of the amount of money they were turning over, convinced that sooner or later Patrice's luck would run out. So they played the game. When Des Moutis won they congratulated him over flutes of champagne. When he lost – and he didn't lose often – they commiserated over a glass of good Scotch. Patrice was happy, healthy and rich. It was surely the golden run he had anticipated that night in Le Grand Cercle with Marie-Thérèse in 1958.

As the entente cordiale continued between the PMU and its biggest customer, the French people were witnessing the dramatic end of the affair between their President and the supporters of *Algérie Française*. By the end of 1960 Charles de Gaulle had privately concluded that the Algerian war was unwinnable and that the only answer was to negotiate independence with the FLN and attempt to get the best deal possible for the French colonists. In public he continued to make soothing noises, declaring in his 1961 New Year address that France would 'protect all her children'. But the beleaguered *pieds noirs* and their allies in the French army had their doubts, and on 30 March 1961 their worst fears were realised when the government confirmed that peace talks with the FLN were under way.

Elite military units in Algeria, including most of the officers and NCOs of the Foreign Parachute Regiments, were incensed by what they saw as the betrayal of their fallen comrades by a President who owed his position as head of the Fifth Republic to the army's backing. The de facto leader of the rebels, General Raoul Salan, recalled to Paris by De Gaulle in 1958, had slipped back into Algiers and now he placed himself at the head of an armed insurrection. Along with the Algerian born air force General Edmond Jouhaud, he led the so-called 'Generals' Putsch' on 22 April with the aim of overthrowing De Gaulle and transferring power to a military cabal.

Rebel tank units were said to be mobilising in the forests outside Paris and ready to move when the signal came. But to the generals' dismay the putsch crumbled as quickly as it had begun. Army conscripts tuning in to their recently issued transistor radios heard the sonorous tones of their President, who wasn't about to step down, beseeching them to do their duty. The vast majority of them stayed loyal forcing Salan, Jouhaud and the other ringleaders to go in to hiding. The Fifth Republic, unlike its predecessors, had stood firm.

But the crisis wasn't over yet. The killing went on at a daily rate in Algeria while some of the disaffected para's and other regulars who'd gone underground joined forces with embittered *pieds noirs* to form the Organisation de l'Armée Secrète or OAS. Patriots to some, right-wing terrorists to others, the OAS dedicated itself to assassinating De Gaulle while also launching a campaign of intimidation and bombing in both Algeria and mainland France.

Public opinion remained split and there were OAS sympathisers in high places, including the upper echelons of the racing community. But De Gaulle's security services were prepared to be every bit as ruthless as their enemies, and by July 1961 numerous rebel officers were in prison awaiting trial in front of a special military court. Their prospects didn't look promising as the government affirmed that enemies of the state, no matter how distinguished or principled, would be crushed.

The violent headlines were on everybody's mind come *le départ*, or the start of the annual *vacances*, on 1 July. Between then and Bastille Day, on 14 July, droves of people left the city for the beaches and the countryside. Extra trains were laid on to accommodate them, and an additional 24,000 Garde Mobile officers put on standby to cope with the expected carnage on the roads. French motorists in that period were alarmingly indifferent to things like speed limits and sobriety, and on every public holiday, be it Bonne Année, Toussaint, Quatorze Juillet or whatever, the highways were littered with burnt and battered vehicles and mangled bodies. To make matters worse the OAS were expected to try to add to the mayhem by ambushing General de Gaulle's presidential Citroën as he and his wife left Paris for their country home in Colombey-les-Deux-Églises, and the police had been ordered to shoot to kill if they saw a suspect car.

In the capital temperatures soared to 35 degrees as the usual throng of tourists, undeterred by the heat and the threat of terrorism, crowded into the Louvre and Notre-Dame and packed the outdoor tables in the restaurants, cafés and bars. The city reeked with the scent of *frites*, sweat and foreign cigarette smoke, and Patrice, who had just become a father for the fourth time, longed to get away. But before he could begin his own family holiday in Brittany, Des Moutis had some serious betting to attend to.

On the night of 30 June–1 July he worked until dawn deciding on his Tiercé selections for the Grand Prix d'Amiens the following day. The race was taking place at Le Tremblay, a picturesque semi-rural racecourse about ten miles outside Paris. The fourteen-runner contest over a mile and three furlongs was the 398th Tiercé since its inception. The hot favourite was a horse of Baron de Rothschild's called Talar, whose rider Roger Poincelet had recently won the Epsom Derby on Psidium, a 66-1 outsider owned by Patrice's old client Etti Plesch.

Talar had winning form on soft ground, and information Patrice received from his jockey suggested he might not be comfortable on the sun-baked turf at Le Tremblay. The gambler decided to leave him out of his calculations and make the 9-1 chance Kopa, trained by René Pelat, the brother of his Biarritz trainer/friend Georges Pelat, his main or 'base' selection. It was an inspired choice. Talar may not have liked the firm ground but he ruined his chance anyway by pulling too hard and dissipating his energy in the early stages. He finished a well-beaten eighth and Poincelet was whistled at by disgruntled punters as he returned to unsaddle, while Kopa cantered to an easy victory with two of Patrice's other selections, Malfaiteur and Tetralogie, finishing second and third.

Des Moutis had started to colour code his various Tiercé permutations to indicate the scale of the profit he estimated he'd make if they won. An all-white permutation represented only a small gain and an all-black a possible return of ten per cent or more, with various shades of grey in between. Patrice believed that the Kopa–Malfaiteur–Tetralogie result was in the category of anthracite or light grey and, from the odds offered on each horse on the morning of the race, he expected to collect three or four times his 80-million-franc stake. As he had also backed Suzy Volterra's horse Dicta Drake, winner of the prestigious Grand Prix de Saint-Cloud on 2 July, it should have been an excellent weekend.

But when Patrice heard the official Tiercé return from Le Tremblay on the radio on the Sunday evening, he discovered that the payout was no more than even money. He would get his stake money back but, instead of a gain in the region of 300 million francs, his winnings would be just 80 million.

Des Moutis was furious. For the estimated return to have contracted so sharply a considerable sum of money must have been bet into the pool on the same horses *after* he had left the Rue Penthièvre. It was a scam. And in Patrice's eyes the only people who could feasibly have perpetrated it were executive employees of the PMU, who he suspected must have looked at his selections after he'd left their office and then backed the same horses for themselves. So much for the charmingly old-fashioned relationship with André Carrus and his staff. The idyll had been shattered. The bureaucrats and *fonctionnaires* had stitched him up.

Early on the morning of Monday 3 July Patrice went to the PMU HQ in the Rue la Boétie. His mood was as dark as the headlines in his daily paper *Le Figaro*. Nineteen people were dead and seventy-four injured after weekend attacks by the FLN in Algeria. Five more had lost their lives in 110mph collisions on French roads *en route* to the south. And the death had been reported of Ernest Hemingway – the Nobel Prize-winning author who had a huge following in France – who had died from a self-inflicted shotgun wound at his home in Ketchum, Idaho. Mourning his loss, the obituary in *Le Figaro* talked of a split personality who had long anticipated 'a rendezvous with death'.

When Des Moutis arrived at Rue la Boétie, the PMU director general and his assistants saw for the first time another side to the personality of the usually composed Centralien. Gone was the aristocratic phlegm and good manners. In its place were expletives and street slang. 'He'd completely lost it,' reported one witness. 'It was as if he'd been stung by a bee.' Patrice got straight to the point, accusing Carrus of double-crossing him in much the same way as President de Gaulle had deceived the Algerian colonists.

The director general's explanation was that a tipster in a popular Marseille newspaper had recommended the same horses in the same order as Des Moutis. This was how Carrus accounted for the 'disappointing' Tiercé return.

Patrice couldn't believe it. 'I have a horror of being taken for a fool,' he railed. 'How many readers do you think this columnist has and what would be their typical bet? Ten francs? Thirty francs? For the odds to have contracted that much all of Provence would have had to follow this man's tips.'

Carrus insisted that betting turnover in departments in the south of France like Bouches-du-Rhône, where Marseille was situated, and the Var and Alpes-Maritimes, homes of Toulon and Nice, was regularly among the highest in the country. He also brought up the result of the 1958 Prix de l'Arc de Triomphe won by the Irish challenger, Ballymoss, from a French horse, Fric, who had also finished second to Ballymoss in the Coronation Cup at Epsom in June. Neither of them was expected to win the Arc by local tipsters because it was thought they would be unsuited by the rain-softened ground. But because the visiting English and Irish punters at Longchamp backed the Epsom combination to a man, the Couplé odds returned by the PMU were unexpectedly short. Carrus said it was an unavoidable aspect of Pari-Mutuel betting.

Patrice was not consoled. If anything the explanations, or excuses, as he saw it, simply confirmed his original perception of the PMU as inefficient, restrictive and untrustworthy. He had wagered 80 million francs, not a sum he could afford to bet lightly, in the expectation that if he won he would enjoy a certain percentage profit. Instead the estimated payout had been slashed and Monsieur Carrus was telling him it was just one of those things.

The director general's deputy Maurice Alexandre found Patrice's behaviour illogical and insulting. He spoke later of what he claimed was the impossibility of PMU officials skewing the pool. Only ten or twelve people would have seen Des Moutis' bets, he claimed. And there was no way such a small group would have had access to the funds needed to depress the odds that much. Especially as they were forbidden to leave their posts at the Rue Penthièvre until 12.45 p.m. and, with no more Tiercé betting permitted after the 1 p.m. cut-off point, they would never have had time to go round *café-tabacs* shovelling on the money. Alexandre's advice to Patrice was that, even for mathematicians – and Monsieur Alexandre was one himself – it wasn't always possible to accurately predict a probable Tiercé return.

Des Moutis – who, according to Alexandre, had 'grumpily' accepted his winning cheque for 160 million francs – wasn't having it. He was convinced that they'd been planning an ambush like this for some time and had kept the necessary 'readies' on hand at the Rue de Penthièvre so that they could step in and make a killing for themselves.

'They have taken me for a half-wit,' he told Alain Ayache that night. 'But soon they will see what I am made of.'

Chapter 9

Des Moutis was convinced that the PMU could no longer be trusted and that elements within the organisation would tamper with his Tiercé bets again, especially if he played above a certain limit. Well, he had a plan that would fix that all right.

Saturday 8 July 1961 was the Prix Aguado at Auteuil, the summer's only Tiercé race over jumps. That morning Patrice went to the Rue Penthièvre as normal and handed over two million francs' worth of bets. It was small change compared to his usual wagering and he had no great confidence in his selections, but he wanted to lull Messieurs Carrus and Alexandre into thinking that the Le Tremblay episode was closed and it was business as usual.

When the result came through that afternoon Foumbam, the favourite in the Prix Aguado, had only finished eighth of the thirteen runners. The winner, Gala, was returned at 4-1 with two relative outsiders taking second and third place. Patrice, who had the trio in the 'any order' rather than the correct order category, made a gain of six million francs.

The next Friday was the 14 July Bastille Day holiday and the Prime Minister Michel Debré's spokesman promised

France it would be '*un jour magnifique*' with no fewer than seven fireworks displays scheduled in the capital alone. The OAS marked the occasion with new *plastique* attacks in both Algiers and Paris, while a 15-year-old Muslim boy was blown up outside Les Invalides when the explosive he was carrying in his pocket detonated prematurely. But despite the security concerns, General de Gaulle, as implacable as ever, was at the wreath-laying ceremony at the Arc de Triomphe at 9 a.m. prompt and later took the salute on Place Clemenceau as paratroopers loyal to the Fifth Republic marched up the Champs-Élysées.

Over the next forty-eight hours an estimated half a million Parisians joined the exodus from the city. The homegrown French rock star Johnny Hallyday was playing at La Baule in southern Brittany, and Jean Cocteau, the ageing artist and writer whose every movement was still reported faithfully in the gossip columns, was *en vacances* in Saint-Jean-Cap-Ferrat. Patrice's family were safely ensconced in Brignogan, far from the heat and the crowds, but he would not be joining them for another week.

On the morning of Sunday 16 July Des Moutis was back at the PMU office in Rue Penthièvre and seemed to be betting heavily again. He deposited a total of 30 million francs on a series of Tiercé combinations on the Prix du Vals des Fleurs at Saint-Cloud. The mile and a half race with a first prize of 30,000 francs – a mere fraction of Patrice's stakes – had seventeen runners and, while Des Moutis claimed that superstition played no part in his transactions, he did believe that, statistically, seventeen-runner races, like the Prix de l'Elevage in 1958, gave him his best chance of a big win.

The only thing the fleet of correspondents employed to give tips in *Paris Turf* could agree on was that it was a particularly open race with little to choose between the two favourites, Green Devil trained by Jacky Cunnington, and Adonius representing the stable of Henri van de Poele. Patrice fancied Adonius, who had run well over a shorter distance in his previous race, and he made him his base selection. But he also liked a colt called L'Uredo, owned by an old bookmaking client of his, Gerry Oldham, a rich financier with horses in both England and France.

Des Moutis did the maths and prepared his bets using the now-familiar colour chart to rate possible returns. Some outcomes were rated a white, some grey, while others were more ambiguous. When he had completed his sums he had a total of eighty combinations based primarily around three horses, Adonius, L'Uredo and an outsider called Foujita.

Patrice was at the Rue Penthièvre by the 8 a.m. opening time. He only submitted thirty of his permutations to the staff there, but each one of them was to be multiplied five hundred times, and the total stake was 20 million francs. The PMU inspectors assumed that was the full extent of the gamble, and Patrice did nothing to put them off. Declining the offer of a *café crème* – he had already drunk two cups of coffee at home before setting off – he left the office around 8.45 a.m. and walked back to where his car was parked behind the Hôtel Plaza Athenée ten minutes away.

The day was already hot and without a cloud in the sky. Slipping on a pair of dark glasses, Patrice settled down behind the wheel of his Mercedes, which he had been careful to fill up with petrol the previous evening, and headed back out towards Saint-Cloud and the western exits from the city.

Over the next three and a half hours he drove like a self-confessed 'madman', roof down, foot down, overtaking vacation-bound family motorists and accelerating away west towards Lower Normandy. He drove through the Sunday market town of Dreux, 73 kilometres from Paris. He drove through Verneuil in the department of the Eure with its pretty medieval churches and Norman half-timbering. He carried on through Argentan, the regional capital of the Orne and familiar to him from childhood, and Vire in the Calvados Bocage country of high hedgerows and narrow lanes. Finally he arrived in the seaside resort of Granville about 12.30 p.m. It was a journey of approximately 200 miles, and he had completed it in roughly three and a half hours. Even the late Aly Khan, a notoriously fast driver, would have been impressed.

Des Moutis had been to Granville many times, often sailing around the coast from Brignogan. The town was busy but not unpleasantly so as the first of its summer visitors enjoyed exploring the beaches, the narrow streets around the harbour and the old fortifications that included ugly remnants of the Atlantic Wall built by the Germans in World War II. The Occupiers had left in a hurry as General George Patton's 3rd US Army began the Normandy breakout in August 1944, but rusting armaments and old concrete pillboxes were still visible seventeen years later.

Patrice's destination was the local PMU bureau in a *café-tabac* near the harbour. When he walked in it was getting on for 12.45 p.m., just fifteen minutes before the *fermeture*, the cut-off time for placing Tiercé bets at *counters* across France.

Fortunately there were only a couple of other punters in the queue in front of him and their business didn't take long. Patrice got to the front and handed the clerk the small matter of fifty *bordereaux*, which had all been filled out the night before, and 48 million francs' worth of stake money. These were his principal bets combining Adonius, his base, with assorted other runners in what he hoped would be the correct order.

The young PMU employee looked at the tickets and the bundle of cash in disbelief. Each combination was to be multiplied five hundred times. This was impossible. This couldn't be happening. Not in Granville. Not to him. He started to say that before accepting a bet of this size he would have to call his superiors in Argentan, but the man standing in front of him with the expensive haircut and the shades and the smart open-necked white shirt, was polite but insistent. 'No need to ring them first,' he said. 'You can ring them after you've registered the tickets. It won't take long.' As the clerk hesitated Patrice slipped a 5,000 franc note across the counter and moments later the young man began to systematically validate Patrice's tickets in the machine.

Fifteen minutes later Des Moutis walked out of the bureau, his business done. He knew that by 2 p.m. the Argentan office would have been called and would in turn have contacted Rue Penthièvre in Paris telling them of the mystery punter in Granville and the scale of his gamble. Carrus and Alexandre would suspect immediately who that gentleman might be. But by then it would be too late for them to pump money in to the pool, depressing the odds, because no more Tiercé betting was permitted after the cut-off point.

The race wasn't off until 4 p.m. so Patrice walked down to a restaurant by the waterfront and proceeded to treat himself to a *grand plateau de fruits de mer* – oysters, *crevettes*, langoustines, *homard*, crab – washed down with a chilled bottle of Chablis Premier Cru, a glass of Calvados and a double *tasse*. Then, after a pleasant ramble around the harbour, he got back in his car and began the long journey back to Paris.

At 5 o'clock he turned on the car radio to listen to the RTF news bulletin and heard that Jacques Anquetil had won the Tour de France, that Gus Grissom was to be the second US astronaut in space, and that Brigitte Bardot was to star with Marcello Mastroianni in the new Louis Malle film, *Vie Privée*. After the news they read out the racing results. Adonius, ridden by Jean Massard, had won the Tiercé race, the Prix du Val des Fleurs at Saint-Cloud, from L'Uredo with the outsider Foujita, another one of Patrice's selections, in third place. The gambler whooped with joy. The combination of numbers 1, 13 and 15 had paid 1,465 francs to a 30-franc stake, and Des Moutis had them five hundred times in the correct order and two thousand five hundred times in the incorrect order. His total winnings came to 289 million old francs less his 68-million-franc stake and amounted to over £200,000 – more like £3.6 million today – which was his biggest haul yet.

The rest of the drive back to Paris was a leisurely Sunday-afternoon cruise through holidaying towns and villages, a nation at play, the shadows lengthening. But coursing through Des Moutis' veins was the glorious adrenaline high, the sense of affirmation and vindication, of a big gamble expertly planned and successfully carried off. He'd said that he would show them and he had.

Chapter 10

The Prix du Val des Fleurs was Patrice's last Tiercé coup that summer. Once his cheque for 289 million francs was safely in the bank, he joined Marie-Thérèse and the family at Brignogan, and then in August they went up to Deauville as usual.

Des Moutis went running along the boardwalk each morning before returning to join his wife for breakfast on the terrace of their suite at the Royal hotel. While others went to the races Patrice played bridge at the Hôtel du Golf, and one evening the couple went to see a Juliette Gréco concert at the Casino. The couple's contentment, it seemed, was complete.

But if Patrice had imagined the PMU would meekly accept his Granville coup as retaliation for the Le Tremblay episode, he was mistaken. In the week following the Prix du Val des Fleurs there was a council of war in Paris. It took place not in the PMU headquarters at Rue la Boétie but in the infinitely grander office of the new Minister of Agriculture, Edgard Pisani.

The department was located in the Hôtel de Balleroy, a palatial nineteenth-century building in the Rue de Varenne that was once the Paris home of the Marquis de Balleroy and his family, ancestors of the disgraced opium addict exposed in 1948. As successive generations of British politicians would discover, the agricultural and farming lobby enjoyed a powerful, not to say unassailable, position in French political life. And, as if to underline the point, the Ministry of Agriculture buildings dwarfed the Prime Minister's official residence, the Hôtel Matignon, further down the street.

In July 1961 Edgard Pisani had only been in his post a few months and was still getting his feet under the table. The 43-year-old, who had grown up in Tunis with part-French and part-Maltese parentage, had endeared himself to De Gaulle and Michel Debré by his patriotic service in the Resistance in World War II. After the war he'd served as a regional administrator before being elected to the Senate in 1954. Newspaper cartoonists mocked Pisani's beard, and Breton farmers complained about his ignorance of rural life, but the minister's skills were political and his chief mission was to ensure that French interests remained at the heart of the Common Agricultural Policy of the European Economic Community – a task he performed very well.

The Ministry of Agriculture was responsible for horse racing, while being answerable to the Finance Ministry about the health of the nation's cut from the PMU. In common with other ministers and Pari-Mutuel officials, Pisani appears to have known or cared little about racing and even less about betting. The Société d'Encouragement had invited him to a meeting one Sunday and, after lunch, he'd asked for some tips so that he could have a bet on the Tiercé. It had to be explained to him that all Tiercé bets had to be placed by 1 p.m. and that it was now after three o'clock.

To ensure that French racing's case was effectively presented at the summit, the Société d'Encouragement president, Marcel Boussac, attended alongside André Carrus, Maurice Alexandre and secretary general Pierre Crespin of the PMU. None of those present were especially enthusiastic about sitting in a stuffy government office – even a grandiose one like Pisani's – a week after Bastille Day, when everyone else who mattered seemed to be *en vacances*. But each of them had one pressing and overwhelming thought on their mind: after the audacity, insolence even, of the Granville stunt, what would Patrice des Moutis do next, and how far would he go? More Tiercé bets multiplied by five hundred? Or six hundred? Or even a thousand? What would be the limit and, if he kept winning, what would be the consequences for their respective constituencies?

Pisani spoke first. He admitted that he was not a specialist, but from what he could see he didn't need to be one. He may not have known much about horses and gambling but it was plain that the PMU was suddenly paying out hitherto unimaginably large sums of money to one man and foregoing revenues to the Agriculture and Finance ministries in the process. In Pisani's view this punter was obviously a crook and had to be stopped before he did any further damage.

Carrus, who spoke next, said that he didn't believe Des Moutis was a crook – at least not on the basis of what he'd done so far. The mild and scholarly Carrus expressed genuine admiration for Patrice's skill and intelligence and for the way he had organised and executed his plans. He was undoubtedly a man with considerable knowledge of racing and form as well as odds, and he had the funds to play with and the nerve to match. What worried Carrus, and his fellow bureaucrats

Alexandre and Crespin, was that, thanks to the scale of Patrice's betting, the character and allure of the Tiercé was now under threat. The seductive appeal of the bet depended on everyone, whatever their means, having a theoretically equal chance of winning the jackpot. If one rich, clever man, wagering huge amounts and multiple bets – and he'd had eighty combinations on 16 July – kept winning it every Sunday, would the rest of the punting population lose interest? What was equally disturbing, added Carrus, was that with so much riding on the outcome, a situation might arise where the big punter might ask himself: why leave things to chance? Why not try to influence the outcome by corrupting a jockey here or suborning a trainer there?

Then it was Boussac's turn. The 72-year-old tycoon had been the dominant figure in French racing for as long as anyone could remember, though by the early 1960s neither his commercial nor his bloodstock empires were as strong as they had been. His business partner Christian Dior had died in 1957, and three years later his successor, Yves Saint Laurent, had left to set up on his own. Boussac's textile mills were facing new challenges from third-world manufacturers, and his stud farms had so far failed to unearth worthy successors to his great stallions of the 1920s and 1930s. But, for all that, he'd retained the aura of a rich and powerful man who expected others to do his bidding, and a non-racing politician like Edgard Pisani was happy to go along with whatever the *grand propriétaire* recommended.

Boussac made it clear that his principal concern about Des Moutis was the possible effect of his activities on the French bloodstock industry. If prize money had to be cut due to a shortfall in PMU income, he said, the health and prestige of French racing would suffer and his fellow owner-breeders – like the new Aga Khan, the Rothschilds and Jacques Wertheimer, who was the part owner of Chanel – would move their best horses to England and Ireland. No doubt Boussac was also thinking of the health and prestige of his own stud and stable. But he was adamant that the link between betting on the Tiercé and the generous purses available to winning owners on French racetracks must be maintained.

The minister was right, he concluded. Des Moutis had to be stopped. But how? Boussac's suggestion, endorsed by Carrus, was that they should change the regulations surrounding Tiercé betting in an attempt to limit the maximum stake. The others all agreed.

Pisani's civil servants were ordered to consult further with Carrus and his PMU colleagues, and three weeks later, on 11 August, they announced their first rule change. From now on the PMU would refuse to register Tiercé tickets that involved more than twenty-five times the same combination of three horses. That would put a stop to bets multiplied by five hundred they presumably thought. Or maybe they just didn't think.

Des Moutis first heard about the rule change when he read a report in an evening paper. The family had returned to Paris and Patrice, Marie-Thérèse and their children were all present in the *salon* before dinner and everyone was reading to themselves. All of a sudden Patrice started laughing, louder and longer than it seemed he'd ever laughed before.

'What is it, Papa?' asked his daughter Nicole. 'Are you all right?' 'Oh yes,' her father replied. 'I'm fine. There are just some people that I find very amusing.'

Des Moutis and Carrus had talked either in person or over the telephone as many as ten or twelve times that year. In the first week of September Patrice rang up the director general's office and said that he'd like to come in and see him again. Carrus, cool but courteous, said he was welcome.

When the gambler arrived at the Rue la Boétie this time, smartly dressed as always in a dark suit and tie and with the ever-present cigarette in his hand, he was at his most charming. Indeed Carrus would have described the Centralien's mood as confident bordering on cocky. But then Patrice thought he had a right to be cocky. 'You might have told me in advance about your new rule,' he began. 'You were going too far,' said Carrus. 'It had to stop. After bets multiplied by five hundred, why not by a thousand next time?' 'Do you want to prevent me from playing altogether?' asked Patrice. 'No, no,' said Carrus, trying not to get irritated. 'You will still be able to multiply your bets by twenty-five. And twenty-five times a Tiercé in the correct order will still be a big win.'

'But you've got it wrong,' said Patrice, smiling. 'What do you mean?' asked Carrus. 'You've got it wrong,' said Patrice again. 'Your minister's rule change should have been twenty-five times per customer ... not per ticket.' Carrus looked flustered. 'I don't know what you mean,' he said. 'It's very simple,' said Patrice, slowly. 'A one-word difference. The new rule should limit each customer to twenty-five times their stake per combination *not* per ticket. If I want to multiply my bet by fifty I just have to present *two* tickets for twenty-five times each ... Do you understand?'

Carrus did understand and he felt foolish but also annoyed to have it spelled out to him by Des Moutis. 'Why don't you ring up the minister now,' suggested Patrice, 'and tell him his mistake? Today's Friday. You could have changed it by Sunday morning.'

Carrus didn't want to ring up the minister, not with Des Moutis standing next to him in his office. And he didn't like Patrice's manner. Why had he been so keen to tell him personally that he'd seen a flaw in the new rule? Was it bravado? Or just childishness? Carrus felt he was beginning to see through the Des Moutis charm and that the gambler was 'like a man determined to seduce my daughter'. Well, Carrus was proud of the Tiercé. He felt it was one of his life's principal accomplishments and he was determined to defend its honour as he would his own.

'I repeat that the change we have made is a reasonable one,' said Carrus, 'and we expect all players to abide by it.' Patrice shrugged and smiled. He already knew how he was going to profit from the new arrangements. And if the PMU wanted to ignore the obvious that was their business. But no one could say they hadn't been warned.

Before he left the director general's office Des Moutis mentioned, as if in passing, that he wouldn't be bringing his Sunday Tiercé bets to the Rue Penthièvre any more. He was sorry to lose his one per cent commission, but from now on he'd bet wherever it suited him. In Boulogne-Billancourt. In Suresnes. In Neuilly. In central Paris. In Finistère when he was away on holiday with the family. Who could tell where he'd be?

Chapter 11

Paris in the autumn of 1961 presented an uneasy contrast between superficial glamour on the one hand and underlying violence on the other. Newspapers and magazines were filled with images of the Shah of Iran and his wife visiting the Paris Motor Show, but the biggest news story of the day was barely mentioned by the French media. Eleven policemen had been killed by the FLN between the end of August and the beginning of October. The murders and injuries to seventeen more officers in turn sparked the brutal suppression of a peaceful demonstration by Algerians in the capital on Sunday 18 October. It would be forty years before the full story would emerge of how up to two hundred Muslims met their deaths at the hands of a rampaging Paris police force who threw many of their victims into the Seine and left them to drown.

Charles de Gaulle never acknowledged the October killings. In his end-of-year address he referred to the one hundred and seventy-three terrorist attacks that had taken place in 1961 and warned that, while he would still attempt to negotiate with the FLN, the Algerian problem would continue to dominate in

1962. The nation, he said, would have to gird itself for further violence.

On a more upbeat note De Gaulle hailed what he claimed was the unique capacity of the French for 'equilibrium and unity', while his Prime Minister Michel Debré outlined optimistic plans for 24 per cent growth in the economy over the next four years. Yet shortly before Debré's announcement, the revenue and equilibrium of the Pari-Mutuel took another hit from Patrice des Moutis.

At the end of November Patrice gambled 480,000 francs on the Prix Georges Brinquant, a Tiercé hurdle race at Auteuil. He wanted to multiply his bets by one hundred, so to get round the new rule change he filled out four series of tickets combining the same three horses and multiplying each bet by the legal limit of twenty-five. That Sunday afternoon Le Ponant II, a 15-1 chance that Patrice felt had been underrated by the tipsters, prevailed narrowly over the favourite Explorateur and an outsider called Blaps. Patrice had the trio in the correct order and his total winnings came to 5,400,000 new francs, the French currency having been officially revalued, with one hundred old francs now worth one new franc.

When Des Moutis got to his office in Neuilly the following morning he put off getting on with the usual risk assessments and insurance claims, and instead rang Carrus. The gambler was in a triumphant mood. 'Well, Monsieur Director,' he said. 'I was a good sport. I told you what would happen.' 'You did what I should have expected,' said Carrus, sounding like a weary schoolmaster vexed by a delinquent but clever pupil who keeps getting the better of him. 'I'm disappointed . . . but not surprised. Now the rules will have to be changed again.' 'How are you going to try to stop me now?' asked Patrice, laughing. 'By putting up barricades outside the *café-tabacs*?'

Carrus declined to answer him. But in the first week of December the PMU announced that they were going to alter their Tiercé rules for a second time. From now on no punter would be able to play the same combination of horses more than twenty-five times whether they presented one or several tickets. Boussac and Pisani both backed the latest change, and the mood in the Ministry of Agriculture was turning ugly. Pisani knew that he'd been made to look ridiculous by the ease with which Des Moutis had been able to exceed the new limit and he wanted to contact *Commissaire* Taupin at the Police des Courses et Jeux and get him to investigate Patrice's methods.

Carrus hoped that he could still appeal to Patrice's better side and respect for government institutions and responsibilities. They were both graduates of the Grandes Écoles, after all, and almost members of the same club. Didn't that stand for something? Carrus called Des Moutis up just before Christmas and, in a fatherly tone, advised him not to overreach himself. Or one day, he warned, you may become the victim of your own greed. Patrice courteously wished Monsieur Carrus a *Joyeux Noël* and then, citing pressure of work, put the phone down.

Des Moutis could see no reason not to go in for the kill. Everything, he felt, was in his favour. Carrus, Alexandre and their *fonctionnaires*, along with the racecourses and Pisani and his civil servants, were all so intoxicated by their Tiercé and the beauty of its creation that they seemed to think it was inviolable. But to Patrice it was no more foolproof than the Maginot Line, the deceptively secure fortification the French army's blinkered strategists thought would protect them from the Germans in

1940. The Wehrmacht had seen the weakness in the stationary French defences and chose to go round them rather than attack head on.

Des Moutis could see a comparable weakness in the latest rule change adopted by the PMU. It stipulated that no punter could have more than twenty-five times the same combination of three horses in any PMU office. But it didn't say anything about punters backing the same combination twenty-five times in a number of different offices.

As the French settled down uneasily to celebrate Christmas, De Gaulle's warnings about Algeria still ringing in their ears, Des Moutis prepared to launch his biggest coup.

Chapter 12

The thoroughbred world of French flat racing at Longchamp and Chantilly was the sport's equivalent of Neuilly and Passy in the 16th *arrondissement*. Jump racing at Auteuil was one rung down the social ladder but still smart.

French trotting racing – where the driver, not jockey, sits on a small sulky, or cart, and the horses must never break into a canter – was more like greyhound racing in the UK. Colourful, cheaper and more egalitarian than the flat but not without its share of *demi-mondaine* high rollers and swells, and just as popular as flat racing and steeplechasing with punters nationwide when it came to trying to win the Tiercé.

The premier trotting racetrack in France was Vincennes, situated in parkland on the edges of Joinville-le-Pont, about ten miles southeast of Paris. The biggest trotting race of the year, the Prix d'Amérique, run at the end of January, drew as big a crowd as the Arc or Grand Prix de Paris, with betting turnover to match.

Vincennes raced regularly throughout the winter months supported by small-change punters clutching a *Paris Turf* in one hand and a beer or a hot dog in the other. On 1 January

1962 the main event was the Prix du Croisé-Laroche over 2,000 metres. Conditions in Paris were dry, sunny and bitterly cold, but the trotters raced on an artificial sand-based surface immune to frost, and the Prix du Croisé-Laroche was to provide the Tiercé race for New Year's Day 1962. It was predicted that, with a bumper crowd on course and thousands if not millions of *café-tabac* punters looking forward to a bank holiday bet, the pool would be one of the biggest of the year.

Des Moutis had no objections to betting on trotting racing. It wasn't a setting in which he'd expect to encounter his smart flat-racing friends like Suzy Volterra and Etti Plesch. If Longchamp and Auteuil were close to the 16th *arrondissement*, Vincennes was nearer to the working-class suburbs of eastern Paris and attracted racegoers to match. But as a gambling medium, trotting presented much the same challenge to Des Moutis as a conventional horse race. And being a former – and still occasionally active – bookmaker as well as a punter, he had almost as many contacts among the owners, trainers and drivers at Vincennes as he did in Chantilly and Maisons-Lafitte.

With the big pool in mind, Patrice rang round his connections on 30 December attempting to glean information about current fitness and form. Then, believing the prospects were fair, he decided to hit the Vincennes Tiercé with everything he had.

If Marie-Thérèse hadn't fully realised it when they first met, or after the racecourse ban in 1953, she must have known by now that she had married more than just an ardent racing lover. Her husband was an obsessive gambler in thrall not only to the adrenalin rush of a successful coup but intoxicated by – and addicted, even, to – the audacity of his battle with the PMU. With each new enterprise the stakes were rising, perhaps dangerously so, as Carrus had warned. But there was no stopping Patrice now. If the PMU and the government were continually going to try to clip his wings, that challenge had to be taken up. Friends could see that he was on a journey with no end yet in sight and, with his confidence surging and the enemy in his sights, he was determined that each new Tiercé gamble should be bigger than the last.

On the morning of 31 December Patrice broke the news to Marie-Thérèse that he would he not be accompanying her and the children on the journey to Brignogan for the traditional *Bonne Année* celebration with her family that night. He cited 'pressure of work' that would unavoidably detain him in the capital. His wife, who set off on the drive to Brittany with their children after breakfast, was naturally disappointed and she may well have been angry. But she cannot have been totally surprised.

Patrice spent New Year's Eve alone. Édith Piaf was performing at the Olympia Music Hall in Paris. Charles Aznavour was at the Alhambra. Princess Grace and Prince Rainier were attending a New Year Gala at the Sporting Club in Monaco, and Jean Gabin and Jean-Paul Belmondo were in Deauville playing old and *nouvelle vague* gangsters in a film based on a Georges Simenon short story set partly in the Normandy hotel. But there were no hotel galas or fireworks and dancing for Patrice. He had withdrawn hundreds of thousands of francs from his bank account and bought half a dozen books of Tiercé tickets from a *café-tabac*. And while others saw in the New Year at parties and in clubs and restaurants, he was at home in Saint-Cloud, working out his selections, filling out his

Tiercé bets, drinking coffee and smoking cigarettes like a cool and solitary existential hero.

'*Bonne Chance, '62*' proclaimed the RTF television announcer at midnight. But Patrice didn't believe in luck. He believed in information and the form book, and he had complete faith in his mathematical system.

Limelight II, the favourite for the Prix du Croisé-Laroche, was a popular and well-known horse who had won the corresponding race twelve months earlier. Back in August he had triumphed in a similar Tiercé race at Enghien-les-Bains. Limelight's driver was also a popular if controversial figure. Roger Vercruysse – or *Verte-Cuisse* (Green Thighs), as he was nicknamed – had a reputation for sometimes inexplicably losing races when he appeared to be on a good thing, and for equally unfathomable victories on rank outsiders. Expecting his horses to always run to form was inadvisable.

After discussions with his sources, Patrice gained the impression that Limelight was neither as fit nor as fancied as some correspondents believed. Indeed, Des Moutis concluded that 1 January was not going to be Limelight's day and that he would definitely not win. Buoyed by a contrastingly strong message for the second favourite, Loustic II, who had finished runner-up over the course and distance on Christmas Day, Patrice struck out the favourite, along with ten of the other nineteen runners, and made Loustic II his base. He also liked a mare called Lobelia, another Tiercé regular with winning mid-winter form, and decided to back Loustic and Lobelia in multiple combinations with the other six horses.

Patrice was going to wager 24,000 francs on each combination, multiplied by twenty-five as decreed by the new

PMU limit. But that was only the beginning. The gambler had pinned a giant map of Paris to his office wall and, equipped with a list of PMU outlets that he'd acquired from Monsieur Calmels at the Café Lutétia, he'd proceeded to underline one hundred of the cafés with a red marker pen. The bureaux were mostly on the western and south-central sides of the city, and on New Year's Day Patrice planned to visit as many of them as he could, on foot, betting 24,000 francs times twenty-five on one of his permutations in each one of them. If he could reach anywhere like one hundred offices he would have bet in the region of 60 million francs and comfortably, but legally, exceeded the PMU shop limit that had been designed specifically to stop him.

Des Moutis set his alarm to go off at 6.30 a.m. on 1 January and by 8 a.m. he was showered, dressed and breakfasted and had driven down to his office in Neuilly and parked his car. The PMU Café Sainte-Foy was only a few steps away, and two minutes after the 8 a.m. opening time Patrice had placed his first 24,000-franc bet and had his yellow ticket punched by the machine. Then, with the list of PMU offices in his pocket, he set off. The hours spent running, skiing and cycling proved invaluable as he hurried from *café-tabac* to *café-tabac*. From Neuilly to the Porte de Saint-Ouen to the Place Clichy – headquarters of the Police des Courses et Jeux; from La Villette to Pigalle and the Grands Boulevards; from Les Halles to the Champs-Élysées.

The sun was shining but there had been a hard frost, and the streets were almost deserted except for a few early risers enjoying a New Year's Day constitutional, and little groups of exhausted revellers belatedly wending their way home. Patrice passed dustbins overflowing with empty champagne bottles and discarded decorations. He passed prowling cats enjoying the unaccustomed absence of lorries and cars. And as he hurried up Avenue de Wagram towards the Arc de Triomphe he passed the entrance to the Club de l'Étoile where youthful partygoers, or *twisteurs*, who had spent the night dancing to Chubby Checker, were just emerging onto the street, refreshed by the hot coffee, croissants and brioches supplied free of charge by the management.

At 11 a.m. Des Moutis stopped at a café for a rum St James but there were still twenty-four more PMU bureaux underlined in red on his map and he couldn't linger. By midday he was working his way from the Place de l'Alma to the Trocadero and back up towards Place Victor Hugo and the 16th *arrondissement*. As the 1 p.m. *fermeture* time approached, he realised he wasn't going to get to all of the hundred bureaux on his list. But he'd only left out eight, which wasn't bad going. Wagering a grand total of 55,200,000 francs, he had backed his main base line combination over one thousand three hundred times, comfortably exceeding the PMU's ineffectual limit.

Cold, tired and hungry, he might normally have gone on to lunch at Le Flandrin for half a dozen oysters, maybe from the Marennes-Oléron Basin, and a *choucroute garnie* or *paupiettes de veau*. But he had promised Marie-Thérèse that he would be at Brignogan in time for a family dinner that night, and he wasn't joking when he'd told Alan Ayache that his wife would lay him out with a rolling pin, or worse, if he was late. There was just enough time for him to dash home, change and pack an overnight bag before getting back in his Mercedes and heading west.

It was five o'clock, the light fading fast, and he was driving past the entrance to the Haras du Pin, the National Stud in

Lower Normandy, when he heard the Tiercé result on the car radio. Maurice Bernardet, the announcer, reported that Loustic II had won the day's big race, the Prix du Croisé-Laroche at Vincennes. An outsider, La Coulances, had finished second and the mare Lobelia was third. Patrice heard later that the favourite, Limelight, and his driver Roger Vercruysse, had dropped back after the first quarter mile and, in racing parlance, had 'made no show'.

La Coulances was another one of Patrice's selections; the mathematician had done it again. Working it out swiftly in his head he calculated that he'd won approximately 492,660,000 francs or roughly £4.9 million in British money. Never before had one player won such a colossal sum from the PMU. Half a billion francs. It would take an average white-collar worker in France twenty-five years to earn that much in wages. It was more than eight times the prize money for the 1961 Prix de l'Arc de Triomphe, and it was more than half the total pool gambled on the Tiercé of 1 January 1962.

Patrice stayed one night at Brignogan. He embraced his wife and hugged his children. He saluted his parents-in-law and welcomed in the New Year, and he ate and drank his fill. And in bed that night with his arms wrapped around Marie-Thérèse and feeling her *froideur* thawing by the minute, he told her they would be going on a vacation very soon. To the sun. Or to the ski slopes. And only to the very best hotels.

They could go anywhere they liked.

Chapter 13

Patrice returned to Paris the next day, and on the morning of Tuesday 3 January – having telephoned ahead first – he made his way to the PMU director general's office in the Rue la Boétie.

Paris was still in a state of high alert. There was a butchers' strike in the capital, but it was not unanimous and Max Prosper, a non-striking butcher in the Rue de Versailles, had been a casualty of the first *plastique* bomb of the year. The device had been set off by the FLN in retaliation for an OAS bazooka attack in Algiers which had killed sixteen and wounded ten.

Tension was also mounting in the office of Monsieur André Carrus. Having first negotiated a security checkpoint at the corner of Rue la Boétie and the Champs-Élysées, Patrice found the director general's inner sanctum crowded with other departmental heads and *fonctionnaires*, including Maurice Alexandre and Pierre Crespin. All of them were talking about the Prix du Croisé-Laroche. When they looked up and saw Patrice the talking stopped. Some of them gasped. Others shook their heads. Des Moutis, loving the audience and the attention, milked the moment for maximum effect.

'It was you,' blurted out one awestruck young official. 'The ninety-two winning tickets. It was all you.' 'Yes,' said Patrice. 'It was me. As I could have told you . . . your second rule change . . . was not very well thought through.' 'How did you do it?' asked another.

Des Moutis took a chair. 'At least this time you didn't have to send four cyclists ninety-two times to the Café Lutétia,' he observed. Then he recounted his grand tour of New Year's Day morning, wagering no more than the legal limit of twenty-five times the same combination in each shop. Carrus and Alexandre looked appalled, but some of De Moutis' younger listeners hung on his every word as if he were a fabled navigator or Polar explorer returning from the ends of the earth and describing what amazing things he'd seen there.

'There is one thing,' said Patrice when he'd finished. 'This time I don't want a cheque. This time I want to be paid in cash.' 'Out of the question,' began Alexandre. 'You are not telling us you are running short? It's not our practice and would complicate things quite unnecessarily. We always issue you cheques. Why the change now?'

'I said I do not want a cheque, Monsieur Alexandre,' replied Des Moutis, raising his voice. 'And if I were you I would think very carefully before refusing to pay me my legal winnings.' 'All right, all right,' interrupted Carrus. 'There is no need for anyone to lose his temper.'

Patrice explained that he didn't want a cheque because he feared his name would be made public and then every tout in Paris would come up to him afterwards and try to tap him for a loan. After fifteen minutes' wrangling, Carrus agreed and, with a sigh, took out his chequebook and made out an official PMU cheque, instructing his bank, Crédit Lyonnais, to 'Pay the Bearer' the sum of 492,660,000 francs.

Patrice left number 83 with the piece of paper in his pocket and walked back to where his car was parked on the Rue de Berri. Circumventing the Champs-Élysées, he carried on along Rue Pierre Charon, turned left on Avenue George V, crossed the Seine on Pont de l'Alma and, twenty minutes after leaving Andre Carrus' office, pulled up outside the PMU's bank, the Crédit Lyonnais branch on Avenue Bosquet.

With his cheque in one hand and a smart, black leather holdall in the other, he took his place in the queue behind an elderly housekeeper arguing about her pension payment. When Des Moutis got to the counter he presented his cheque to the cashier. The young man looked at it in evident, jaw-dropping amazement, reading and re-reading it several times. It reminded Des Moutis of the PMU clerk in Granville.

The cashier looked up suspiciously at this unknown man in a black trenchcoat who he would always remember leaning sideways against the counter and fixing him with what seemed to be an ironic look. It was the same trademark Des Moutis expression, one eyebrow raised, with which he had greeted Carrus at their first meeting a year earlier.

'Please, Monsieur. Do you have some form of identity?' asked the cashier. 'You are not very trusting, my friend,' said Patrice. 'The cheque is all in order. It says "Pay to Bearer" and I have signed the back, as is common usage.' 'But it's an enormous sum, Monsieur,' said the cashier. 'Enormous, no doubt,' agreed Pat. 'But you can give me the notes in extra large denominations. That'll make it easier to carry.' The cashier hesitated. 'If you will excuse me one moment, Monsieur,' he said. 'I will be back shortly.'

A couple of minutes later the young man returned, preceeding a plump, bald, well-tailored man who introduced himself as the branch manager. Smiling unctuously he invited Patrice into his office. 'It was a very important cheque,' explained the manager. Never before in his thirty years at the bank had he seen a personal cheque for such a sum. If the gentleman would just show him one piece of identity there in the privacy of the office to put his mind at rest, he said. It would be strictly between the two of them.

'Monsieur le Directeur,' replied Des Moutis. 'It is a cheque written out to the bearer. The bearer is me. You have my identity. Do you want to pay me or not?' 'I am so sorry, Monsieur,' said the manager. 'But I must ask for a written confirmation from my client, the Pari-Mutuel Urbain. I am sure you understand.'

Patrice was angry when he left the bank. But he decided to leave his car outside the branch and walk back to the Rue la Boétie, and by the time he'd crossed the river and walked up Avenue George V and across the Champs-Élysées he'd calmed down. When he walked into Carrus' office the director general looked even less pleased to see him than he had been earlier that morning. 'What is it now?' he asked wearily.

'Your bank won't pay,' Patrice said to Carrus. 'Maybe your account doesn't have that much money in it?' 'That's absurd,' said Carrus. 'What on earth are you talking about, man?' Patrice repeated what had happened in the Avenue Bosquet, and at once Carrus got on the phone to the Crédit Lyonnais, confirmed the validity of the cheque and agreed to supply a written confirmation that Patrice would bring back with him by hand.

It was past midday when Des Moutis arrived at the branch a second time. He handed over the letter that had been typed by Carrus' secretary stipulating that the PMU cheque for 492,660,000 francs, dated 3 January 1962 and made out to the bearer, should be paid in full to the gentleman presenting the note. This time the plump manager wasn't smiling.

'I am sure,' said Patrice, 'that in your thirty years at the bank you have never had to pay out such a sum either.' The manager look pained.

As Des Moutis leaned against the wall of the manager's office smoking a Gauloise, a team of clerks trooped in and out bringing the 492 million in large denominations. When Patrice had counted it all he threw the bundles nonchalantly into his open valise, while more bank officials gathered at the office door to watch. Patrice could feel their eyes popping out of their heads. He stood up, buttoned his trenchcoat and, with a nod and a smile towards the manager, strolled out through the branch and out onto the street. He could feel the eyes still following him from the doorway as he opened the car and put the black holdall on the front passenger seat of the Mercedes. Then, with a last look back at the bank staff, he got into the car and drove away down Avenue Bosquet towards the Boulevard Saint-Germain, to lunch with Marie-Thérèse at Brasserie Lipp, and on towards his destiny.

Chapter 14

Edgard Pisani was emphatic. The Pari-Mutuel, said the minister, was an integral part of France's financial infrastructure and, unless they were checked, the assaults of Patrice des Moutis threatened its health and wellbeing, as well as undermining the authority of the state. The challenge had to be faced down.

Marcel Boussac's view, warning of the consequences for French racing and breeding, was equally sombre, and André Carrus, Maurice Alexandre and Pierre Crespin all agreed that drastic steps had to be taken.

On 16 February 1962 the PMU announced a third change to the rules surrounding Tiercé betting. From now on no one would be permitted to have more than 60 francs on any Tiercé combination, multiplied a maximum twenty-five times, whether they were placing their bets in one café bureau or a multitude of bureaux. To underline how far they would go to back up this change, it was also specified that any attempt to breach the new rule would constitute a criminal offence.

When Patrice heard about the latest development he was incensed. To him it was further evidence of the cowardice and incompetence of the PMU monopoly and a diabolical restriction of the rights of French punters whatever their means. He wasn't prepared to leave it there either, though for the moment, sated by his colossal New Year's Day triumph, he lay low.

As winter turned to spring there were no fresh Tiercé coups and no new big winners emerging centre stage, allowing the PMU management to wonder if they were finally rid of Patrice des Moutis, and whether their latest measures had closed him down. In truth they had merely lost him, temporarily, to Megève and Val-d'Isère, to the beaches and warm seas of Senegal and, on his return, to long hours spent running, cycling, sailing and playing tennis.

Patrice and Marie-Thérèse, who wanted for nothing, could truly echo the words of Françoise Hardy's song 'Tous les Garçons et les Filles' about having 'a happy heart without fear of tomorrow'. But outside the charmed world of the 16th arrondissement France continued to be in the grip of conflict. In March the government declared that an accord had been reached with the FLN, and in an April referendum more than 90 per cent of French voters approved the terms negotiated for Algerian independence. A second plebiscite, which took place in Algeria in July, resulted in an even bigger majority in favour. But by then hundreds of thousands of pieds noir had already begun heading for the exit. Many of them were fearful of FLN warnings that there were two ways for them to leave the country: with a suitcase, or in a box. In the end the authorities in Paris graciously allowed them two suitcases each but most of the Harkis, or Arabs, that had remained loyal to France, were abandoned to their fate.

In Paris there was relief but no rejoicing that the war was officially over. The Prime Minister Michel Debré, angry at what he regarded as the surrender of Algeria's oil and gas reserves, resigned and was replaced at the Matignon by Georges Pompidou, an urbane ex-banker who had once taught literature at the Lycée Henri IV. Edgard Pisani remained at Agriculture, and Valéry Giscard d'Estaing, a smoothly self-promoting aristocrat, was appointed as the new Finance Minister.

The OAS continued to try to disrupt the Algerian settlement despite the arrests of many of their leaders. In April the air force general, Edmond Jouhaud, was captured, tried and condemned to death, and then the kingpin, Raoul Salan, was arrested and put on trial for his life in the Palais de Justice in Paris. The setting was suitably grave and public interest intense. But to the outrage of the Élysée Palace, the tribunal was swayed by Salan's past military service and sentenced him to life imprisonment rather than a firing squad. Jouhaud, who spent nearly five months on death row, subsequently had his sentence commuted too.

Still the remnants of the OAS refused to give up, and in August they came as close as they ever would to killing the President. On the evening of Wednesday 22 August De Gaulle's black Citroën DS, preceded by motorcycle outriders and followed by a back-up car, was on its way from the Élysée to Villacoublay airfield near Versailles from where the General and Madame de Gaulle were due to fly by helicopter to their country home at Colombey-les-Deux-Églises.

As they passed through the suburb of Petit-Clamart the convoy drove into an OAS ambush organised by a blue-blooded French airforce officer, Lieutenant Colonel Jean-Marie Bastien-Thiry, who was part of an autonomous group calling itself the

Old General Staff. The OAS had two cars and their gunmen were armed with sub-machine guns. Over one hundred and eighty rounds were fired by the attackers and several of them pierced De Gaulle's car, passing within inches of his head, and blew out a rear tyre. Miraculously neither the General, who remained unmoved, nor his wife, who was understandably shaken, nor any of his aides-de-camp was injured. The convoy carried on safely to the airfield where De Gaulle was heard to remark that the OAS were very poor shots.

Behind the presidential façade De Gaulle was outraged by the threat to his wife and innocent bystanders, and he ordered the Interior Minister Roger Frey to set the hardmen of the Corsican 'Action Service' on the would-be assassins' trail. Bastien-Thiry was quickly tracked down, tried and convicted, and this time De Gaulle wasn't tolerating any merciful interventions. On 11 March 1963 the 35-year-old air force officer was shot by a military firing squad at Fort d'Ivry. The execution provided a gripping opening scene to *The Day of the Jackal*, the debut novel of Frederick Forsyth, who was working for Reuters in Paris at the time, and was a stark reminder of the sweeping powers of the Fifth Republic.

If peaceful citizens longed for idle pleasures to distract them from the long-running Algerian psychodrama, they had the usual array of sport, showbusiness and crime to choose from. But then at the end of the year elements of all three combined in a spectacular homegrown racing and gambling scandal that would run and run.

The designated Tiercé race for Sunday 9 December 1962 was supposed to be a hurdle race at Auteuil but in the preceding week heavy rain hit Paris, clogging gutters with the last remaining fallen leaves, saturating the ground in the Bois de Boulogne and rendering Auteuil unraceable.

On Thursday the 6th the PMU announced that Sunday's Tiercé had been switched to a trotting race at Vincennes: the Prix de Bordeaux, to be run over 2,500 metres for a first prize of 70,000 new francs. On Friday 7 December twenty-three runners were declared for the contest, but the following day no fewer than six were withdrawn, which was unprecedented in the eight-year history of the Tiercé. Then, on the morning of the race, came the news that a horsebox belonging to the trainer Robert de Wulf and transporting one of the favourites, Mon Cher, had broken down 80 kilometres from Paris, leaving just sixteen runners to face the starter. Fortunately for De Wulf, Mon Cher wasn't his only entry. He was also running a strongly fancied contender called Meiningen, who was already safely stabled at Vincennes.

The *Paris Turf* tipsters liked the chances of Normandie, a recent course winner driven by Roger Vercruysse, along with Obedience, who was in the care of *Verte-Cuisse*'s brother Mathieu. Among the others under consideration were Mars II and Milo d'Amour, who had both finished strongly last time out. But it was Meiningen, owned by Madame Bérénice Moreau and driven by the suave Bernard Simonard, who was reported to be particularly fit and well.

Carrus was not in Paris on 9 December. The PMU director general had gone to a family reunion in Bordeaux. Alexandre was not in the Rue Penthièvre office either. He was busy playing bridge, the one pastime he had in common with both Carrus and Des Moutis. The man left in charge for the day was the secretary general, Pierre Crespin, who – unusually for a senior *fonctionnaire* – was not a graduate of the Grandes Écoles. A neat, precise man in his early forties, Crespin had a small moustache like Carrus, but there the similarity ended. Whereas the director general could recall and recite past results and gambles off the top of his head, Crespin depended on his meticulous files and card indexes, and had a reputation for exactitude.

The Prix de Bordeaux was the fourth race at Vincennes and was not due off until 3 p.m. The news of Mon Cher's non-participation had come through about one o'clock. Half an hour later Crespin received a call from the PMU regional centre at Lille reporting some unusual betting patterns on the race. Several dozen Tiercé tickets had been registered all backing exactly the same combination of five horses and all wagering the maximum 60-franc stake multiplied by four. Among the five selections were the favourite Meiningen, Mathieu Vercruysse's mount Obedience and an outsider called Nemrose, who were all picked to finish in the first three in the correct order and any order.

Crespin told his staff to ring round the other regional headquarters and ask if they were seeing similar moves for the same five horses. Within the hour they started ringing back. First on the line was the greater Paris region. Then Bordeaux. Then Lyon. Then Marseille. All of them reported significant numbers of bets on the same combination, to the same stake and multiplied by four. As Pierre Crespin digested the information he began to realise he was watching a carefully orchestrated plan. Someone was mounting an attempted coup. Crespin rang Vincennes racecourse and warned officials there to be on the lookout for unusually large and identical bets on the numbers 3, 4 and 2 combination – Meiningen, Obedience and Nemrose – and to report back to him at once if they saw anything untoward. Then he sat back to wait.

The conditions at Vincennes were atrocious. The temperature had risen during the morning and a pale sun was shining, but there were still sheets of water on the track and some of the drivers wanted the meeting called off. By three o'clock, after three races had been run, the course was like a quagmire. Even the customary pre-race canters left the horses and drivers splattered with mud, and by the time the runners in the Prix de Bordeaux had gone a few hundred metres, the drivers' silks were unrecognisable.

What was also striking about the race, as the correspondent for *Le Figaro* reported the next day, was that within a hundred metres of the start the majority of the runners appeared to have no chance of winning it. In the *Le Figaro* columnist's words it was '*une course qui laisse une drole d'impression*' – a race which left an odd impression. Was it the going? he wondered. Or was it something else? Everyone would have their own opinion.

One professional's view was that it was still a relatively early stage in the winter trotting season and a number of the runners were having their first race for some months. In the circumstances their owners and trainers wouldn't have wanted them to be subjected to too hard a race first time out and the drivers would have been instructed accordingly. It was assumed that regular punters, familiar with the sport, would understand that these horses would 'come on for the run' and were best passed over on this occasion.

That was certainly the case with a trotter called Oscar RL, who was anchored near the back of the field the whole way but who would go on to finish second in the much more valuable and prestigious Prix d'Amérique the next month. There was also scepticism about the performance of Mars II, who belatedly made up ground to finish fourth and looked as if he could have been first or second under a more robust drive. His pilot, Domingo Perea, said afterwards that he'd been blinded by the mud on his goggles and couldn't see where he was going.

But there were no fitness or steering problems for the market leaders Meiningen and Obedience, and the race swiftly developed into a match between the two, with Meiningen eventually prevailing by half a length. Trundling home in third place and dragging the mud with him was the 28-1 outsider Nemrose, whose driver was a popular Vincennes character called Michel-Marcel Gougeon, better known as 'Minou'. Students of form agreed it was a remarkable performance by the long shot who had finished plumb last in his previous two races and had supposedly been carrying an injury. Other than Mars II and the fifth-placed Milo d'Amour, who was also given a lot of ground to make up, the rest of the runners, including Roger Vercruysse's mount Normandie, were unsighted.

The time of the race turned out to be almost three seconds slower than the next event on the card, which was run over the same distance and in identical conditions. But the slog through the Flanders mud, as some journalists were describing it, had thrown up exactly the outcome predicted with such unanimity by those groups of like-minded punters in Paris, Lille, Lyon, Bordeaux and Marseille. Numbers 3, 4 and 2. Meiningen, Obedience and Nemrose resulting in a Tiercé return of 399.50 new francs to a three-franc stake for placing them in the correct order, and 79.90 for listing them in '*désordre*'.

As news of the outcome reached Pierre Crespin in his office in the Rue Penthièvre he thought again of those unusual betting patterns. The secretary general was naturally suspicious. Was the result a legitimate coup and nothing to be surprised about in the extreme conditions? Or had the finishing order been determined in advance? Crespin talked again to the management at Vincennes and rang Carrus in Bordeaux on a pre-arranged number. Carrus advised him to refrain from making any public statements until a full inventory of the race had been compiled, as he feared that premature talk about race fixing would only damage the sport and erode confidence in the PMU.

On the Monday morning Crespin relayed the director general's views to an anxious Maurice Alexandre in his office at the Rue la Boétie. But at 11 a.m., while the two men were still procrastinating, some dramatic news came in from Lyon. A local newspaper, Le Progrès, was reporting that on the Sunday morning a team of three men and one woman had gone round the city in a taxi visiting thirty PMU offices. In each one of them they had placed identical bets on the same combination of five horses in the Prix de Bordeaux: 2, 3, 4, 13 and 14. Their total winnings were believed to be in the region of 105 million new francs, though there was a suspicion that the unnamed punters may have breached the new rule about twenty-five being the maximum number of permissible tickets on any one Tiercé combination.

When Crespin called the main PMU office in Lyon, he was told that the three men and one woman had returned in a car early that morning requesting immediate payment. But the PMU senior management had recently introduced another new rule, or procedure, stipulating that winnings of 10,000 francs or more would only be paid by cheque, and that claimants would first have to supply proof of their identity. When one of the punters in the Lyon office had been asked to identify himself, he had hesitated and then said that he'd come back later.

The story was picked up rapidly by radio stations and the national press and by lunchtime there were reports of a similar operation in Lille, where three men and a woman in a car had visited thirty PMU *café-tabacs* on the Sunday and had, again, placed identical bets on the same Prix de Bordeaux combination. Early editions of the evening paper *France-Soir* were running headlines about '*un Gang du Tiercé*' that might have executed the perfect scam at the expense of 'the poor victim', the PMU.

Carrus had arrived back at headquarters that afternoon to be told that a number of other Tiercé winners had turned up at the Rue Penthièvre office also seeking to be paid. Pressed by officials as to where they had placed their bets, they admitted they had struck them in Lyon, insisting they just happened to be passing through there over the weekend. The Rue Penthièvre staff were told to ask the punters to return the next day with more ID and, according to one clerk, some of them had guilty expressions on their faces as they left the building.

By mid-afternoon on the 10th, PMU bureaucrats had finally completed a full assessment of the Prix de Bordeaux Tiercé. They had established that eighty-three winning punters had filed exactly the same bets, each of them wagering 3,600 francs, split between six different permutations, and winning 300,000 francs apiece. There had also been a series of winning forecast bets on the first two finishers resulting in additional gains of four million one hundred thousand new francs or roughly £400,000 sterling.

That there had been some kind of collusion or pre-arranged plan between the eighty-three punters seemed beyond the shadow of a doubt. How many of them had placed the bets themselves and how many had entrusted others – in Lyon, Lille and elsewhere – to place their bets for them? It remained to be seen whether they were truly all part of a team under the direction of a mastermind. And if so, who was he? Well, the PMU officials had a pretty good idea who it was, and initial enquiries seemed to have given them good reason. Among the eighty-three identical winners were the brother-in-law, tailor and good friends of the PMU's old acquaintance, Monsieur Patrice des Moutis.

Some of these lucky punters had already come to the notice of the PMU in the summer of 1961 when they were found to have backed the same horses in the same Tiercé races as Patrice. This time they seemed to have been players in a massive operation reaching to all four corners of France, and to the PMU directors it bore all the hallmarks of the latest and most audacious attempt by their old rival to circumvent the rules. But *this* time, Carrus reasoned, Des Moutis had broken the law.

The fourth rule change, introduced by Edgard Pisani earlier that year, was quite clear. No punter, whether they were betting in one PMU outlet or several, could have more than a 60 francs times twenty-five maximum bet on any Tiercé combination. And if it could be proved that the eighty-three winners of the Prix de Bordeaux were not betting solely for themselves but were proxy punters for Patrice des Moutis, then they, and the elegant gentleman from Saint-Cloud, could face criminal charges. There were also grounds for suspicion that the syndicate had bribed some of the owners and trainers to withdraw their runners the day before, and had then paid the drivers to fix the outcome of the race.

Maurice Alexandre was all for going straight to the Police des Courses et Jeux, but the first instincts of Carrus and Crespin were to try to bury the affair if at all possible so as to avoid a scandal. In the case of Carrus, there also seemed to be some last lingering sympathy for a man he had initially liked – admired, even – and a desire to keep the law out of his affairs. But then the decision on Patrice's future was taken out of the director general's hands.

On 13 December Edgard Pisani and his fellow ministers at Interior and Finance ordered that payment to the suspicious Prix de Bordeaux Tiercé winners should be blocked pending further investigation. That same day the Société de Vincennes, the racecourse management company, lodged an official complaint with the public prosecutor's office, alleging that the eighty-three winning punters had violated the rules of the Pari-Mutuel Urbain on the orders of Patrice des Moutis, and accusing Des Moutis of attempted conspiracy to defraud. Only at this early stage of proceedings French law required that the accused could not be named in public so the official legal document lodged with the prosecutor merely referred to an accusation '*contre X*'.

The parties may not have realised it at the time, but it was the beginning of a legend – the birth of an almost-mythological figure who would intrigue and enthral not just the racing world but all of France in the years to come. Who was this mysterious Monsieur X they asked? And was he a hero . . . or was he a thief?

Chapter 15

The tabloid newspapers, always happy to knock the government and state bureaucracy, loved it. Monsieur X, they declared, must be a brilliant man to have had the brains and courage to fashion such an ingenious scheme. He was surely the 'Tamer of the Tiercé' – not a thief but a Robin Des Bois Moderne who had dared to take on the PMU, the 'infernal machine' invented to part the 'little people' from their money.

In *café-tabacs* across the land where the self-same little people dreamed every Sunday of a life-changing win, everyone was talking about it. Had the Prix de Bordeaux consortium really breached Article 8 of the PMU rules on maximum stakes? And what about the trotting drivers? If there was a plot were they complicit in it? Reporters kept returning to the fact that soon after the start there were already no more than two runners in with a winning chance with the others seemingly 'disinterested' in the outcome, as Gerard Daudan, special correspondent for *L'Aurore* put it.

The press pack descended on Vincennes at the next meeting and confronted the drivers with various accusations. Bernard Simonard, the driver of the Prix de Bordeaux winner Meiningen, disclaimed all knowledge of any chicanery. The 34-year-old, a suave figure with big hair, a houndstooth jacket and a red polo-neck jersey, stood up well under cross-examination, but some of his fellow drivers were less comfortable. When Minou Gougeon was unable to explain the remarkable improvement in form of the third-placed Nemrose his trainer brother Jean-René – known as 'the Pope of Vincennes' – retaliated by refusing to speak to the press about anything. His fellow trainer Jean Riaud and a thunderously muddy Roger Vercruysse also went on the attack and violently ejected one journalist from the weighing room.

The *syndicat* of trotting race owners and breeders were equally indignant, and put out a statement protesting the honesty and probity of their sport. But simultaneously there was a rumour that 'Monsieur X' – whoever he might be – had been tipped off by an informant on the Vincennes management committee about six runners and their drivers who would be prepared to finish out of the places in the Prix de Bordeaux if the incentive was big enough. Or was it three runners who could be induced to finish in the first three? The story got more exaggerated each time, as a payment of a million new francs was alleged to have changed hands to secure a deal.

When Patrice des Moutis, who had not been publicly named and had yet to be questioned about the race, was told of the rumours, he described them as 'delirium'. His official position, reiterated repeatedly to Marie-Thérèse, whose brother was one of the winning punters, was that he hadn't personally wagered so much as a centime on the race and had merely offered 'advice' to a group of friends. For the moment he was staying at home in Saint-Cloud, biting his tongue and still somehow hoping to preserve his anonymity. He had managed to avoid identification after his earlier big Tiercé coups, with the sums of money won reported in the papers but never his name. But with the stakes getting higher all the time how much longer would it be before he was exposed?

The PMU meanwhile were trying to improve their image. Spokesmen talked up the Tiercé's role as a vital source of profits for the French economy, while also underlining its contribution to the health of French racing, which had received 716 million francs from the Pari-Mutuel in 1961.

An official Police des Courses et Jeux enquiry into the Prix de Bordeaux was now underway, headed by Patrice's old adversary, *Commissaire* Taupin. He was to place evidence before Judge Georges Raynaud, a senior figure at the Parquet de la Seine, who in turn instructed Judge Pierre Simon to take day-to-day charge of the case.

Taupin wasted no time briefing against his old foe, talking darkly of a mastermind who was one of the best *techniciens* of the Tiercé, well known in the racing milieu and in the capital. This man, claimed Taupin, was a former Centralien and engineer who had used his mathematical knowledge to make a series of spectacular gains on the racecourse and, on his advice, millions had been wagered on the Prix de Bordeaux. He painted a lurid picture of a huge conspiracy to isolate up to nine runners, leaving it so much easier to win on the rest. *Les tricheurs*, or fraudsters, he claimed, some of them from Paris, some from Marseille, preferred to stay in the shadows. But under PMU rules those of them who failed to present their winning tickets by close of business on Friday 14 December would lose their money anyway.

As the drama continued into a second week public interest showed no signs of abating. Britain's Conservative Prime Minister Harold Macmillan was meeting with President de Gaulle at Rambouillet in what would turn out to be a futile attempt to persuade the General not to veto British membership of the Common Market. 'London must bow to the demands of the Six,' proclaimed Agriculture Minister Edgard Pisani in an uncompromising declaration of intent. The Australian jockey Neville Sellwood, who had died in a fall at Maisons-Laffitte in November, was posthumously awarded the Cravache d'Or, or Golden Whip, which is presented every year to the champion flat-racing jockey. And there were juicy crime stories for the nation to feed on too, like a spectacular jewel robbery in Cannes, and the discovery of a headless body in a suitcase in the left-luggage office at Austerlitz station in Paris. But not even murder, nor the sight of the Duke and Duchess of Windsor at the premiere of *Follow Me*, a topless revue starring the Bluebell Girls at the Lido, could displace Monsieur X and the Gang du Tiercé from the front pages.

On 17 December twelve of the eighty-three winning punters who had had their payments blocked announced that they had retained the Paris lawyers, Messieurs Alessandri and Sarfati, to represent them and bring a counter-action against the PMU. With much fulmination and outrage they also attempted to hit back in the propaganda war by parading one of the so-called 'little men' beloved by the papers. Marcel Legluer, a barman from Rue Saint-Benoît, had won 360 francs on the Prix de Bordeaux Tiercé, picking the correct horses out on the Sunday morning. But he too had had his winnings blocked. Did Monsieur Legluer, a respectable married man, really look like a fraudster? And was this the behaviour of a reputable and trustworthy organisation? If there was a plot, claimed the punters, it was a conspiracy to defraud the public by the PMU.

By January 1963 a combination of leaks, briefings and innuendo had begun to establish in the public's mind that Patrice des Moutis – Centralien, mathematician and Neuilly insurance broker – and Monsieur X were one and the same man. Pressed to comment by the papers, Patrice was sticking to the line that he hadn't wagered a sou on the race himself and had merely been acting as a 'technical advisor' to a group of friends. Some of them were family, like his brother-in-law Henri; some were long-standing acquaintances, like his tailor at Sulka on the corner of Rue de Rivoli; and others were punters he had known for years, like the professional gamblers 'Julie' Carrax, Jacques Guyadet, René Lacoste and Jean Seuret. They had wanted to try to win the Tiercé. He had suggested that the Prix de Bordeaux at Vincennes might be a good opportunity, as less than half the runners were likely to be fully fit. But if they had all followed his recommendations to the letter . . . well, that was entirely their choice not his.

Then on 7 February came a dramatic announcement from *Commissaire* Taupin and his team working under the direction of Judge Simon. Of the eighty-three punters whose winnings had been blocked and who were allegedly all 'friends' of Patrice des Moutis, no fewer than forty-five of them had a criminal record. Included among them were the Pigalle pimps, the Perret brothers, who were associates of the Bande des Trois Canards or Three Ducks gang, one of the most notorious bands of racketeers in Paris.

The police appeared to savour the revelation, whereas some of the initial admirers of the dashing Monsieur X were left confused and perturbed. What on earth was the connection between Des Moutis – old boy of the Lycée Janson de Sailly and the École Centrale, husband of Marie-Thérèse Queret and resident of Neuilly-sur-Seine and Saint-Cloud – and men of this type? Were they really his friends? And was he now their partner in a fraudulent enterprise? Or was there another more nuanced explanation?

When Des Moutis was running his bespoke bookmaking service in Paris in the 1950s it's highly likely that he sometimes came into contact with the rival illegal businesses run by the *Milieu* or French Mafia. They too had their own wealthy clients who didn't all come from the underworld. Maybe they laid off bets with one another and even shared a few big-hitting punters? Maybe they got on rather well? Would it have been so surprising if the Breton aristocrat was one of those urbane, sophisticated men of the world, found equally in Paris, London and the USA in that era, who were to varying degrees fatally attracted to bad company? To the nocturnal world of clubs, gangsters and les mauvais garçons?

It was a theme that would recur continually throughout the rest of Patrice's life.

Chapter 16

In the first week of January 1963 Des Moutis was summoned to appear before Judge Simon in his chambers in Nanterre on the northwestern edges of Paris. Under French law suspects are first interviewed at length by a judge or investigating magistrate who can ask all manner of questions – including about a suspect's biography and family background – to establish whether or not there may be a case to answer.

By now there were three interrelated investigations into the Prix de Bordeaux involving both Taupin's men at the Police des Courses et Jeux and the Brigade Criminelle of the Police Judiciaire from the Paris police headquarters at 36 Quai des Orfèvres. They were not only trying to determine if there had been a conspiracy to break the PMU rules on maximum stakes, and whether the winning punters had acted independently and of their own volition; they were also enquiring into the trotting race drivers and trainers to find out if the race had been run entirely on its merits.

Patrice, who had a lawyer present, was twice cross-examined under oath for a day at a time by Judge Simon. Throughout the interrogation he stuck to his story that he had not personally placed any bets on the Prix de Bordeaux – indeed, he claimed he'd been away in London when the race was run, flying on the Sunday afternoon – and had merely been acting as an advisor to a group of friends. When the full list of runners was published on 7 December, he said, he had been asked for his views on the race. He'd responded that if they were serious about trying to pull off a really big Tiercé win they should attempt to recruit more punters – each of them wagering no more than the twenty-five times 60-franc maximum permitted stake – and spread their bets out around the country.

He admitted that he'd been delighted when he'd heard that his friends had won, and defended their actions as a perfectly reasonable attempt to get round the outrageous PMU limit, which he said should be overturned and would not be tolerated in any proper free-market betting system.

When Judge Simon asked him about the apparent involvement of the Bande des Trois Canards, he replied that his friends had obviously taken his advice about numbers and gone out and recruited right and left. If some of the extra punters had an address in Pigalle, what was that to do with him? The judge should go and ask them about their bets in person. Judge Simon said he intended to do just that.

In Patrice's presence, *Commissaire* Taupin told the judge that he believed Des Moutis had given stake money to each of the eighty-three successful players, in a flagrant breach of PMU rules. The proxy punters, or straw men, were to get a share of the profits in return for helping Des Moutis exceed the limit on maximum stakes. He also believed Patrice had drawn up the list of PMU bureaux to be hit nationwide and, along with his lieutenants, had recruited known gangsters to take part in the operation because they were prepared to run the risk of being involved in a criminal conspiracy. Patrice's motive, he alleged, was pure greed combined with malign hostility towards the PMU. Pressed again about his role by the judge, Patrice continued to insist that he hadn't personally bought a single ticket.

As the hours ticked by, Des Moutis remained effectively a prisoner in the prosecutor's office, and an increasingly conspicuous absentee from the family home. Mindful of how angry his wife would be getting, he challenged the judge to either raise the stakes or fold. 'If you want to keep interrogating me,' he said, 'why not charge me?' So they did.

In the third week of April – a month after the execution of Jean-Marie Bastien-Thiry – Des Moutis and fifty-one of the Prix de Bordeaux winning punters, including his 'lieutenants' Jules Carrax, Jacques Guyadet, René Lacoste and Jean Seuret, were informed that they were to be officially charged with fraud and conspiracy to defraud. As well as the three separate police enquiries there was also the countersuit being brought against the PMU by some of the punters, and the whole judicial process rapidly became enmeshed in the objections and obfuscations of clever lawyers and bogged down in legal minutiae.

It would be eight years before Patrice finally faced his accusers in court. In the meantime the legend of Monsieur X continued to grow in the public's imagination. The majority of café-tabac punters interviewed in the immediate wake of the Prix de Bordeaux expressed sympathy and even admiration for Des Moutis, and no love for the Pari-Mutuel. The gambler's earlier Tiercé triumphs were now also public knowledge, and he was acquiring an aura of diabolical cunning, which could work to his advantage as long as he was seen as a lone individual refusing to be cowed by the state rather than as part of a criminal conspiracy. But even as early as 1963, some of Patrice's friends, like Alain Ayache, feared for his long-term safety and counselled caution in taking his campaign against a powerful state-backed institution too far.

The qualified respect that Carrus had once felt for Des Moutis was not shared by other elements within the PMU, who were already doing their best to undermine Patrice's image, reminding anyone who cared to listen that Monsieur X's supposed friends included gangsters and pimps. Worrying connections, surely, for a Breton-Norman gentleman and resident of Saint-Cloud? It was a calculated attempt to appeal to France's conservative Catholic element who were always sensitive about law and order issues. And a not so subtle hint that the government of the Fifth Republic, having pretty much finished off the OAS, could now afford to turn its attention to the threat represented by lawbreakers of a different hue.

Chapter 17

In Paris in the early 1960s the Bande des Trois Canards were almost as infamous as the Kray brothers were in London. And just as the twins retained a base for the 'firm's' activities in the heart of the East End, the Trois Canards were indelibly associated with Pigalle. But the leaders of the gang were not from Paris. Like other *Milieu* in post-war France, they had migrated to the capital from the hot south.

The Rue de la Rochefoucauld is a long, narrow street winding its way north from the Church of La Trinité through the 9th *arrondissement* and on towards the heart of Pigalle. Despite some recent gentrification, it's remained a multi-ethnic area of small, local shops and businesses albeit with organic groceries and *boulangeries* replacing the more old fashioned *crémeries* and *fruiteries* of the 1950s. Number 46 is a music shop which sells and repairs saxophones, trumpets and trombones. Number 48, next door, used to be a tourist dive selling Johnny Walker Black Label for 15 Euros a shot. But back in the 1950s and 1960s, number 48 Rue de la Rochefoucauld was the Bar Cabaret Les Trois Canards and the headquarters of the gang of the same name.

The original leaders of the gang were three meridional boys made good or, depending on your point of view, made very very bad. Eugène Matrone, Gaëtan Alboreo and Marius Bertella were all born and brought up in Marseille, the French sons of Italian parents. Seasoned hoodlums by their early teens, the trio moved up to Paris in 1951 and swiftly established a presence in Pigalle. The principal racket in the area was prostitution and the pimps were mostly *pieds noirs* like the French-Algerian, Jimmy Mignon, and the half-Jewish Perret brothers, whose mother Leonie had fought with the Americans in World War II.

The Perrets had a bar of their own, the Cabaret le Soleil d'Alger on the Rue Bergère, and, like most of the *pieds noirs* racketeers, they also dabbled in loan sharking and illegal gambling. But acutely aware of territorial divisions, they stuck to the southern half of the *quartier* around the Rue du Faubourg-Montmartre. The northern sector, stretching on up towards Montmartre itself, was the territory of the 'Unione Corse' who had businesses all across the city. Number 48 Rue de la Rochefoucauld was situated almost exactly halfway between the two camps.

The new boys intimidated the *pieds noirs* but showed respect to the Corsicans who, like themselves, had gravitated to Paris after the war. In return for that loyalty and regular tithes from their businesses, Matrone, Alboreo and Bertella were able to run an ever-more profitable organisation, expanding into legitimate commerce like the wine and spirits trade as well as extorting protection money from other bar and café owners and retailers.

Marius Bertella had bought the Trois Canards in 1951 from Baro Ferret, a *manouche* or gypsy guitarist who had played with Django Reinhardt in the 1930s. Ferret, a big handsome man with dark eyes and slicked-back hair, had been a black marketeer during the Occupation and continued to pimp and fence stolen goods well into the post-war era.

Nighttimes at the club were hot and noisy with the *manouche* bands playing bebop in the upstairs room, an eclectic crowd dancing to the music, and the drinkers spilling out onto the street. Well-to-do Parisians looking for a vicarious late-night thrill often turned up by car after dinner, boasting of their familiarity with the red-light district and overtipping the doorman until he let them in. Brushing shoulders with the underworld after dark was sexy and exciting, enabling members of *le Gratin* to feel like Broadway swells visiting the Cotton Club in 1920s Harlem, briefly swapping the formality of their world for something edgier and more alive.

But there was another side to the Trois Canards that the Pigalle 'tourists' didn't see. Down below the bar was a cellar where members of the French Gestapo had tortured their victims during the war. The cellar was still in use, and unfortunate business associates of the Canards who had fallen behind with their payments were sometimes taken down there and subjected to similar beatings and mutilations. Men like Nono Griglia, a *hôtels de passe* owner from the Rue des Lombards, who suffered at the hands of the gang in May 1964 and whose body was later found stripped and scarred in the forest in Saint-Germain-en-Laye.

Their well-deserved reputation for violence helped the Canards take over more of the neighbourhood's illegal pursuits, including street bookmaking and the clandestine card games, where the *Milieu* were the bank and took a commission from winning players. Stakes were high and participants came from the worlds of sport, politics and finance, as well as the underworld, and the Canards laid on generous amounts of alcohol and food while providing credit at a price. *Commissaire* Taupin and the Police des Courses et Jeux wanted to know if Des Moutis had ever been present at one of these occasions despite his preference for Le Grand Cercle and protestations that his game was not poker but bridge.

By 1963 new waves of Marseillais, Toulonnais and Nicois emigrés were finding their way to the Rue de la Roche-foucauld, and the Bar Les Trois Canards functioned like a Grande École of crime, awarding newly arrived southerners their higher education certificate and *une bonne place* in the criminal hierarchy. The top earners in the *Milieu* remained the Corsicans, who retained the privileges they'd enjoyed inside France since the dying days of World War II. With the Marseille docks under their control, and no fear of disruption by the government, the Corsican Godfather Antoine Guérini and his brothers had been shipping opium from Turkey to Marseille and the US for years. But after the French military defeat at Dien Bien Phu in 1954, and the collapse of French power in the region, there was a dramatic increase in the amount of opium derivative trafficked from Indo-China, and emerging challengers to the 'Emperor of Marseille' began to see the potential profits to be made from refining the opium in laboratories in Provence and manufacturing it into pure heroin to sell to the American market. The rivals felt they should have a share of the casino gambling business too, and it wasn't long before war broke out between the old and younger generations.

At 5.30 a.m. on Sunday 14 April 1963 the club manager Jean-Baptiste Andréani had just left Le Grand Cercle in Paris after another long but profitable night. Baptiste was driven back to his apartment on the nearby Avenue Foch but, as he got out of his car, a vehicle pulled up behind him and two shotgun blasts were fired from an open window. Baptiste was hit in the legs and the base of the spine. He survived but he never walked again, which was apparently the intention. 'They meant to seriously wound not kill' said the Cercle's financial director Jean-Baptiste Deorli, who arrived on the scene, perhaps not coincidentally, just as the attackers were driving away.

The shooting was allegedly ordered by the Gaullist and Corsican businessman Marcel Francisci in retaliation for Baptiste's refusal to give him a share of the profits from Le Grand Cercle. But the word in the racing and gambling fraternity was that the Bande des Trois Canards had decided to throw in their lot with Francisci and had supplied a gunman for the attack. Baptiste's assailant was said to be a relatively junior member of the Canards called Jacky Imbert, also known as Jacky le Mat, or Jacky the Madman, in Provencal dialect.

Imbert, who was born in Toulouse in 1930, had done time for beating up his mother-in-law's violent lover, and had also served with the French army in Algeria. After being discharged for persistent breaches of military discipline, he'd settled in Marseille before making his way to Paris in the 1950s and coming under the tutelage of the Canards. Loyal, brave and a natural leader, he'd teamed up with another ambitious young southerner called Gaëtan 'Tany' Zampa and had been involved in break-ins, armed robberies and debt collection. But the pair always maintained that Paris was just a staging post and that one day they would go back to Marseille and become Godfathers in their own right.

Imbert was a punter who loved both horse and trotting racing and, along with the Perrets and other members of the Trois Canards, he was rumoured to have been among the proxy winners of the Prix de Bordeaux. Despite the PMU propaganda and the alarm expressed by some of the more sensitive souls in the 16th *arrondissement*, it wasn't that unusual for gambling gentry like Des Moutis to mix with the underworld. Even without the illegal bookmaking connection, the racing world was a bit like a nightclub where social and class barriers could be blurred, and bold characters intermingle for pleasure and profit. Marius Bertella, whose father had been a jockey, was himself an ardent betting and racing enthusiast and participating in Patrice's Prix de Bordeaux plot would have appealed to the Canards as a suitably audacious way to beat the system.

But there was a catch, as Des Moutis and his friends would have been wise to remember: men like Bertella, Imbert and the Trois Canards didn't always bet on horses just for the fun and a bit of sport. Sometimes they preferred races where they knew the result in advance. Especially when they had dirty money that they needed to launder.

Chapter 18

With Patrice and his lieutenants attempting to fend off accusations of an unhealthy connection to the Trois Canards, and the police continuing their enquiries in Pigalle, the Prix de Bordeaux investigation bumped along. In the meantime the fame of Monsieur X received another semi-serious boost from the owner of a national magazine.

In December 1965 Charles de Gaulle was elected to serve a second seven-year term in the Élysée Palace. The President only deigned to place his name on the ballot paper on 5 December, with a week to go until the first round of voting. In a run-off on the 20th he beat the Socialist candidate François Mitterand, a Machiavellian politician of unfathomable depth who had cropped up regularly in the short-lived administrations of the 1950s.

In a foretaste of more recent elections, not everyone was enthused by the choice of candidates on offer. Jean-Jacques Servan-Schreiber, the dynamic founder of the weekly news magazine *L'Express*, and another former pupil of the Grandes Écoles and the Lycée Janson de Sailly, felt the staid electoral race needed livening up. He suggested that an unnamed 'Monsieur

'X' should run for the presidency on an independent ticket. The profile of his ideal candidate sounded a lot like the Socialist mayor of Marseille, Gaston Defferre, who did run unsuccessfully for the Élysée four years later. But in racing circles there was much amusement that Servan-Schreiber's Monsieur X could presumably also stand for Patrice des Moutis, and why not? Had not the Tamer of the Tiercé displayed exactly the kind of ingenuity that was needed to liven up De Gaulle's France and oppose the tyranny of the over-mighty state?

Friends of Patrice said that Servan-Schreiber himself found the notion entertaining – anything to sell a few more copies of his magazine, after all – and was sure that, if elected, racing's Monsieur X would offer a progressive modern alternative to the status quo. There was light-hearted talk in advertising circles of promoting a Monsieur X brand of olive oil, mustard, and even refrigerators which would be 'ice cool' like the gambler.

In the end Gaston Defferre didn't stand as an independent candidate, and Des Moutis didn't join the hustings in his place. Neither could he copyright the Monsieur X name or demand payment, as he was still denying authorship of the audacious Prix de Bordeaux Tiercé scheme that Monsieur X was meant to have devised. But Patrice, who had met Servan-Schreiber socially, thoroughly enjoyed it when people kept asking him what his first act would be when he moved in to the Élysée Palace. 'Abolish the PMU' was his answer.

President de Gaulle's view of Monsieur X was not revealed, though it's probably safe to assume that Le Vieux Charles was not amused by the stunt. In his final pre-election address to the nation the General had praised the 'grace and stability' he claimed to have restored to *La Belle* France and asked for the people's endorsement to complete his 'Sunday mission'.

Des Moutis meanwhile, who as Monsieur X received a few write-in votes on spoiled ballot papers, was cautioned by family and friends to refrain from any further Sunday Tiercé missions as long as Judge Simon's enquiry persisted.

In Patrice's eyes it was the authorities who were playing dirty in June 1965 when the PMU informed the Finance Ministry of his record January 1962 Tiercé coup and request to be paid in cash. Gambling winnings were not liable to taxation in France but the Pari-Mutuel were convinced that Des Moutis had something to hide. The Finance Minister, Valéry Giscard d'Estaing, passed the matter on to the Trésor Public, the French equivalent of the Inland Revenue, and the case ended up on the desk of the chief inspector of taxes. Old returns were dug out, going back to 1957 when Patrice's Grande École contemporary Felix Gaillard was Minister of Finance, and questions asked about Patrice's income from his insurance business. The inference was that Des Moutis could have been disguising taxable earnings as gambling profits. After a lengthy inquiry the taxman declined to take it any further, but not without an implicit warning that the government bureaucracy he worked for might not be so tolerant in the future.

Marie-Thérèse was hugely relieved that the investigation was at an end, whereas her husband brushed it off as a heavy-handed attempt at character assassination. But even so he seems to have seen the wisdom of steering clear of the PMU for the time being, while also promising to keep his distance from any of the new *demi-mondaine* friends he might have made in Pigalle and at the Grand Cercle.

If Patrice's life had been a film or theatrical performance, it had just about reached the equivalent of the intermission. The second act would be shorter than the first, though just as dramatic. But for the next few years he was content to play the respectable *haute bourgeois* game and go back to being the quintessential insurance company risk assessor, business partner of his brother Gilbert, devoted husband of Marie-Thérèse and loving father of four. Whatever reservations the long-suffering Gilbert may eventually have had about his brother's activities there was no suggestion that the children were anything other than adoring admirers of their dazzling papa.

French racing may have been off limits to him but not so events across the Channel and, whenever the orderly façade became too much and he needed to satisfy his craving for a gamble, Des Moutis flew over to England to see his good friend Peter O'Sullevan. The man who 'sees all, knows all and tells all the inside news', according to his *Daily Express* byline, was both a French speaker and a consummate punter and together he and Patrice backed many of the top French horses that ran at the big English meetings in the 1960s. Horses like the 1963 Epsom Derby winner Relko, whose owner François Dupré was also the proprietor of the Hôtel George V, and the peerless 1965 Derby and Prix de l'Arc de Triomphe winner Sea-Bird II, who was reckoned to be the finest thoroughbred of the twentieth century.

Sea-Bird ran in the colours of the Lille industrialist Jean Ternynck and was trained at Chantilly by Etienne Pollet. A proud, imposing man at the summit of his profession, Pollet liked to have a decent bet on his horses when he was lining them up for a big race, and Des Moutis, like Peter O'Sullevan, had often helped him to 'get on' with the London bookies. But as the investigation into the Prix de Bordeaux continued to drag on, allowing the whispers and rumours to foment, Pollet was one of the first senior French racing figures to snub Patrice in public.

It happened in the summer of 1967, when Pollet ran a four-year-old colt called Great Nephew in the Eclipse Stakes at Sandown Park. A small, exclusive group of French owners, trainers and gamblers were flying over to London together in a private plane from Le Bourget. When Patrice arrived at the airfield and saw Pollet, the trainer averted his eyes, and when Des Moutis got on the plane Pollet got up from his seat and went and sat on his own in a single seat at the back of the cabin. The two men never spoke to each other again.

Fortunately for Patrice his English racing and bookmaking friends were more tolerant and he was greeted warmly on his arrival at Sandown. The diminutive Geoffrey Hamlyn, who for fifty-six years was the main betting correspondent of the *Sporting Life*, got to know Des Moutis well during this period and was always impressed by his intelligence and charm, despite feeling some unease about what he called his 'host of dubious connections'. In his autobiography, published in 1994, Hamlyn wrote that Patrice 'enjoyed a fair measure of success on our racecourses despite his lack of fluent English. He understood enough to know that his movements were followed eagerly in the betting ring and occasionally he would turn round to the tic-tacs – the men whose hand signals relayed money from pitch to pitch – and say "Ah oui. Monsieur Patrice, he is backing the favourite."'

Another of Patrice's good English friends was the book-maker Victor Chandler, the youngest son of Bill Chandler, who had founded Walthamstow Greyhound Stadium and went from being a street bookie in Hoxton to becoming one of the richest men in London in the 1930s. Victor, who was born in 1924 and was almost the same age as Patrice, shared the Frenchman's enthusiasm for good food and wine and bespoke tailoring, and his family business was a repository of racing history, with some of the best connections on and off the track.

Sometimes Chandler laid Patrice's bets on French horses, or backed the same horses for himself and his firm. Sometimes Patrice passed on bets from his French clients and, if the clients lost, Chandler and Des Moutis shared the profits. But theirs was more than just a business arrangement and, in 1969, Chandler asked Patrice to help him keep an eye on his errant son. 'Young Victor' Chandler, as he was known to family and friends, was 18 years old and had just left school after two years at Millfield, where he'd been able to pursue his interest in betting and racing without any problems with the authorities. The headmaster, R. J. 'Boss' Meyer, was himself a client of the Chandler firm but a singularly unsuccessful one, and his gambling losses continually outstripped the school's fees.

Young Victor would eventually go on to become a famous gentleman bookie – a bit like an English version of Des Moutis – laying odds to an exotic cast of characters, from the artists Lucien Freud and Francis Bacon to West End gangsters and peers of the realm. But in 1969 his plans were still fuzzy and unformed beyond a vague desire to live in Europe and work in a casino. So to begin with, the prodigal went to Paris to live in a Left Bank apartment with his father's former French au pair. After a series of scrapes, some romantic, some financial, the relationship broke up and Victor senior arranged for his son to move into the Saint-Germain-des-Prés house of an old friend, a *comtesse* and racehorse owner, who was also a friend of Des Moutis.

The teenager spent his days learning French at the Institut Catholique and bunking off whenever he could to go to the races. Lester Piggott, another one of his father's old friends, rode in France nearly every weekend between April and October, and sometimes the great jockey could be prevailed upon to give Young Victor tips. But the highpoints of Chandler's Paris odyssey were the invitations to Sunday lunch with Patrice and Marie-Thérèse at their home in Saint-Cloud.

By the late sixties the couple had moved into a large and strikingly modern house near the bottom of the hillside facing out across the Seine. The big white villa, with electric gates and a lift from the garage up to the upper floors, felt more like a house on Mulholland Drive in Los Angeles than a traditional Parisian residence. There was a large garden and a pool and an upper sun deck with a ravishing view across the rooftops towards the Bois de Boulogne and the city.

Chandler was in awe of Patrice's Gatsbyesque confidence and style, while Marie-Thérèse seemed every inch *la grande femme*. Some Sunday mornings Victor met his host in the Parc de Saint-Cloud where the 48-year-old Patrice, who was now a grandfather, would appear in a monogrammed sky-blue tracksuit at the end of another five-mile run. The chauffeur-driven Mercedes would be waiting nearby to ferry the pair back to the house for champagne before lunch.

Des Moutis would discuss horses, bets and forthcoming races and seemed to Victor to be the epitome of the rich and successful professional gambler he himself longed to become.

His conversation was rapid, urgent and punctuated with frequent interjections like 'Are you with me?' and 'You follow?' When they touched on the Tiercé, Patrice was adamant that it was the PMU that was behaving like the Mafia and that the French betting system was one big restrictive practice prepared to go to any lengths to ensure the punter could not win.

He told Victor about the Greek shipping owner Constantine Goulandris, who won 720 million old francs on a Tiercé race at Auteuil in May 1967. A notoriously superstitious gambler who, according to Patrice, spent all his time touching wood and fingering his rosary, Goulandris stayed at the Plaza Athénée whenever he was in Paris and did his betting in a PMU bureau near the Place de l'Alma at the bottom of Avenue George V. He often lost heavily but on that one occasion when luck went his way the PMU blocked his gains, accusing him of breaking the limit on maximum stakes and backing the same combination several hundred times. They also hinted that Monsieur X might have been involved in some way, which was completely untrue. Patrice believed the PMU were bluffing and that they would never have taken a rich and extremely well-connected Greek financier to court but, to his disgust, Goulandris folded in the face of family pressure and meekly cancelled his bet. Des Moutis, by contrast, was adamant that he would fight Messieurs Carrus, Alexandre, Crespin and their minions every step of the way.

With his tailormade suits and shirts and his short, well-cut hair, Patrice may have seemed like an unlikely 1960s rebel. But Young Victor Chandler gained a clear impression of a man who relished his outlaw status and was prepared to take his battle with the Pari-Mutuel to the very limit of what was legal and beyond.

Patrice's rebellious fervour chimed with the spirit of the age. In May 1968 the Fifth Republic had tottered and nearly fallen in the face of the *événements*, the wave of student demonstrations backed up by strikes involving millions of workers. The tumult was directed partly against capitalism and traditional bourgeois values but also against the authoritarianism and egoism of France's ageing President. De Gaulle briefly left the country to confer with General Jacques Massu, the controversial 'victor' of the Battle of Algiers and commander of the French forces in Germany. The old paratrooper urged the President to return to Paris and reassert control while also pressing him to offer an amnesty to those officers still in prison as a result of the failed Algerian putsch of 1961.

With half a million demonstrators in the Place de la République on 11 June, and army units once again said to be mobilising outside the city, a revolution was only narrowly averted. The Gaullist party won a crushing victory in subsequent parliamentary elections but the mandate of Le Vieux Charles had been fatally eroded and, after losing a referendum on constitutional change the following April, the 78-year-old suddenly resigned.

The former Premier Georges Pompidou was elected President in De Gaulle's place and moved smoothly into the Élysée Palace. Giscard d'Estaing, who had warned of the dangers of 'brutal suppression' of the nation's youth, remained at Finance, and Roger Frey continued as the Interior Minister and France's top cop. Pompidou's first Prime Minister was the progressive Jacques Chaban-Delmas, yet another graduate of the Grandes Écoles and – like Jean-Jacques Servan-Schreiber and Félix Gaillard – contemporary of Des Moutis, who talked optimistically of plans to create a 'new society' in France. But Pompidou was never entirely comfortable with Chaban's more radical ideas, for fear they would seem too much of a rupture with the Gaullist past. He was prepared to buy off the trade unions to lessen the likelihood of them taking to the streets again in nationwide protests. But he also wanted to reassure France's rural, conservative majority that student rioters and others who flagrantly broke the law would be punished just as surely as they had been in the era of the Marquis de Balleroy and Loulou the *beau chasseur*.

It may have been no coincidence then that less than a month after Pompidou had taken office, the interminable investigation into the Prix de Bordeaux entered a new phase. On 10 July 1969 Judge Maurice Landreau, a colleague of Judge Simon and Judge Raynaud, ruled that Monsieur X and seventy-five of the winning punters – the other eight had died since 1962 – should definitely go on trial for fraud and conspiracy to defraud.

A crucial influence on Judge Landreau's deliberations, not revealed to the public at the time, was the discovery that Des Moutis had withdrawn a large sum of money from his bank account the day before the race and had travelled down to Lyon with Jules Carrax, Jacques Guyadet, René Lacoste, Jean Seuret and Seuret's girlfriend Marie Louise Baumann on the Saturday afternoon. He may have flown to London a day later but, with other players with Paris addresses travelling to Lille, Bordeaux, Marseille and other cities to place bets at the same time, it looked very much to the Judge as if Monsieur X had been much more than just a technical advisor, and was indeed the architect of the ingeniously devised plot.

The PMU put out a statement welcoming the judge's decision and claiming that, throughout the long enquiry, they had acted to protect the integrity of the Tiercé and the interests of the 'little' punters. But Des Moutis, whose lawyers were still pursuing a parallel civil claim against the PMU, declared himself to be 'stupefied' by the ruling and slammed the PMU's actions as the 'fraudulent attempt' of a monopoly to withhold payment.

As Young Victor Chandler had observed first hand, Patrice was consumed with a passionate and over-arching anger and had no intention of backing down. It had been nearly five years since his last big gamble on French soil but, within days of the July court ruling, he began to work on a new scheme to take the battle back to the enemy.

Chapter 19

Toussaint, or All Saints' Day, falls on 1 November and is a public holiday in France. Traditionally families mark the occasion by laying flowers on the graves of the dear departed, even as reckless bank holiday motorists add to the death toll on the roads. As on other fête days, the PMU mark the occasion by staging a Tiercé race with one of the biggest pools of the year. 1 November 1969 was a Saturday, so the gambling highpoint of the weekend was going to be the Prix Georges de Talhouet-Roy at Auteuil on the afternoon of Sunday 2 November. A hurdle race for three-year-olds over 3,500 metres, or approximately two miles and five furlongs, it was worth 80,000 new francs to the winner, considerably less than the day's feature event, the prestigious Grand Prix d'Automne. But for most of the thirty thousand holidaying spectators packing into the stands at Auteuil and for millions more watching at home on television or listening on the radio, the Prix Georges de Talhouet-Roy was *the* betting race of the weekend, with blanket coverage in the sporting press.

Fifteen years after its drab and poorly supported debut at Enghien the Tiercé was booming. Approximately 90 million francs was being gambled every Sunday as the concept of an innocent flutter achieved unprecedented heights of respectability, with serious and merely recreational punters from all walks of life chancing their luck.

The popular singer Enrico Macias, a Jewish *pied noir* who was born Gaston Ghrenassia in Algeria but changed his name when he moved to France in 1961, had recorded a hit song about the Tiercé entitled 'Les Millionaires du Dimanche'. The upbeat tone was echoed by newspapers like *Le Figaro* running lyrical articles hymning the transformation of Sunday mornings in small towns and villages across the land. Everywhere, it seemed, there were hopeful punters queuing up at their local PMU *café-tabac* in between Mass and their customary visits to the *pâtisserie* to buy a *tarte aux pommes* for Sunday lunch.

The Monday morning reports of Tiercé winners and losers were equally gushing, whether saluting a baker from Douarnenez who'd won twenty times his stake money for a total gain of 100,000 francs, or rueing the fate of a racehorse owner and high-stakes gambler who'd dropped thousands of francs on multiple combinations.

Des Moutis was planning to win thousands of francs on the Prix Georges de Talhouet-Roy Tiercé and, despite the ongoing Prix de Bordeaux investigation and Judge Landreau's ruling that he must go to trial, he believed that this time he had a foolproof plan. On the evening of Saturday 1 November thirty especially invited guests – some of the men in flared trousers with flowered shirts and cravats, the women in Pierre Cardin miniskirts and patterned tights – arrived at Patrice and Marie-Thérèse's villa in Saint-Cloud. Neighbours would remember the fleet of cars in the driveway and lining the street outside, including a dozen Citroëns, two Mercedes and an Alfa Romeo, all of them with Paris plates.

The guests were a mixture of friends and relations, including Patrice's Breton cousin Bernard and his nephew Yves, office colleagues from Neuilly, and other businessmen or *hommes des affaires* Patrice saw regularly as part of his Paris working life. They were all there voluntarily and ready to play the Tiercé with their own money after first hearing the resident Saint-Cloud form expert summarise the race and outline his selections. What could possibly be illegal about that? The group would be behaving no differently to punters following a tipster's advice in *Paris Turf*.

Some among the eminently respectable gathering may have been nervous about the court case hanging over Patrice's head for organising proxy betting on the Prix de Bordeaux. They may also have been wondering if their host still had any links to the Bande des Trois Canards but, if so, they were too polite – or perhaps just too intent on making money – to ask. In fact the original Trois Canards gang had broken up in 1965. The leader Marius Bertella had supposedly gone into retirement, buying a stud farm in Normandy in the valley of the Orne not far from where Des Moutis spent his childhood summers. One of the Perret brothers had been killed in a feud with the Zemours, another *pieds noirs* clan who packed a bigger punch. And Gaëtan Alboreo, Eugène Matrone and the other Canards had gone back to Marseille where the young pretenders 'Tany' Zampa and Jacky Imbert had pursued their aim of ousting the Guérinis and taking over the French Connection heroin-smuggling trade from Marseille to the US. The *Milieu* had by no means given up their interest in horse and trotting racing, but nobody was talking about gangsters or illegal card games that Saturday night in the Rue de Béarn.

The arrivals were welcomed by Marie-Thérèse at her most vivacious, in company with her two eldest daughters, Patricia and Nicole who appear to have been enthusiastic participants in their father's schemes. So far from seeing anything criminal or reprehensible about his actions they applauded him for his nerve, along with their older and more studious brother François who was away at college.

The guests were all shown into the family *salon* with its numerous deep sofas and armchairs and occasional tables. The author Richard de Lesparda described the scene in his 1970 account *La Maffia du Tiercé*, observing that you could have fitted more than a hundred punters into that Saint-Cloud *salon* without difficulty. In one corner of the room a simple but delicious buffet supper had been laid out, and everyone helped themselves to lobster *bisque*, *poulet froid avec mayonnaise* and a selection of salads and cheeses washed down with bottles of Bordeaux red from Patrice's cellar.

The host and centre of attention was seated at a long coffee table piled high with racing papers, notebooks and pages of form. De Lesparda remembered that when Patrice was finally ready to address them all there was an electrifying atmosphere which Des Moutis – who loved an audience – milked as skilfully as an experienced performer making his entrance at the Comédie-Française.

Patrice and several others present had actually lost money on their two previous Tiercé attempts. Thirty thousand francs had gone astray on 26 October, and another 16,000 francs that very Saturday afternoon. But Des Moutis assured them that they were like horses or jockeys just coming into form at the right moment and that he had every confidence that 2 November would be their day.

The first thing to remember about the Prix Georges de Talhouet-Roy, Patrice said, was that it was a race for three-year-olds only, the youngest age at which horses compete in hurdle races, and that a number of the fourteen runners – six colts, four fillies and four geldings – were unknowns with little or no previous form. The likely favourite Primo de Solera, predicted to go off at odds of around 9-2 in *Paris Turf*, was one of seven of the runners to have contested the Prix Magne, a race over the same course and distance on 18 October. Primo de Solera, who was to be ridden by Jean-Paul Ciravegna, one of Auteuil's less famous jockeys, had been successful that day. But as a result he now had to concede weight all round, and Patrice suspected that might be too much of a burden.

There were a lot of tips for a horse called Clown, who had been third in the Prix Magne and was now receiving weight from Primo de Solera, which ought to give him an edge. But Patrice didn't seem to rate either Clown or his rider Jean-Jacques Declercq. Neither was he enthusiastic about Start, a colt who had finished second in the earlier contest and was the mount of Jean-Claude Biard, known as 'Bibi', who had a reputation as a bit of a wild boy and bon viveur. But then most of the French jump jockeys in the late 1960s lived hard and fast lives, none more so than the card-playing gambler Michel Jathan, who was a gin rummy devotee.

Jathan was riding Patrice's base selection Maestro II, whose young trainer Gérard Philippeau was himself a former jockey and one-time rider for Patrice's Biarritz rugby and bullfighting friend Georges Pelat. Bayes' Theorem and all that talk about logic and probability was all very well, but Patrice's faith in Maestro's chances had been boosted by a private conversation with Pelat who, despite having a runner in the race himself, had passed on a big tip for the once-raced Maestro.

What might politely be called 'stable sources' had also put Patrice onto the unraced Rio Verde, who was owned by the immensely wealthy art dealer Daniel Wildenstein, whose collection included works by Monet, Degas and Van Gogh and whose Paris office was in the Rue la Boétie, the same street as the headquarters of the PMU. Wildenstein was the richest and most influential owner in French jump racing in 1969, and his horses were trained by the Egyptian born Maurice Zilber, who had come to France seven years previously.

Des Moutis had noticed that Rio Verde had also been entered in a claiming race the following week – claimers, or 'selling races', as they were known in England, being for the lowest standard of horses, with the winner automatically put up for auction straight afterwards. If Zilber felt Rio Verde was no better than a claimer it was reasonable to assume that it would struggle in a better class of race like the Prix Georges de Talhouet-Roy. But after numerous telephone calls to and from Zilber's yard in Chantilly it was clear to Patrice that the claiming race entry was a smokescreen by the wily trainer designed to give a false impression of Rio Verde's ability and ensure it went off at better odds at Auteuil.

Of the remaining runners Patrice was quite interested in Amyrol, who was also having his first run over hurdles and whose owner-trainer Richard de Tarragon was related to a Jockey Club member of Patrice's acquaintance. De Tarragon had an impressive strike rate from relatively few runners, and Patrice had been assured that his stable would be backing their horse on Toussaint.

Extraordinarily the Des Moutis household still had five different telephone-betting accounts with the PMU in 1969, including one for Patrice, one for Marie-Thérèse and one each for Patricia and Nicole and, despite the Prix de Bordeaux inquiry and their troubled history, the PMU management had not yet bothered to close them down. Patrice explained to his guests that a portion of his bets on the Talhouet-Roy would be going on by phone, and that in an attempt to cover multiple combinations he himself was going to submit 283 different Tiercé coupons, wagering the maximum permitted stake on each line. As long as one of them paid at least 800 francs to a three-franc stake in the correct order he was sure to be in profit.

For everyone else, some two thousand Tiercé *bordereaux* had been assembled at the house, Patrice having methodically bought them all at various PMU outlets the previous day. The thirty-strong group were told to fill in their legal share there in the *salon* that evening and then take them to their local PMU *café-tabacs*, including the Café Sainte-Foy in Neuilly and the Café Clemenceau in Saint-Cloud, the following morning.

Under Patrice's supervision twenty-eight of the guests, two of the couples acting as one, proceeded to fill in sixty-six tickets each, pledging to wager the 60-franc maximum multiplied by four on a combination of Maestro II, Rio Verde, Amyrol and a classy ex-flat racer called Verpen, another runner making his hurdling debut, in the correct order and any order. It was a lengthy process and, as everyone toiled away, the air in the room was soon thick with cigar and cigarette smoke just as in a PMU *café-tabac.* But glasses were kept refilled throughout the evening as Patrice, the ringmaster, went from guest to guest correcting an error here, helping with a detail there, and stiffening the resolve of anyone suddenly assailed by doubt.

Sunday 2 November dawned grey but mild, and Patrice was up early as usual. Using one of his daughter's PMU telephone accounts to place a Tiercé bet for his cousin Bernard and nephew Yves, and then driving over to the Café Sainte-Foy in Neuilly to place a cash Couplé bet for himself – predicting the first two in the Talhouet-Roy in the correct order or any order – on Rio Verde and Maestro II.

That afternoon Patrice put on his monogrammed sky-blue tracksuit with the white piping and drove down to the Bois de Boulogne, leaving his car outside the restaurant in the Jardins de Bagatelle.The leaves on the horse chestnut trees were a blaze of russet and gold as Des Moutis jogged two and a half miles through the woods to the perimeter of Auteuil racecourse. Late arrivals were still making their way into the track's recently modernised grandstand but Patrice joined the other illegal bookmakers, touts and would-be gatecrashers gathered on the gravel outside. His appearance back among the undesirables, after an absence of some seven years, was the cause of much excitement and immediate speculation that Monsieur X – or 'the Saint', as some of his devoted followers now called him – was about to pull off another coup.

Auteuil is a flat, looping, criss-crossing track, and Patrice stationed himself on a bench overlooking the top left-hand turn just after the grandstand. Other than being on the balcony of one of the apartment buildings on the far side of the course it was as good a viewing position as an excluded spectator could hope for. And with the aid of the racecourse commentator and the binoculars he'd brought with him from home – having jogged through the Bois with them in their case slung around his neck – he was able to follow the action well enough.

The second and third races came and went followed by the Grand Prix d'Automne, and it was almost half-past four by the time the regular Auteuil starter, Colonel Illiers, sent the fourteen runners in the Prix Georges de Talhouet-Roy on their way. The unfortunately named Clown seemed destined to live up to his name: after jumping the first of the twelve hurdles, where one of the outsiders came down, he was already 20 metres behind the others, and his jockey Jean-Jacques Declercq made little effort to improve his position as the race continued on its way. It was noticeable too that Start, ridden by Jean-Claude Biard, was well behind from the outset and never made up ground.

Running past the stands on the first circuit, a 13-1 shot called Ritoly was in the lead with the favourite Primo de Solera going well in fifth place, and six or seven others all still in there with a chance. They jumped the hurdle opposite Patrice's vantage point and then swung left-handed to gallop away down the back stretch beneath the trees alongside the Avenue du Maréchal Lyautey. Clearing the third-last obstacle, Maestro II had made significant ground up on the outside of the field but Ritoly was still in the lead with Primo de Solera now in second place and Rio Verde moving into contention in third.

Swinging round the Passy turn into the long home straight, a majority of the punters in the stands were roaring on Primo de Solera and his jockey. '*Allez, Ciravegna*,' they cried. '*Allez, Allez.*' It was still Ritoly in front as they jumped the last but, as old Auteuil hands like Des Moutis knew only too well, it's a stiff run

RIGHT
Patrice des
Moutis.

BELOW
Patrice at the
window of his
office in Neuilly.

OPPOSITE Patrice at
home in St Cloud with
his youngest daughter
Olivia.

ABOVE Spectators at
Longchamp, 1952.

BELOW Runners taking
the water jump at Auteuil,
November 1951.

ABOVE LEFT Madame Suzy Volterra: racehorse owner, society hostess and friend of Monsieur X.

ABOVE RIGHT The Mexican-born actress, racehorse owner and Deauville femme fatale, Maria Felix-Berger.

BELOW Prince Aly Khan and Rita Hayworth, May 1949.

ABOVE The Normandy Hotel, Deauville.

LEFT Vintage advertising signs in Provence, including one for the PMU.

BELOW Some of Patrice's 'Commandos' outside the main PMU office in Lyon, 15 December 1962.

ABOVE Packed stands at Auteuil for the 1960 Grand Steeplechase de Paris.

BELOW RIGHT The singer Enrico Macias in 1964.

OPPOSITE Glamorous female race-goers at Auteuil, May 1957.

ABOVE A punched Tiercé bet, 1962.

ABOVE Marcel Boussac (left) confers
with President Charles de Gaulle at
the Grand Prix de Paris at Longchamp,
June 1960.

ABOVE Pierre-Désiré Allaire: owner,
trainer, gambler and friend of Alain Delon.

LEFT French Agriculture Minister, Edgard
Pisani, meets a constituent in Paris 1965.

ABOVE Jean Paul Belmondo and Alain Delon in *Borsalino*.

BELOW Baro Ferret (seated, left) and Django Rheinhardt (seated three from the left) in the Bar Cabaret Trois Canards, Paris 1945.

The actors Marcel Bozzufi and Fernando Rey in the 1971 film *The French Connection*.

Punters trying out the first automatic Tiercé machine in Paris, April 1970.

Patrice's friend Alain Ayache holding copies of his tipping sheets *Spécial Dernière* and *Le Meilleur*.

ABOVE Daniel Wildenstein (in glasses on the right) leading in Allez France and Yves St Martin after their victory in the 1974 Prix de l'Arc De Triomphe at Longchamp.

BELOW Winter trotting race at Vincennes.

OPPOSITE Patrice and his son Francois accosted by a journalist as they take a lunchtime walk during his trial, December 1971.

ABOVE Valery Giscard d'Estaing and his future Interior Minister, Michel Poniatowski, in 1972.

BELOW Inside the Palais de Justice, Paris.

ABOVE Inside a cell block in the Fresnes Prison in Paris.

BELOW Front gate of the Fresnes Prison.

OPPOSITE TOP Pierre Costes at home with his wife Annie.

RIGHT Patrice's imprisonment is front page news in *L'Aurore*, February 1975.

eur X'' en prison

arde à vue dans les locaux de la police des jeux, M. Patrice des Moutis, écroué, hier soir, à la prison de Fresnes.

atrice des Moutis : trop uvent impliqué dans des

tamment Pierre Costes, Cravache d'Or, ainsi qu'à deux entraîneurs.

Depuis, tout le monde a d'ailleurs été libéré, sauf plusieurs parieurs arrêtés à Marseille et Toulon, et transférés à Paris.

Courses douteuses

Jusqu'alors, le nom de M. des Moutis ne figurait pas dans la procédure. Mais les inspecteurs de la brigade des jeux, sans faire preuve de beaucoup d'imagination, soupçonnèrent M. X... d'avoir participé à l'affaire. Il avait, en effet, été trop souvent impliqué dans des courses douteuses.

La grande affaire de M. X... fut celle du Prix de Bordeaux, couru également un 9 décembre, mais en 1962. M. des Moutis avait fait jouer des sommes

d'un non-lieu dans le Prix de Valencey.

Patrice des Moutis, ingénieur de l'Ecole centrale, expert en assurances, a toujours soutenu qu'il était un technicien des courses et que ses méthodes étaient scientifiques et non pas malhonnêtes. Il trichait pourtant en faisant jouer par des prête-noms des sommes supérieures au maximum légal au préjudice des petits parieurs.

Bronzage

Cette fois, il est mêlé à une affaire beaucoup plus grave puisqu'il est enfin démontré que le Prix Bri- de Abattue était truqué.

Lorsque les policiers se sont présentés au domicile de M. des Moutis, mardi soir, celui-ci revenait des sports d'hiver. Le bronzage lui donnait bonne mine, mais il avait pourtant l'air accablé lorsqu'il quitta le cabinet du juge d'instruc-

ABOVE
Jockeys in the weighing room at Auteuil including Jean-Pierre Philipperon (standing) in green and yellow silks and Jean-Pierre Ciravegna (sitting) in yellow, blue and red.

LEFT
Monsieur X.

from the final jump to the finish at the Bois de Boulogne track, and the complexion of a race can change dramatically in the last 200 metres. To the bitter disappointment of his vocal supporters it was Primo de Solera who was beaten first – no doubt anchored by the weight as Patrice had predicted – as Michel Chirol riding Rio Verde battled it out with the fast-finishing Maestro II, with the long-time leader Ritoly engulfed by the others and dropping back. Chirol dug deep in the Wildenstein colours but, as they passed the post, it was Maestro and Michel Jathan in first place by a nose with a head separating Rio Verde from the staying on Amyrol in third. A rank outsider called Azure finished fourth.

Des Moutis had done it again. Maestro II, who had won at the second attempt, had been his base selection, and Maestro, Rio Verde and Amyrol his three recommendations in the correct order and any order. Jumping down jubilantly from the bench, he paused briefly to acknowledge the salutes and tributes of his admirers and then, as one witness described it, ran off back into the Bois like a tracksuited Robin Hood making his getaway in Sherwood Forest.

When the full Tiercé return on the Prix Georges de Talhouet-Roy was declared the Maestro II, Rio Verde and Amyrol combination, numbers 10, 14 and 12, were found to pay 3,781,90 francs to a three-franc stake in the correct order and 659,70 francs in *désordre* or any order. Patrice's family, friends and fellow backers, some of whom had watched the race on their television sets, listened to it on the radio or seen the result on the teleprinter service of France-Presse, were ecstatic. Each of the twenty-eight punters had won nearly 90,000 francs for a stake of 17,000, and the total payout to the group, including Patrice's successful Couplé bet on Maestro and Rio Verde, which netted him a gain of 850,000 francs, was not far short of three and a half million.

That night everyone returned to Beverley Hills-sur-Seine and the *salon* in the white villa rocked as never before as the winners celebrated their good fortune. They rolled back the rugs, turned up the music and danced, drank and smoked until the early hours of Monday morning.

Patrice was up at 7 a.m. on 3 November despite having had no more than a few hours' sleep. As always he loved the early mornings in the big modern house, with their sense of order and comfort spiced with the anticipation of things to come. There was some tidying-up to do that day and he dutifully emptied ashtrays and cleared away bottles and empty glasses before drinking two cups of black coffee and taking Marie-Thérèse's breakfast tray upstairs to their bedroom.

There was a red sky over Paris as Des Moutis drove through the Bois de Boulogne and on through Passy to Le Flandrin on Avenue Henri-Martin. In the restaurant section the waiters were hoovering and already laying up for lunch, but the café tables at the other end of the terrace were for those neighbourhood regulars who came in every morning for *petit dejeuner* or just a *café crème*. Patrice took another espresso standing up at the bar, enjoying the smells of freshly ground coffee and croissants, and chatted briefly with the manager before going over to the PMU counter at the back.

The 1962 rule change required all winning punters to furnish proof of identification before their cheques would be issued. Patrice had placed Tiercé bets in Le Flandrin for his cousin and nephew so he showed the cashier his counterfoil coupons along with ID cards for Bernard and Yves. The names and details were recorded and the standard practice was that the cheques would be posted to their address – in this case Patrice's address as they were both staying with him for the holiday – later that day.

After leaving Le Flandrin, Des Moutis went back up to Neuilly to the Café Sainte-Foy and presented his own ID card to process payment of the cheque for his Couplé winnings. Then when he got upstairs to his office next door he rang the main PMU telephone betting line to confirm the balance on his account and ask for a payment of 70,000 francs to be sent to him by cheque straight away.

The rest of Monday passed uneventfully. On Tuesday morning Patrice left home before the postman had arrived, and around 11 a.m. he rang Marie-Thérèse at the house to see if the cheques for his cousin and nephew had come in that day's post. She said they hadn't.

At lunchtime Patrice went into the Café Sainte-Foy, where they had a cheque ready for him for his Couplé gains. But when he went down to Le Flandrin later that day the cashier told him that the other two cheques had not yet been issued. The 70-year-old André Carrus had officially taken a back seat at the PMU the previous year and some of his day-to-day responsibilities were now being shared by Maurice Alexandre and André's younger son, Pierre who, along with his brother Jacques, was determined to ensure that the legacy left to the Carrus family by Albert Chauvin continued to thrive.

According to the cashier in Le Flandrin, neither Alexandre nor Pierre Carrus had yet had time to sign the cheques to Bernard and Yves. Yet the cheque Patrice had just been given for his Couplé winnings in the Café Sainte-Foy had been countersigned and dated by Pierre Carrus the previous day.

Patrice's suspicions were immediately aroused and he sensed intent to refuse payment.

The PMU had been faced with upwards of thirty punters holding a mass of identical winning tickets for the Prix Georges de Talhouet-Roy Tiercé. Among them was their old *bête noire* Des Moutis, his wife, daughters and colleagues from his Neuilly office. Patrice knew that the eyes of the PMU management lit up with panic every time he won so much as a centime. They would know that he must have been the architect of this latest coup and maybe now they would try to infer that his wife, daughters, colleagues and friends were not independent punters betting with their own money but part of a gang betting at Patrice's direction to enable him to get round the limit on maximum stakes. In which case, unless he moved quickly, they were quite likely to allege another conspiracy to defraud and attempt to block payment.

While Des Moutis was still trying to assess the situation, the PMU cashier at Le Flandrin rang him at his office and told him that the cheques to his cousin and nephew had now been issued and were in the post. But Patrice was only slightly reassured. He feared that unless he and his co-winners moved fast to cash any cheques that had been sent, the PMU's bank, the Crédit Lyonnais, would refuse to honour them.

It generally took five working days for a cheque to clear in France, but in certain circumstances – if, for example, the depositor was paying in a sufficiently large sum – clearance could be obtained within twenty-four hours. According to Patrice's account, what happened next is that he contacted an unnamed collaborator, who was one of the thirty winning Prix Georges de Talhouet-Roy punters, and suggested that they try to round up as many of the cheques that had already been issued as they could possibly get their hands on. If the cheques were all made over to Patrice he could deposit a sufficiently large enough sum with his bank for them to guarantee payment the next day. He would then pay the others their winnings in cash and any PMU stoppage would have been forestalled. It may have seemed his best bet but, whether through arrogance or lack of foresight, it was also a dangerous one, placing himself in the spotlight as the main beneficiary of the gamble.

A frantic Tuesday-afternoon tour of friends' offices and houses followed, yielding around fifteen cheques which, Patrice advised the bearers, should be made over to him. The others all did as instructed, in one case even endorsing a PMU cheque that had been made out to his son, and Patrice then took them to his bank near the Rond-Point des Champs-Élysées and asked for rapid clearance. After some deliberation the bank, who knew Des Moutis well, advised him that the funds should be in his account by the end of the following morning.

So far so good, thought Patrice. But when he returned to the bank at midday on the Wednesday, he was told that the PMU's Crédit Lyonnais branch on Avenue Bosquet had refused to co-operate, claiming that they had not yet received authorisation from Rue la Boétie to fast-forward payment. The bank suggested that Monsieur des Moutis should perhaps contact the PMU himself and ask them to issue the necessary instructions. With little confidence that would work, Patrice tried to get through to someone official on the PMU's telephone-betting account line only to be told they too had been unable to issue his cheque for 70,000 francs as they had yet to be given the all-clear by the deputy director general.

Increasingly desperate to get his hands on the money, not just for himself but on behalf of everyone who'd been part of the gamble, Patrice called up a friend who did a lot of business with Crédit Lyonnais and asked him if he could use his contacts to find out what exactly the bank and the PMU were up to. At 5.30 p.m. on Wednesday 5 November the friend rang back to say that, although the PMU had paid the cheques to Patrice for his individual Couplé win and the two to his cousin and nephew, the Crédit Lyonnais had been instructed to block the payment of thirty-four other cheques that had been issued to winning punters, including all of those endorsed to Patrice.

As Des Moutis was about to discover, the PMU and the Paris police – not just *Commissaire* Taupin this time but the Brigade Criminelle from the Quai des Orfèvres – had already begun an investigation into the Prix Georges de Talhouet-Roy, starting with the running and riding of Clown. The gelding's trainer Jacques Dubois and jockey Jean-Jacques Declercq were being asked to explain why their horse had got off to such a bad start and had then made 'little effort to rejoin the peloton' (the rest of the field).

As a frustrated Des Moutis waited anxiously for his payout the PMU continued to study the result. Then, on 12 November, they officially confirmed that while they had paid out 1,100,000 francs of Tiercé winnings to people they considered to be legitimate punters, they had blocked further payments of over three million francs because they had been asked to issue the cheques to 'persons in the entourage of the same turfiste, Monsieur X, believed to be the brain behind the Prix de Bordeaux'. And Article 8 of PMU rules expressly forbade any punter to wager more than sixty francs on any combination of three horses in one or any number of PMU bureaux.

That same day the Auteuil Société des Steeplechases deposed two charges of fraud and attempted fraud before Judge Landreau, who was now widening the scope of his initial inquiry, which had already lasted seven years, to include the Prix Georges de Talhouet-Roy.

Some of Patrice's friends, so bullish and excited over the Toussaint weekend, were furious to find their winnings had been snatched away from them. Others, suddenly remembering those Trois Canards stories about the Prix de Bordeaux, were fearful of being prosecuted for conspiracy to defraud. But Des Moutis remained calm and, as if to demonstrate there was no fraud and that he had nothing to hide, he called up the Brigade Criminelle personally and invited them to send someone out to talk to him and to see his list of punters and winning bets.

On 14 November Divisional Commander Marcel Leclerc arrived at the insurance company offices in Neuilly. Unlike the thin and disapproving *Commissaire* Taupin, the detective from the Quai des Orfèvres was a big, down-to-earth farmer's son who'd joined the force after his military service in 1960. Leclerc cheerfully accepted Patrice's offer of a drink and a cigarette and produced the list of names he'd been given by the PMU, who had described them as co-conspirators abetting Patrice's illegal betting on the Prix Georges de Talhouet-Roy. Des Moutis put a line through four of the names saying that they had nothing to do with it, but didn't deny the involvement of the rest.

Leclerc pressed Patrice about the fifteen punters who had signed their winnings over to him and wanted to know the name of the man who had helped him round up the cheques. Patrice declined to reveal the punter's name but insisted again that everyone involved had been betting of their own volition and with their own money and that the only crime committed had been the fraud perpetrated by the PMU and Crédit Lyonnais in withholding payment.

Leclerc congratulated Patrice for predicting the result of the Prix Georges de Talhouet-Roy so accurately and talked about his own, mostly losing, bets on the horses. How did Patrice get it right so often, he wondered? Des Moutis talked modestly about logic and probability and the long hours he spent studying the form. When Leclerc left the two men shook hands amicably and agreed to talk again soon. But the detective returned to his colleagues at the Quai des Orfèvres, the French Scotland Yard adjacent to the Palais de Justice on the Île de la Cité, sceptical that the punters who had endorsed their cheques to Monsieur X had done so to facilitate quick clearance by the banks. Leclerc believed it was part of a pre-arranged plan to circumvent Article 8 and act as proxy punters on Patrice's behalf.

By Monday 17 November the PMU and the Société des Steeplechases had been talking to the press, and the lurid headlines began. 'New Tiercé fraud,' they screamed. 'Monsieur X implicated.' Reporters camped outside the white villa in Saint-Cloud and a photographer climbed over the fence and halfway up a weeping willow tree in the garden in an attempt to get a picture of Patrice and Marie-Thérèse inside the house.

One journalist trying to flesh out his story for the evening paper, *France-Soir*, got an off-the-record quote from a PMU executive at the Rue la Boétie. 'It's been ten years,' the man said, 'but this time . . . X is finished.'

Chapter 20

The Prix Georges de Talhouet-Roy was escalating into another scandal on a par with the Prix de Bordeaux, and some considered it all the more shocking given that, only that summer, Judge Landreau had confirmed that Monsieur X and his confederates in the earlier affair must go to trial. As far as the PMU management were concerned, that should have closed Des Moutis down, yet only a few months later their fish seemed to have wriggled off the hook.

'He's back,' punters were saying in the grandstands at Auteuil, Enghien and Saint-Cloud, and in the café bars in Pigalle – all of them marvelling that Monsieur X was now at the centre of not one but two contested Tiercé races, both the subject of judicial enquiries, with the fate of nearly eight million new francs hanging on the outcome.

Some government ministers and public figures were again professing alarm that a small group of gamblers betting in large sums could so substantially increase their chances of winning at the expense of the 'little' punters with their minimum stakes. The theme was taken up enthusiastically by the PMU's friends in the press. 'That's enough,' railed the magazine *Weekend*. 'The Tiercé must not fall into the hands of racketeers. This is Paris in 1969 not Chicago in 1930.' *Tiercérama*, a weekly tipping sheet, questioned the supposed scientific basis behind the high-stakes wagering of 'Monsieur Demoutis' (sic) and his friends. The process had yet to be satisfactorily explained, they said, hinting that it might have more to do with race fixing and corruption than mathematical theorems. The right-wing weekly *Minute*, founded in 1962 during the Algerian War, went even further, recommending prison for Patrice. 'This Tiercé affair must be the last,' declared its correspondent Saint- Aubin. 'Let's hope the individual responsible will soon be put in a place where he can do no further harm.'

All of these articles found their way to the insurance office in Neuilly, where it was said that Patrice's anger at some of the insinuations was loud enough to make the glass rattle in the window panes. The last shreds of the privacy and anonymity that he had tried to hang onto ever since his first Tiercé coup in 1958 had now been stripped away. His name and address were all over the papers and the PMU's propagandists were trashing his reputation and portraying him as a master criminal. It was time, Des Moutis decided, to try to regain the initiative and accept some of the numerous invitations he'd had from radio and TV programmes begging for an interview.

The first outing was not a success. The television producer Gilbert Larriaga had telephoned asking Patrice if he was prepared to appear on Channel 2's fifteen-minute Sunday-afternoon racing programme. Patrice agreed but, at his insistence, his face remained in shadow, which was a mistake and made him appear sinister. The interviewer was the respected racing presenter Léon Zitrone, who Patrice knew well, but he seemed at pains to avoid awkward questions. 'Dear, Monsieur X,' he began affably, 'might you be able to give us your tips for today's Tiercé?' 'Willingly, dear Monsieur Z,' replied Patrice. But aside from offering his views on the day's racing, Des Moutis found himself with little more than a couple of minutes in which to get across his arguments about the justice, or lack of it, of his treatment by the PMU.

Nobody at the Rue la Boétie had been prepared to come on the programme, affecting disdain for what they termed 'adversarial debate'. *Minute* had also declined despite having been invited to send a representative to 'liven things up', as the producer put it. As a result, both Patrice and the viewers were left frustrated and hungry for more. But in the course of several lengthy radio appearances over the next week Des Moutis fared much better.

In the space of twenty-four hours he responded to questions by the journalists Jean Claude Turjman and André Theron on France Inter and André Arnaud in the studio of Europe 1. Each time he assured his interrogators that his fellow punters on the Prix Georges de Talhouet-Roy had been betting of their own free will and with their own money, adding that his lawyers were busy preparing a counterclaim against the Sociétés des Courses, or racetrack management companies, who had initiated the process of withholding payment. Contrary to what the listeners may have heard, he said, he was not so much the Big Bad Wolf as a victim of the PMU's bureaucratic fraud.

Aware that public opinion could still go either way, Patrice then agreed to take part in a live discussion on Radio Monte-Carlo beginning at 9 a.m. on Sunday 23 November. Squeezed around a table in a black leather booth in the station's Paris studio was Patrice, the Radio Monte-Carlo racing correspondent Bernard Campaux, the station's editor-in-chief Claude Maurel, and Daniel Lahalle, a respected sports writer and regular columnist for *France-Soir*. As Maurel later testified, the programme was a resounding success. It had been scheduled to run for approximately forty-five minutes, including audience phone-ins, but proved so popular with so many listeners in the Monte Carlo, Marseille, Nîmes and Montpellier regions wanting to put a question to Monsieur X that it was allowed to run on for nearly two hours.

Everybody wanted to ask Patrice about his methods, and he began by explaining that, contrary to some of the myths that had grown up around him, he had no one single specific method. Every Tiercé race was different, he said, and every one had to be approached anew. Yes, there was the famous mathematical equation involving the possible number of Tiercé combinations in proportion to the number of runners. But the important thing was to first eliminate six or seven runners on the basis of form, weight, going preferences and so on, thus reducing the overall number of combinations that needed to be played, and then play all the rest.

When asked by Daniel Lahalle for his definition of the Tiercé, he said it was all about buying a dream, a description that would surely have found favour with André and Pierre Carrus and the PMU. For preference, he said, he favoured jump racing over the flat, adding that whatever the race it was important to play the horses rather than the jockeys, and he agreed with Bernard Campaux that he himself was not a typical Tiercé punter but more of a speculator or professional gambler. And when asked what else he liked to bet on he admitted 'a little weakness' for the old French card game, Scarlet and Black, which was played in Monte Carlo and in French casinos including Le Grand Cercle in Paris.

Patrice confessed later to Marie-Thérèse and friends like Alain Ayache that he had been fascinated, but also a little nervous, to find out what the listeners thought of him. He needn't have worried. There wasn't a single hostile caller, only admirers like the lady from Cavaillon ringing in to say how shocked she was by the disgraceful way the PMU had treated him. Thanking her sincerely for her support, Patrice stressed again that when he lost, the PMU happily kept his money without any recourse to an inquiry but, when he won, they automatically cried fraud.

After about an hour and a quarter Patrice was offered a restorative glass of rum St James as the producer Maurice Gardett, who was in a studio in Monte Carlo, interrupted to say that after hearing the case for the defence the audience were now going to hear from the prosecution. Having spurned the opportunity to appear on television with Léon Zitrone the previous weekend, the PMU deputy director general Maurice Alexandre had agreed to be interviewed by Radio Monte Carlo, but only as long as he was in a separate studio to Patrice. The station had co-operated by sending a radio car to the Rue la Boétie, and it was from there that Alexandre now joined in the discussion.

Every inch the smooth-talking executive, he started by assuring listeners that the PMU was at the service of all punters everywhere, including ones in the studio of Radio Monte Carlo. At which point Patrice interrupted to praise, with heavy irony, the great rapport the PMU had with him personally. Alexandre refused to rise to that, describing Patrice as a punter of 'great talent' who analysed races 'very astutely' but then claimed that there were certain 'technical problems' regarding Patrice's betting which he wouldn't go into as they would not be of great interest to the Radio Monte Carlo listeners.

Des Moutis butted in again to say that Alexandre was welcome to discuss those 'technical problems' with him at any time. Alexandre resorted to lofty *politesse*, observing that Patrice had talked for over an hour and would he please now allow him to get a word in too. Concerning the Prix de Bordeaux, continued Alexandre, there was evidence of certain infractions of Article 8 of the PMU rules, and there was a suspicion of a similar fraud in relation to the Prix Georges de Talhouet-Roy. At the sound of the word 'fraud' a furious Des Moutis interrupted yet again. 'You have no right to use that word,' he demanded. 'The law will be the judge of that,' replied Alexandre. 'But of course, my friend,' retorted Des Moutis sarcastically.

The Radio Monte Carlo racing correspondent, Bernard Campaux, wanted Alexandre to respond to Patrice's point, which had been picked up by a majority of the phone-in listeners, that the PMU seemed quite happy to accept Monsieur X's bets and keep his money when he lost but when he won they cried foul and refused to pay out. 'You have put it perfectly,' said Patrice, before Alexandre could reply. 'Myself, my wife and my daughters still have telephone-betting accounts with the PMU. Despite all this talk of fraud they haven't closed any of them because they know I'm their biggest punter and when I lose – and I do lose sometimes – they profit. If there is a Mafia du Tiercé it's a Mafia run by the PMU, who are permitted to defraud punters whatever their means and withhold payment to winners in order to line the pockets of the French government.'

'We are not interested in telephone-betting accounts,' rejoined Alexandre coolly. 'Only instances where the identity of winning ticket holders suggests to us they have been party to corruption.'

'Monsieur Alexandre,' interjected Daniel Lahalle, 'if, when he leaves this studio, Monsieur X goes on to play today's Tiercé and his friends follow his tips, will you accept their bets or will you turn them away?' Alexandre's reply was icily polite: 'In any case where we see evidence of malpractice,' he said, 'we will take that evidence to the prosecutor.'

In spite of Alexandre's efforts the response to the programme in the days and weeks that followed was overwhelmingly supportive of Des Moutis and critical of the PMU. One female phone-in listener, sounding completely smitten with Patrice, picked up on the Robin Hood theme, like the illegal bookies at Auteuil, depicting him as a *Robin des Bois Moderne*, fighting a battle on behalf of all oppressed citizens struggling against bureaucratic tyranny. The description caught on, even though the analogy was a difficult one to sustain given that Patrice's avowed aim was to scoop as much of the Tiercé pool as possible, effectively taking from the rich *and* the poor, in the guise of the mug punters with their three-franc minimum stakes, and award the proceeds to himself, his family and his friends. But with the exotic title adding to his mystique, the Des Moutis legend continued to grow with a fulsome piece in *Paris Match* acclaiming his success as the incarnation of the dreams of gamblers everywhere.

The positive coverage inspired a near-rabid response from Saint-Aubin in *Minute*. 'Monsieur X a Saint?' he railed. 'Monsieur X a poor innocent victim of the PMU? Do not be taken in. Monsieur X is a dangerous personage and war against him is totally justified.'

The PMU seemed to agree, as in the week following the Radio Monte Carlo programme they launched three missiles in Patrice's direction. First they issued a letter informing him that his telephone-betting account and those of his wife and daughters were now officially closed. They also contacted the Société d'Encouragement and asked them to write to the Jockey Club in England and the Turf Club in Ireland and urge them, in a spirit of reciprocity, to extend the 1953 racecourse ban on Des Moutis to all British and Irish tracks. Their Anglo-Irish friends obliged, meaning there would be no more happy away days for Des Moutis to Epsom, Ascot, Sandown Park and the Curragh.

The PMU's alarm over Patrice's popularity was shared by civil servants working for Valéry Giscard d'Estaing in the Finance Ministry. The state's share of the Tiercé and other PMU pools now amounted to between three per cent and six per cent of their total tax revenue and they couldn't allow their cut to be jeopardised by the actions of a rich gentleman gambler from Saint-Cloud. The chief inspector at the Trésor Public was instructed to look again at the tax returns of Monsieur X, and there was talk of a new 30 per cent levy being introduced on 'excessive' profits from betting on horse and trotting racing.

Patrice spent an exhausting year trying to maintain that punters were already taxed at base thanks to the deductions taken out of the PMU pool before paying winning bets. A further charge, he claimed, would not only be unfair but counterproductive, depressing betting turnover and reducing the state's take. He won the argument but the costs of his war with the authorities were mounting and, with his gains continually blocked, his income from gambling was diminishing. Two or three fraud cases were now pending, and if Des Moutis couldn't beat the PMU and the government fairly in open court, in what direction might he turn next?

Chapter 21

Still Patrice tried to get around the legal limit on maximum Tiercé stakes, and for his next attempt he returned to the setting that had yielded a bonanza pay-off eight years earlier.

Early on the morning of Sunday 25 January 1970 Des Moutis, clad in his best dark suit and tie, left Saint-Cloud in his black Mercedes 220 and drove 15 miles along mostly empty peripheral roads to Orly airport on the southern side of Paris. It was a sad day for Patrice as he was on his way to the funeral of an old skiing friend who had been killed in an accident on the Oreiller-Killy piste in Val-d'Isère and was going to be buried near his family home outside Divonne-les-Bains.

At Orly Des Moutis boarded a 9 a.m. flight to Geneva and, settling down in his seat in the Air France Caravelle, he turned again to the reading matter that he had been studying for the last twenty-four hours. The *Paris Turf* form guide and tips for the Prix d'Amérique, the Prix de l'Arc de Triomphe of trotting racing, which was due to take place that afternoon at Vincennes. The forty-sixth running of the world's richest trotting race promised to be one of the biggest betting events of the year in

France, with a Tiercé pool to match Toussaint and Quatorze Juillet, and Des Moutis was intent on winning it.

The thirteen-runner contest over 2,600 metres featured two popular favourites: Upsalin, the 1969 victor, representing the local owner-trainer Henri Lévesque, who'd won the race five times before; and the brilliant mare Une de Mai, who had triumphed in the Prix de la Côte d'Azur at Cagnes-sur-Mer on 13 January. She was to be driven by her trainer Jean-René Gougeon, elder brother of Minou Gougeon who'd partnered the outsider Nemrose in the Prix de Bordeaux and who would now be steering Une de Mai's stable companion Toscan. The two Gougeon representatives were both co-owned by their breeder, *Comte* Pierre de Montesson, and the larger-than-life trainer and gambler Pierre-Désiré Allaire, who was a friend of Frank Sinatra and renowned as one of the biggest punters at Vincennes.

It was safe to assume that the great majority of Tiercé bets on the Prix d'Amérique would include both Upsalin and Une de Mai and, if either of them won and the other one finished in the first three, it would be a small payout. But if one of them were to lose and not even be placed the payout would be much bigger. In defiance of the form experts, Patrice had concluded there was a strong possibility that Une de Mai would not win. It wasn't just that she had never shown her best form at Vincennes. It was also that, as a mare, her value could only increase by so much if she was successful, as she could only be in foal to one stallion per breeding season. But if her stable companion Toscan – representing the same owners – were to win, his value as a sire would quadruple at the very least given that he would be able to cover dozens of mares each year.

Patrice des Moutis had no doubt that such thoughts would have crossed the minds of worldly owners like Allaire and the *Comte* de Montesson. Maybe he had actually been tipped off by them to back Toscan and not the mare. Allaire was a big punter, after all, and well known to Patrice back in his bookmaking days. But whatever his reasons, when Des Moutis decided on the six or seven runners he was going to rule out completely, Une de Mai was one of them, whereas Toscan was to be his base selection alongside Upsalin, the American challenger Snow Speed and two improving French trotters. Tony M was a local horse in good form and expected to relish the step up in distance from his last run, while Des Moutis knew that Tidalium Pelo had been quietly aimed at the Prix d'Amérique all winter.

Patrice had a hire car waiting for him at Geneva airport. It was no more than a thirty-minute drive north to Divonne-les-Bains and, shortly after crossing the French border, he stopped at a stately old spa hotel and rang Marie-Thérèse in Saint-Cloud. He would later claim that in the course of the conversation, intended to reassure his wife that he had arrived safely, he just happened to pass on a few tips for the day's big Tiercé race, unaware that she might share them with friends. For her part, Marie-Thérèse didn't deny that she was not alone in the house that Sunday morning. In fact, she was surrounded by about a dozen friends and family members, including her daughters Patricia and Nicole, for whom a bet on the Tiercé had become almost as much of a weekend institution as going to Mass, or the market in Garches and then out to lunch. And after writing down Patrice's recommendations for the Prix d'Amérique Marie-Thérèse said it was perfectly natural for her to share them with the assembled company and then telephone a few other friends and tell them to back the same combinations.

By the end of that Sunday morning Madame des Moutis and her nineteen companions had visited either the Café Clemenceau in Saint-Cloud, the Café Sainte-Foy in Neuilly, or Le Flandrin on Avenue Henri-Martin, and had each played Patrice's core permutation of Toscan, Upsalin, Tony M and Tidalium Pelo to a 720-franc stake multiplied by twenty. All with their own money, they said, and all of their own volition. Patrice, over 300 miles away in Divonne-les-Bains, didn't place a single bet in his own name, and had to wait until after the funeral service and interment to hear the result.

It was an extraordinary race. Snow Speed, renowned for breaking fast, tried to grab an early lead behind the autocar that was leading them in at the start. The American horse was yanked back suddenly by his driver Gerhard Krüger and, in the process, Upsalin, who was positioned just behind him, ran into the back of Snow Speed and the resulting collision knocked both runners out of the race. An enormous sigh went up from the crowd, many of whom were faithful fans of the 1969 winner.

Des Moutis may not have been expecting such a dramatic opening salvo but his suspicions about Une de Mai and Toscan proved uncannily accurate. Sweeping left-handed around Vincennes' top turn for the final time, Une de Mai was in a good position on the inside rail. But then her driver, Jean-René Gougeon, seemed to 'open the gate', to ease her out at a crucial moment enabling her stable companion Toscan, who was tucked in behind, to surge through the gap. Toscan and Minou

Gougeon came away strongly to win the race by three lengths, with Tony M staying on into second place and Tidalium Pelo just keeping Une de Mai out of third. Minou Gougeon wept tears of joy afterwards, but his brother Jean-René stayed out of sight in the weighing room.

The numbers 10, 2 and 11 Tiercé paid 1,555.50 francs for a three-franc stake in the correct order, and 311.10 francs in any order, and Marie-Thérèse and her family and friends had won 31,000 francs apiece, or over 600,000 francs in total. But that was not all. Madame des Moutis, on her husband's advice, had also won the small matter of four million francs, or around £400,000, from a series of Couplé bets matching Toscan with Tony M and Tidalium Pelo.

As Patrice digested the outcome on his flight home that night he had the satisfaction of knowing that, while luck may have been on his side at the start, his decision to leave out Une de Mai had been fully vindicated and that, acting on his advice, his wife and friends had made money.

Except that they hadn't.

On the morning of Monday 26 January, Marie-Thérèse and her fellow winners went back to the three PMU cafés where they had placed their bets. All of them provided identification, as required by law, and all claimed their winnings, which they were told would be issued by cheque as per usual and posted to them later that day. Some among the group of twenty were not used to taking large sums of money out of their bank accounts to bet on horse and trotting racing and were keen to make good the withdrawals and bank their profits as soon as possible.

But when Tuesday morning's post arrived there was no sign of any cheques from the Pari-Mutuel Urbain. The one exception being a payment for Marie-Thérèse's handsome Couplé win which had been sent out by the Café Clemenceau in Saint-Cloud.

One irate claimant went over to the Rue la Boétie to enquire what was going on only to be told that Maurice Alexandre, Pierre Carrus and Pierre Crespin were not available. In their place an anonymous *fonctionnaire* declared that, just as punters had five days in which to present their winning claims, the PMU had five days in which to pay out.

On Wednesday morning, 28 January, there were still no cheques in the post, and when Thursday also yielded a blank the twenty punters, led again by Marie-Thérèse – but with Patrice presumed to be advising them now in the background – recruited a court bailiff to go back to the three PMU *café-tabacs* and demand their cheques. The cashiers in Le Flandrin, the Cafe Sainte-Foy and the Café Clemenceau all insisted they had not yet received the cheques from the PMU's head office.

The bailiff, Maître Desagneaux, went straight to the Rue la Boétie where he was received by a visibly discomforted Pierre Crespin. The secretary general claimed that it had not yet been possible to pay the twenty winners because fifteen of them had been among the group of punters under investigation regarding the Prix Georges de Talhouet-Roy the previous November. One of those punters was Madame des Moutis and, while Monsieur Patrice des Moutis was not one of the claimants, the Vincennes stewards and the PMU needed to be satisfied that the Prix d'Amérique Tiercé winners were not party to another 'fraudulent' attempt by Monsieur X to circumvent PMU rules. Accordingly, Crespin continued, the Prix d'Amérique winnings had been blocked and he intended to relay his suspicions to the Public Prosecutor who was already investigating the Prix Georges de Talhouet-Roy as well as the Prix de Bordeaux.

When Maître Desagneaux reported Crespin's comments to Marie-Thérèse, Patrice and the other winners in Saint-Cloud were incensed. One of them, an elderly aristocratic gentleman not used to being accused of fraud, wanted to 'call out' René Ballière, the President of the Société de Vincennes, and challenge him to a duel. Des Moutis managed to calm the gentleman down, assuring him that he and the other nineteen winners were not the real target of the PMU's actions. He was the one they were after, he said, and he should be the one fighting the duel. It was all part of a calculated attempt to destroy him, borne out of years of pique and resentment over his various Tiercé coups. Des Moutis added that his lawyers were confident that the PMU's conspiracy claims would never stand up in court, especially in the case of the Prix d'Amérique as none of the others had signed their cheques over to him.

Meanwhile Patrice's friend and loyal supporter Alain Ayache was doing his best to continue the fight on Patrice's behalf. In the autumn of 1969 Ayache and two other journalists – Georges Angey and Raoul Tubiana – had started a new weekly racing and betting magazine called *Spécial Dernière*. It occasionally featured the Des Moutis Tiercé recommendations, under the byline of 'Monsieur X', and with the first official published photograph of Patrice looking dashing yet enigmatic in a suit and tie and dark glasses.

The Monsieur X column was a big hit with the public, and within a few months of its launch the magazine's readership was up to 350,000 and still growing. At the end of January 1970 *Spécial Dernière* ran an article by Charles Angers that savaged the PMU in general and its treatment of 'Madame X' and the other nineteen Prix d'Amérique winners in particular. The PMU's behaviour, it said, implied that any perfectly normal winning bets could be deemed suspect in their eyes enabling them to withhold payment with only the most threadbare legal justification. It amounted to outrageous treatment and unacceptable intimidation of punters everywhere.

When Angers asked Marie-Thérèse for her response to the PMU's threats she replied firmly that their latest attempt at intimidation would have no effect on her and that if she saw another good opportunity to play the Tiercé she would take it. Marie-Thérèse Queret, it seemed, had evolved from being a silent and not always approving witness of her husband's gambling and illegal bookmaking to a willing and determined participant every bit as scornful of the PMU as Patrice.

But despite the outward display of sang-froid in the Des Moutis household, Patrice's mood – especially when he was on his own with his closest friends – had become noticeably darker. He told Ayache that he felt that 'now the times are working against me', with investigations multiplying by the day. As well as the Police des Courses et Jeux inquiry into the betting patterns on the Prix d'Amérique and the Prix Georges de Talhouet-Roy, the Brigade Criminelle were investigating the running and riding of Clown and Start in the Auteuil race and also looking into the incident at the start of the Prix d'Amérique and interviewing the trotting drivers Gerhard Krüger and Jean-René Gougeon.

The collision had instantly ruled Snow Speed and Upsalin out of the race, thus reducing the number of potential winners to eleven, but, as Des Moutis had pointed out to Marcel

Leclerc at a meeting over coffee in the Sainte-Foy, Snow Speed and Upsalin had been two of his original Tiercé choices. Did it make sense therefore that he would have colluded in some scheme to ruin their chances, as the police and the PMU were inferring? He also denied having profited personally from the Prix d'Amérique outcome, maintaining that he had just 'passed on some tips' to his wife, who had 'apparently' passed them on again to her friends. As for Marie-Thérèse's big Couplé win, he insisted that had been a bet of her own choice with her own funds. Leclerc smiled and nodded but patently didn't believe him.

Despite Patrice's denials of wrongdoing, the publicity surrounding the Prix d'Amérique, coming so soon after the Prix Georges de Talhouet-Roy controversy, was enveloping him in what he described as 'an odour of sulphur'. Leclerc, Taupin and their colleagues were turning up uninvited at too many smart houses. And one by one certain former friends and acquaintances – some of whom had been so excited to be in on the Prix Georges de Talhouet-Roy gamble the previous autumn – were snubbing Patrice and Marie-Thérèse and closing the doors to their 16th *arrondissement salons*. The bedroom doors of the admiring female racehorse owners, for whom Monsieur X had once been such an enjoyable afternoon companion, were closing too. 'So sorry, my darling. But all those policemen. It's too much scandal.' Just as bad was the number of former clients of the Neuilly insurance office that were taking their patronage and their money elsewhere, adding to the pressure on both Patrice and his brother Gilbert.

Des Moutis was spending a great deal more than he was earning, and it wasn't as if he could try to redeem the situation with another spectacular Tiercé coup. The days of his 'happy Sundays', as the singer Enrico Macias called them, of the great Granville and *Bonne Année* gambles, were, he reluctantly concluded, over. The PMU were determined that he should not win. Not like before. Not ever again. At most now he could place one Tiercé bet multiplied by twenty in his own name, and only one, on any combination of three horses. Any more bets placed on the same horses by himself or his wife or his daughters or friends and the gains would be blocked, a whistle would be blown and *Commissaire* Taupin and the Police des Courses et Jeux would come running.

With the bills mounting and his income falling, it seemed that all Patrice could do was wait for justice to pronounce on the Prix de Bordeaux and decide the fate of the seven million francs' worth of winnings that had yet to be released.

Chapter 22

On 20 February 1970 the Chambre d'Accusation ruled that the Prix de Bordeaux case should be tried not in a civil court but in the 13th Correctionel or Penal Court, in the Palais de Justice in Paris. It was a momentous decision and one that smacked of political interference. Monsieur X was to be called to account in the highest and most august courthouse in the land, the place where swindlers, murderers and traitors like the OAS Generals Edmond Jouhaud and Raoul Salan had been brought to hear their fates. Correctional Tribunals ranked below the Assize Courts that normally tried murder cases and armed robberies but they still had the power to impose a sentence of up to ten years imprisonment. It was no longer just about money or reputation or pride. From now on Patrice's freedom was at stake.

The legal timetable, though, was still excruciatingly slow, and the court proceedings were not actually due to begin until 1 December 1971. Patrice des Moutis and his lawyers had almost two years in which to prepare their case, and Patrice was determined to fight the PMU with all his might. *Spécial Dernière* weighed in with more articles scornful of PMU rules set up specifically to stop Des Moutis, even as Patrice was busy accumulating fresh evidence of what he described as 'PMU stupidity' to place before the court.

On Sunday 1 February 1970 Des Moutis and a card-playing friend of his Philippe Loic, who was also one of the Prix de Bordeaux and Prix Georges de Talhouet-Roy punters, had each placed a small Tiercé bet on the Prix de Nevers at Vincennes. Patrice wagered 1,200 francs multiplied by twenty and Loic bet just 300 francs multiplied by five. Crucially both men filled out identical coupons combining the same three horses and placed their bets together in the Café Sainte-Foy.

The result, in which a favourite trained by Pierre-Désiré Allaire was surprisingly unplaced, was exactly as Patrice had predicted, with his selections finishing first, second and third in the correct order. The payout was 5,484 francs to Patrice, the smallest sum he'd ever won on the Tiercé, and an even more modest 1,371 francs to Philippe Loic. But, while the Café Sainte-Foy PMU bureau issued Patrice's cheque the next day, Loic's winnings were withheld. A few days later he was informed by the bailiff, Maître Desagneaux, that the PMU had blocked payment due to suspicions – based on earlier Tiercé races – that he was a proxy punter for Monsieur X.

Far from being angry, Patrice was positively delighted. The PMU, he said, had fallen into his trap. The absurd ruling, with its supposition that he would employ another punter to help him win the colossal sum of a thousand francs, or approximately £100 sterling, made a mockery of their case and he would say so in court.

A victory to Des Moutis perhaps, but mockery gave way to fury in August 1970 when Patrice, Philippe Loic and Jules Carrax won 20 million francs each, from three individual Tiercé bets on the Grand Handicap de Deauville. They had studied the race together, shared their thoughts as punters often do, and then gone and backed the same horses – along with Lester Piggott's victorious Prix Morny mount My Swallow – on the Sunday morning. When they went to collect their winnings from the PMU bureau in Suresnes, where they had placed their bets, they had to display their ID cards as required by law. The bureau manager, Monsieur Oliveiro, had been about to hand over the cheques, but when he realised that one of the three identical winners was the notorious Monsieur X, he froze with alarm. At which point Patrice reached across the counter and simply plucked the cheques out of Oliveiro's hand as if he were picking an apple off a tree. Nodding politely, the three punters walked out of the office and went back to Patrice's villa in Saint-Cloud.

That afternoon Monsieur Oliveiro turned up at the Des Moutis house in a wretched state. He had been in touch with PMU head office, he said. Protocol demanded it when paying out such large sums. When he'd told the management that one of his big three Tiercé winners was Monsieur des Moutis and that he'd taken his cheque, Pierre Crespin had flown into a rage. Now they were threatening to sack him and close the Suresnes PMU branch altogether unless he personally recovered or made good the 20 million francs.

Patrice des Moutis invited Oliveiro into the *salon*, poured him a large Scotch and wrote him a personal cheque for twenty million francs there and then. Half an hour later, after the tearful Oliveiro had left, thanking them all profusely, Patrice rang the office in Rue la Boétie. The PMU senior management had refused to see him in person any more, saying there could be no face-to-face meetings between them until after the trial, so their only contact was by telephone. Des Moutis, his tone cold and contemptuous, kept it short. Poor Monsieur Oliveiro is guilty of nothing, he said to Pierre Crespin. The man responsible is me. I have repaid the money and if you know what is right you'll lift the threat to close the Suresnes bureau and assure Monsieur Oliveiro his job is safe. The following day the PMU's Suresnes branch opened as normal and Antoine Oliveiro went back to work.

Spécial Dernière seized on the Suresnes and Prix de Nevers stories and ran another scathing editorial denouncing the PMU as an unprincipled monopoly, happy to raise millions for the state and the French racing industry while confiscating stake money and withholding the payment of perfectly legal winning bets. The magazine's readers responded by continuing to write in enthusiastically to Monsieur X, asking for his advice on everything from next Sunday's Tiercé to the best home for their savings and pensions, which he urged them *not* to invest in betting on horse racing.

Whatever the 16th *arrondissement* smart set now thought of the infamous punter in their midst, a poll of *Spécial Dernière* readers at Vincennes found that 81 per cent of them were still on the side of racing's Robin Hood in his battle with the PMU. And if it was really true that he had enlisted a band of co-conspirators to help him pull off the Prix de Bordeaux coup, what of it? They liked him all the more for his audacity, not less.

The adventures of Monsieur X had struck a chord, particularly with the young, in an era that was naturally more sympathetic to stories of charismatic outlaws and rebels than authority figures. In February 1970 *Butch Cassidy and the Sundance Kid* had opened to general acclaim in cinemas across Europe, and a few months later the French had their own version in the shape of the gangster epic *Borsalino*. The colourful portrait of aspiring mobsters in Marseille in the 1930s starred Jean-Paul Belmondo and Alain Delon – the Paul Newman and Robert Redford of French cinema – and, like *Butch Cassidy*, combined wit and slick storytelling with an infectiously memorable soundtrack. Not for the first time, Des Moutis was compared to Belmondo by some, while his alter ego Monsieur X was compared to the more emotionally detached Delon.

If French cinemagoers, like audiences in Britain and the US, enjoyed watching their favourite filmstars playing gangsters, some of the stars of that era liked mixing with gangsters in real life. In London the actor Stanley Baker was a good friend of the West End godfather Albert Dimes, and in New York and Las Vegas Frank Sinatra and the Rat Pack mixed openly with Mafia made men. In Marseille Alain Delon was sometimes seen in the company of the Corsican godfather Marcel Francisci and was on friendly terms with the younger Canards, Tany Zampa and Jacky Imbert.

In his book *Stars and Truands* the reformed French criminal Thierry Colombié recalls how Delon gave Zampa a wolfskin coat which the racketeer liked to wear in winter when strolling round Marseille's Vieux Port. Colombié also described the even closer links between Delon and Jacky Imbert, who were united by their joint passion for trotting racing. By 1970 Jacky le Mat, who had first met Delon when working as a stunt driver, was building a promising alternative career as a trotting-race driver at Marseille's Borély racetrack. And Delon, who followed Jacky's betting tips whenever he was in town, had chosen Imbert's racing patron Pierre-Désiré Allaire to train the trotting horses he was starting to breed with his partner, the actress Mireille Darc, at Allaire's Puy-Sainte-Réparade Stud near Aix-en-Provence.

Gangsters and filmstars, showbusiness and racing – it all seemed to go together as part of an ageless and quintessential mix. But by the early 1970s the gangsters of the Côte d'Azur, including Francisci, Zampa and Jacky Imbert were mixed up in another kind of business that wasn't harmless at all. With the Guérini family out of the game after Antoine Guérini's assassination in Marseille in 1967, the younger *Milieu* leaders were now the chief shareholders in *Le French*, or the French Connection, drugs trade between Indo-China, Provence and the US. By 1970–71 the business was worth, literally, millions of francs and the bosses and senior executives of the organisation needed an increasing number of ways to launder the proceeds so as to be able to pass the cash off as legitimately acquired earnings. And what better way of doing that, for men who were all gambling enthusiasts anyway, than through betting on horse and trotting racing.

The underworld had fixed races before going back to the days of François Spirito and Paul Carbone, the templates for the Belmondo and Delon characters in *Borsalino*, and there was nothing new about jockeys stopping the occasional favourite to benefit some grateful patron. But by the spring of 1971 Marcel Leclerc and his colleagues in the Brigade Criminelle at the Quai des Orfèvres in Paris were beginning to wonder if the Corsicans and their Marseille friends hadn't embarked on something much bigger. Something involving the wholesale corruption of jockeys and trainers and the fixing of races, especially Tiercé races, in such a way that might conceivably involve – however reluctantly – the people's favourite and Robin des Bois . . . Monsieur X.

Chapter 23

Marseille's main racecourse, the Hippodrome de Borély, is on the eastern edges of the city within the grounds of the Parc Borély, with its lakes and miniature château. Flanked by a mix of tall, modern apartment buildings and landscaped greenery, the track overlooks the sea, and there's a fine view of the Mediterranean ferries and cargo boats coming in and out of the bay. To the southeast lies the rugged limestone Massif protecting the *calanques*, or fjord-like inlets, that line the coast towards Bandol, while to the west the skyline is dominated by the 135-foot tower of the church of Notre-Dame de la Garde with the Vieux Port beyond.

Borély races between March and December each year, staging mixed programmes of flat, jumps and trotting racing. The fixtures may not have the same social cachet as racing at the Paris tracks, or Deauville or Chantilly, but there's a Grand Prix or two and the prize money, thanks to Pari-Mutuel subsidy, is never less than generous.

On Saturday 27 February 1971 Borély staged an eight-race card featuring the Prix d'Entressen, a nineteen-runner trotting race over 2,100 metres, or rather more than a mile and a quarter. A Marseille punter called Louis Mattei won one million one hundred thousand francs from a 180,000-franc bet on the Trio, a simplified version of the Tiercé, in which players have to name the first three home in any order. The respective odds of the first three finishers in the Prix d'Entressen were 27-1, 8-1 and 35-1, and Mattei's gains represented no less than 70 per cent of the total pool wagered on the contest.

Since the 1960s most racecourses had been equipped with camera patrol film technology providing a filmed record of a race should stewards subsequently decide to hold an inquiry. There was no camera patrol film at Borély in February 1971 or at least no film of the Prix d'Entressen. But it was noticeable to professionals watching in the stands that the first three left the other nineteen runners behind right from the start and that, when some of the chasing pack tried to make up ground, an intervening group of four or five horses and drivers seemed to be acting as a shield for the leaders. 'Every time I tried to overtake them one of them swung in front of me to block my way,' claimed one unnamed driver. Another said, 'I had the distinct impression that certain drivers were defending others and did not ask for the maximum effort from their horses. I was disgusted.'

The racecourse stewards saw no reason to enquire into the race on the day, and Louis Mattei was issued with a PMU cheque for his winnings within forty-eight hours. But the size and scale of the betting alerted the Police des Courses et Jeux, and within a week they had begun an investigation. Their enquiries yielded more rumours and stories among Borély's regular 'faces' who believed that there had been 'an arrangement' and that the Prix d'Entressen had been a fixed race. The drivers of some of the favourites had supposedly been paid to stop their runners from figuring in the first three so as to boost the odds on the Trio payout, while other drivers had been enlisted to ensure that the shorter-priced runners didn't break ranks. It had been a skilled team effort, and the driver of one of the horses protecting the lead of the first three had been Jacky Imbert.

The tip-offs also claimed that the three horses who made up the winning combination had been selected not by Louis Mattei … but by Patrice des Moutis … and that the currently cash-strapped Monsieur X had been one of several beneficiaries of the outcome.

The information about a possible PMU 'meridional' angle, as it was being called, was passed on to the Brigade Criminelle in Paris, though the possible involvement of Des Moutis was not yet released into the public domain. But a few months later the violent death of a young jockey shed further light on French racing's dark underside and hinted at more, as yet unexposed, links between Monsieur X and his PMU feud and the *Milieu*.

On 8 May 1971 the body of Jean-Luc Durry was found in a friend's house, the Villa Lolita, in Cannes. The 20-year-old rider, who was lying curled up on a bed, fully dressed, with a gun dog at his feet, had supposedly shot himself in the head with a single bullet from a .22 rifle. It was a shockingly premature end to what had once promised to be a brilliant career. Durry had left school at the age of 14 to go to the apprentice jockeys' college in Maisons-Laffitte. He'd started riding on the flat a year later and was quickly hailed as an exceptional talent. In 1967, only his second season with a licence, he partnered forty-six winners, and the great French champion jockey, Yves Saint-Martin, anointed him as a future successor.

In 1969 Durry won the prestigious Prix Ganay at Longchamp riding in the colours of Madame Strassburger, widow of the American breeder and newspaper owner Ralph Strassburger, who had been one of French racing's senior figures. But young Durry was already going through agonies trying to control his weight, the bane of so many jockeys' lives, and the situation wasn't helped by his heavy drinking. As he got bigger he was forced to switch from the flat to jump racing – where the minimum weight for a rider is higher – beginning at Clairefontaine near Deauville in 1970. Initially he looked so stylish over hurdles and fences that he was retained to ride for Daniel Wildenstein and Maurice Zilber, which should have been the making of him.

Durry, though, couldn't resist partying and playing cards with the bad boys of the weighing room, allegedly running up huge debts in the clandestine card games so generously organised by the *Milieu*. He was also left distraught when an affair with Sandra Pyers, the daughter of the Australian jockey Bill Pyers, who was riding on the flat in France for Wildenstein and Zilber, suddenly came to an end. When Durry was drunk one night he got hold of a gun, went and stood in the street outside Pyers' house in the village of Lys near Chantilly and fired several rounds through the windows.

With his debts mounting, his riding increasingly erratic, and rumours that he was losing his mind, Durry was advised to take a short break from racing and the Paris circuit. In better times he had spent a winter on the Côte d'Azur riding the winner of the Grand Prix de la Ville de Cannes at Cagnes-sur-Mer and, with a friend and ex-jockey Robert Laouira making the arrangements, it was to Cannes that he returned in the spring of 1971.

After Durry's death one of his former racing colleagues described him as 'not equipped to defend himself', while others said he was the 'victim of several adventures' and in 'serious trouble' in his professional life. But he left no suicide note and there was little official effort made locally to establish the full circumstances of his death or question what he was doing with a gun dog and a .22 rifle in May when the hunting season in the south of France runs from early September to February. Privately investigators for the Police des Courses et Jeux and the Brigade Criminelle refuted the assumption that he had killed himself. They believed that Durry had been stopping horses to pay his creditors, who included 'B movie types with Midi accents and smart tailoring' (the Midi being all of the south of France from the Pyrenees to the Italian border) and may have been shot to stop him talking about those activities to the authorities. A bullet in the back of the head was, after all, a favourite *Milieu* method of execution often dressed up, improbably, as suicide.

It was also pointed out that Durry had ridden fancied but beaten runners in a number of controversial Tiercé races, including several where Des Moutis had backed the winners. One detective journeying down to Cannes to look into Durry's last days even went so far as to allege that Monsieur X 'may not have had tears in his eyes' on receiving the news of Durry's death.

PMU lobbyists like the right-wing magazine *Minute* seized on these leaks with relish. Their columnist Saint-Aubin portrayed Patrice as 'not so much a prisoner of bad company' as a gambling mastermind, unhinged by his feud with the PMU and 'more than open to the underworld's advances'. It was a determined attempt again by the PMU's advocates to depict Des Moutis not as a Robin Hood or saint but as the accomplice of racketeers, and a return to the line of attack that had originally linked him to the Perret brothers and the Bande des Trois Canards.

Now it was finally time for the conflicting claims about Monsieur X, his friends and his motives, to be publicly tested in court.

Chapter 24

A vast overpowering monument to imperial grandeur, the Palais de Justice is right in the heart of Paris on the western side of the Île de la Cité next door to the Conciergerie, the former prison turned museum where Marie Antoinette and other aristocrats were held prior to their execution in the Revolution.

The aristocratically bred Des Moutis and his lawyers approached the main entrance on Boulevard du Palais early on the morning of Wednesday 1 December 1971. Patrice was following in the footsteps of some of the most famous criminals in French history. Serial killers like Dr Marcel Petiot, who murdered at least twenty-three people during World War II. Traitors and collaborators like Marshal Pétain and Pierre Laval, heads of the wartime Vichy government. Fellow 16th *arrondissement* charmers like the murderer Georges Rapin who styled himself 'Monsieur Bill'; and rebels and OAS leaders like Edmond Jouhaud and Raoul Salan.

Unlike those prisoners, who were brought to the law courts in handcuffs and under guard, Des Moutis at least arrived a free man. But once he'd passed through the wrought-iron gates and climbed the steps leading up to the massive Second Empire façade, it would have been hardly surprising if his confidence momentarily wavered as he made his way through the high-ceilinged vestibule and along the corridors to Courtroom 13. The character and dimensions of the building seem designed to crush the spirit; the worn grey stone and bare walls reflecting the pain and despair of the hundreds of former defendants and their families – some innocent, some guilty – who have passed that way before.

Court 13, on the first floor of Staircase D, was on the criminal, as opposed to the civil, side of the building and linked by passageways and tunnels to Police Judiciaire headquarters at the Quai des Orfèvres. The courtroom itself was tall with high windows – precluding much of a view of the river and the city outside – and lit by four chandeliers. On either side of the central aisle there were about a dozen rows of wooden benches for witnesses, families and members of the public and the press who, as well as representatives of all the leading French newspapers, included foreign correspondents like Patrick Brogan of *The Times* and others from New York, Sydney, Madrid and Milan.

As is customary in France there was no jury. The president of the court and his two fellow judges entered through a door at the back of the room and took their seats on a raised podium at the front, the Scales of Justice inscribed on the wooden panelling above their heads. The competing teams of lawyers, looking like penguins in their black gowns and white ruffs, stood or sat on either side of the aisle conferring with their clients.

Des Moutis was officially charged with breaking the rules of betting by wagering more than the legal limit on the 1962 Prix de Bordeaux at Vincennes, and with fraud and conspiracy to defraud by recruiting eighty-three friends and other punters to bet in his name across France. Fifty-one of the original eighty-three Tiercé winners stood accused with him (although only a handful of them were in court), and of flouting a law dating back to 1891 prohibiting fraudulent betting on behalf of a third party.

From the outset Patrice seemed determined to put on a good show and not to let either his fellow accused or his supporters down. Questioned at length by President Arnaud and the other judges, the 'Superman du Tiercé', as Jean Laborde called him in *L'Aurore*, argued his case with fluency and *élan*. He denied being part of a conspiracy and referred to the absurd PMU response to his modest win on the Prix de Nevers with Philippe Loic in 1970 as evidence of their paranoia and hostility. As regards the Prix de Bordeaux, he continued to maintain that he had just 'helped out some friends', though he admitted that in a four-year period between 1958 and 1962 he had won over 15 million francs from Tiercé betting. 'How did you do it?' asked Arnaud. 'Do you want a tip?' asked Patrice, smiling. The judge laughed – everyone laughed – and for a moment the courtroom relaxed.

Treating the judges like old friends, Des Moutis explained how he systematically ruled out certain runners on the basis of form, class, going and other considerations. He had been the PMU's best customer, he said, but only his successes were ever mentioned, never his losses. But now, having laid out huge sums on legitimate winning bets, he couldn't get his stakes back let alone his gains. At the same time, the publicity leading up to the court proceedings had ruined his career as an insurance expert as former clients were continually being told by the PMU that he was a criminal.

In their reports the next day most press observers agreed that Patrice had performed 'drolly and with aplomb in the face of justice' and that the courtroom audience had been on his side. One female correspondent for *Le Figaro* was impressed by how handsome Des Moutis was, with his dark hair and 'profile like Belmondo'. She was struck by the depth of his hostility to 'his enemy' the PMU yet also puzzled that he'd continued betting with them for so long when he held such a damning view of their conduct. 'In court he looks rich and well,' she said. 'Yet he tells us, "I am ruined."'

Patrick Brogan of *The Times* was intrigued by the £750,000 worth of winnings and stake money he estimated the PMU would have to repay to Des Moutis if he was acquitted. He also explained to his English readers that the PMU was 'a state body with a turnover of around £500 million a year', from which the government 'keeps about £69 million' – an unimaginable state of affairs in Britain, where bookmakers were the main beneficiaries of betting, and the government and horse racing some way in arrears. But Brogan praised Des Moutis as 'the only man in France to know about horses, know about the laws of mathematics and to have the necessary capital to beat the system'. The PMU, he noted, claimed to be defending the interests of the ordinary punter. '"If it all goes to Monsieur X",' they say, '"there will be nothing for the little man."' But *The Times* correspondent was sceptical and felt the real nub of the case was the determination of the French Finance and Agriculture ministries to 'hang onto their very generous slice of the cake'.

2 December began with the cross-examination of a man the prosecution described as 'one of Monsieur X's principal

lieutenants'. The heavyweight Parisian Jules Carrax, who admitted having spent all his life around horses and racing, said he was used to plain speaking and that, in his opinion, the Prix de Bordeaux was the 'biggest fraud of the century'. Some of Patrice's supporters gasped and looked nervously at one another until Carrax went on to say that the fraud was the one perpetrated by the PMU in refusing to pay out to the winning players. One day soon, he added, he was going to put a bomb under PMU headquarters in the Rue la Boétie, and good riddance to the lot of them.

The judges didn't like the sound of that, and neither did Patrice's lawyer, Maître Kelignec, who was quick to switch the focus back to the more elegantly spoken Des Moutis, who claimed that the rule changes on maximum stakes introduced by the PMU discriminated against the 'little punters' just as much as himself, as a little punter could never become a big winner if there was an arbitrary ceiling on how much he or she was allowed to bet. He also told the court that it was 'a gambler's duty to try to find a weak point' in a race and a set of odds. 'But not by breaking the rules?' interjected President Arnaud. Once again Patrice insisted that he hadn't broken the rules because he hadn't personally had 'a sou' on the Prix de Bordeaux and therefore couldn't possibly have been in a conspiracy with the other accused. In what seemed an attempt to elicit Arnaud's sympathy, he said he hadn't bet much himself for some time now because the PMU rules were so rigged in favour of the house.

The court sat again on Saturday 4 December, when Marcel Boussac and the Société d'Encouragement director Jean Romanet lamented the damage that would be done to the health and well-being of French racing and bloodstock if Tiercé fraud was permitted to continue. Once again Boussac depicted a flight of the biggest owners, like Daniel Wildenstein and the Aga Khan, to Newmarket and County Kildare. Or, perish the thought, French breeders might sell their best stallions to the Americans and take the money. Then the counsel for the PMU called Pierre Crespin and Maurice Alexandre, who recounted the suspicious betting patterns they had encountered on Sunday 7 December 1962 and lamented again the disgraceful attempt to break the rules. Honest punters everywhere were the losers, they said. 'But there is never a losing year for you, is there, Monsieur?' countered Des Moutis as Alexandre resumed his seat.

Each day the proceedings broke for lunch and Patrice and his lawyers hurried out of the building and off to one of the many restaurants nearby on the island or on the Boulevard Saint-Germain and the surrounding streets. There, in a haze of cigarette smoke and over a hastily consumed *steak frites* or *omelette aux fines herbes*, accompanied by a couple of glasses of red, they discussed how things were going and planned their strategy for the next session.

On Saturday afternoon it was the turn of the now 72-year-old André Carrus, the Grand Patron of the PMU and their star witness, to contrast his unimpeachable integrity with the slipperiness of Monsieur X. In an exchange that onlookers described as 'the latest episode in the rivalry of the two Grandes Écoles', the veteran Polytechnicien began by saying that he'd had to listen to the claims of Monsieur des Moutis and his friends about the Prix de Bordeaux for several days now and that he would like to add a few observations of his own.

Carrus defended the rule changes introduced on his watch by the former Minister of Agriculture Edgard Pisani as 'absolutely necessary' to protect the little punters from speculators. Most of the eighty-three identical winning tickets on the Prix de Bordeaux Tiercé, he said, were written by the same hand. The hand of Patrice des Moutis. Was that really the action of a man who professed not to have had a single centime on the outcome? The Police des Courses et Jeux, he went on, had established that Des Moutis took 400,000 francs out of his bank account the day before the race and, while they had not been able to obtain conclusive proof of a conspiracy with the other punters, he believed that everything pointed in that direction. President Arnaud seemed less sure but, as he adjourned the court for the weekend, he advised all parties to be ready to make their concluding statements the following week.

The general impression was that over the first four days Des Moutis had fared well, but when the proceedings resumed on Monday 6 December Maître Archevêque and Maître Legrand for the PMU, and Maître André Lenard for the racecourse management companies, tore into Patrice's character and testimony. Lenard, in particular, painted a lurid picture of Monsieur X as a criminal mastermind, assisted not so much by lieutenants as four 'sergeant-majors' who had recruited a group of punters that included twenty-one fugitives from justice and others who appeared to be insolvent. Yet this same band, said Lenard, had mysteriously found the necessary funds to travel from Paris to Lyon, Lille, Bordeaux, Marseille and other cities to bet the maximum permitted sum on multiple combinations of the same five horses. In Maître Lenard's account there was no doubt that Patrice was a fraudster in the legal sense of the word, and a man who had sent his 'commandos' out across France to find a way to get around the PMU rules and wager money on his behalf.

The use of the word 'commandos' to describe Des Moutis' fellow gamblers was highly inflammatory. At the end of the Algerian War in June 1962 a special military tribunal of the Fifth Republic had dealt with the case of a former paratrooper turned OAS gunman called Roger Degueldre, whose team of hardened killers had been known as the 'Delta Commandos'. The tribunal sentenced Degueldre to death, and he was executed by firing squad at the Fort d'Ivry like the Petit-Clamart plotter Jean-Marie Bastien-Thiry eight months later. Applying the term 'commandos' to the Prix de Bordeaux punters led by Des Moutis seemed like a deliberate attempt by Maître Lenard to associate the diabolical Monsieur X with another enemy of the state, now dead and buried.

Lenard also returned to the PMU's rather sanctimonious theme that 'the little punter' had to be protected and, to better dramatise his point, listed the scale of Patrice's betting in various of his Tiercé coups to date. In January 1962 he had wagered in excess of 55 million old francs for a total gain of 492 million. Lenard affirmed that Des Moutis had also supplied the bulk of the 300,000 new francs gambled on the Prix de Bordeaux, netting a total profit of more than six million francs. Monsieur X, he said, was an unprincipled speculator with a vested interest in trying to influence the outcomes of races he had a major stake in and, if the court wished to make an example of such a character, the only appropriate punishment for Des Moutis was prison.

It was a brutal, hard-hitting display that left Patrice and Marie-Thérèse seething. Maître Kelignec and his Paris colleague Monsieur Bondoux tried to rebut Lenard's diatribe and to reassert Patrice's claim that the PMU was a bureaucratic 'monster' accountable to no one. Kelignec was also one of the advocates appearing for the 'Marseillais' – a group of punters from the Midi who were accused of being some of Patrice's so-called 'commandos'. But where was the evidence against them? asked Maître Kelignec. There was no conclusive proof that Des Moutis had given them money to bet on his behalf and therefore no legal grounds for claiming they had entered together into a conspiracy.

At 6 p.m. on Friday 10 December President Arnaud, comparing the proceedings to a horse race, declared that the closing stages of this contest would have to wait until he had had time to reflect on the conflicting arguments. Judgement, he said, would be reserved until the New Year.

In fact, it was to be two months before the participants returned to Courtroom 13 to hear Arnaud's verdict. In the intervening period racing was held up at Auteuil due to a strike by *gauchistes*, the left-wing members of the trade union representing PMU operatives, while the film *The French Connection*, starring Gene Hackman as a New York detective pursuing a wealthy Marseille drug smuggler, opened in Paris.

A crime of a more traditional type made the headlines too when it was revealed that a million francs' worth of jewels belonging to the society hostess Madame Antoinette Amythauen had been stolen from her sleeping car on the *Orient Express*. The theft added topicality to the publication of the memoirs of 'Monsieur Alexandre', the former hairdresser to *le Tout-Paris* who had counted Madame Amythauen as one of his best clients. The celebrity hairdresser brought his autobiography out on 18 February 1972, the same day that the former bookmaker to *le Tout-Paris*, Patrice des Moutis, was back at the Palais de Justice at 9 a.m.

Jean Laborde of *L'Aurore* was struck how full of confidence Patrice seemed, and apparently ready to 'bet the maximum' on his liberty. Laborde and his fellow journalists had mostly been expecting Des Moutis to be convicted. But to their surprise, delight and to the disgust of the PMU and the racecourses and their lawyers, not to mention the ministries of Agriculture and Finance, President Arnaud ruled that Patrice's role in the Prix de Bordeaux and that of his four lieutenants was 'not proven'.

The shock verdict came at the climax of a two-hour address by Arnaud as he read his fifty-page judgement to the court. At the beginning of the judge's exposition he seemed to be inclining towards a conviction as he described what he called the 'Tour de France undertaken by Monsieur des Moutis and his friends' to buy Tiercé tickets in Marseille, Lyon, Bordeaux and Lille, and the attempt to recruit 'straw men' – proxy punters – to place bets on their behalf. But the president then made it clear that he could not accept the subjective hypothesis – put forward by the PMU and the Police des Courses et Jeux and their advocates – without positive proof.

Arnaud said it was hard to choose between the two versions of Patrice's behaviour. On the one hand there was the well-founded suspicion that he had been the chief conductor of a carefully orchestrated plan. But on the other, the judge questioned whether he would have willingly involved family members like his brother-in-law if he thought it might end with financial penalties and even the possibility of imprisonment. All for what, to a non-gambling man like himself, seemed horse and trotting racing's 'precarious chance' of a profit.

So, continued Arnaud, he was giving Monsieur des Moutis and his co-accused the benefit of the doubt as it was not proven that he had gained personally from the venture. Neither had it been established beyond all reasonable doubt that the Prix de Bordeaux had been fixed.

However – and here Arnaud paused ominously – the absence of a penal judgement did not mean that Monsieur des Moutis was not to be condemned. The court, said the president, was in no way blessing his conduct or expressing any kind of approval of his behaviour. He should feel no satisfaction at the outcome and there should be no glorification of his attempt to win an enormous sum of money without effort or risk. Comporting himself like the sternest headmaster admonishing a pupil for letting himself down and letting the school down, Arnaud deplored 'the lamentable example set by a former student of one of our Grandes Écoles'. Being an inveterate gambler, he said, was nothing to be proud of, least of all lending his 'considerable talents' to such a vile and ignoble enterprise.

Patrice sat in silence, head bowed, until the president's tongue-lashing had finished. In conclusion Arnaud acknowledged that the PMU and the racecourses would no doubt wish to take the case to appeal. For the moment, therefore, he ruled that the disputed Prix de Bordeaux winnings and the funds gambled by the accused should remain in the custody of the Treasury.

'Monsieur X given the benefit of the doubt' shrieked the newspapers the following day. One of the few dissenting voices was that of an editorial in *Le Figaro*, which noted that, despite the severity of the president's verbal dressing-down, Des Moutis had expressed no regret and made no act of contrition for his behaviour in court. Neither did he promise not to launch another commando-style raid in the near future. Was that wise? the paper wondered. And was this really a victory for Des Moutis or just the beginning of a long pursuit?

Le Figaro's reservations were not shared by Patrick Brogan, who was given a generous amount of column inches to hail Patrice's acquittal in *The Times*. 'Monsieur X is a national hero,' exclaimed the London correspondent. 'Five million Frenchmen back the horses every week on the simple system, the Tiercé, devised by the Pari-Mutuel Urbain, an institution in France just as the pools are in Britain.' What inspiration those punters would have to resume the fight, said Brogan, now that Monsieur des Moutis had discovered a sure-fire formula for winning. 'The French state betting board will have to pay out over six million francs to Monsieur X and the others who beat the book in 1962,' he enthused. And referring to the stalled enquiries into the Prix Georges de Talhouet-Roy and the Prix d'Amérique, he reckoned the PMU 'will also have to pay out half as much again on bets placed on races in 1969 and 1970'.

But would they? Patrice may have seemed full of bravado as he and his fellow defendants and their lawyers descended the steps from the Palais de Justice and headed off for a celebratory lunch in Lapérouse on the nearby Quai des Grands Augustins. But while Des Moutis was relieved to have escaped jail, and gratified that his opponents had failed to convincingly make their case, he knew too it was not the end of the story. The insurance business in Neuilly was still ailing, it was almost impossible for him to place a legitimate bet on horse and trotting racing and, without the winnings plus stake money from the Prix de Bordeaux and the other contested races, his financial position seemed unlikely to improve. On top of that the government of the Fifth Republic was indisputably still gunning for him.

Some observers with long memories said the flavour of the case, if not the details, reminded them of the so-called 'Stavisky Affair' which had gripped the nation forty years earlier. Serge Alexandre Stavisky was a charming but fraudulent 'financial consultant' with an extravagant lifestyle and friends in politics and high places. Unlike Des Moutis, who strenuously denied the allegations against him, Stavisky was patently a fraudster who at one point had worked as a nightclub manager and, at another, had dabbled in illegal gambling. He made his money by selling fake bonds to gullible investors, including life insurance companies advised by government departments, while enjoying the protection of his network of influential contacts.

Stavisky's trial for fraud, which began in the Palais de Justice in 1927, went on for six years, and he managed to be granted bail no fewer than nineteen times. In the process he captured the public imagination, not unlike Monsieur X, with opinion divided strongly between those in favour and those against. It didn't end well, though. Although he was brought up in France, Stavisky was a Russian Jew who had been born in the Ukraine. A change in the political weather in the early 1930s resulted in his friends in the French Radical Socialist government coming under attack from anti-semitic and right-wing opponents for their links to the embezzler. Faced finally with exposure, Stavisky went on the run and his body was found in a ski lodge in Chamonix in January 1934. He'd been shot in the back of the head – not unlike Jean-Luc Durry – and the official verdict was suicide, leading the satirical newspaper *Le Canard Enchaîné* to joke that, given the distance the bullet had travelled, he must have had a very long arm.

Rumours persisted for years that Stavisky had been killed by the police at the behest of the government, and Patrice's friends feared that the longer his feud with the state continued the greater the danger that he could suffer a similar fate. Across town in the head office of the PMU and in the offices of the ministries of Agriculture and Finance, *fonctionnaires* were already preparing to take their case to the Court of Appeal, their lawyers working even harder than before to establish a conclusively damning portrait of Monsieur X that would lead to his imprisonment or worse.

The fish had wriggled off the hook once again. But for how much longer?

Chapter 25

The French judicial system coughed, spluttered, and spewed out more writs, counter-suits and depositions. But it wasn't until 4 June 1973 – fifteen months after the Arnaud panel's verdict – that the Prix de Bordeaux saga finally reached round three and what most participants hoped was the final chapter.

The French Court of Appeal, which sat in a different part of the Palais de Justice to Correctional Court 13, is a unique jurisdiction and only certain lawyers, prosecutors and magistrates are qualified to work there. Maître André Lenard, representing the PMU and Vincennes racecourse, was one such advocate, and a familiar figure in the court's closed legal community. Once again he drew on all his experience and considerable forensic skills to pour scorn on Patrice's version of events in December 1962, and this time Lenard's reasoning – backed up by the efforts of Maître Archevêque and Maître Legrand – found a sympathetic response.

In the period between the two hearings Patrice had been doing his best to maintain the image of a relaxed man about town with no fear of conviction and nothing to hide. He was still the sophisticated Parisian stopping off for morning coffee in the Café Sainte-Foy, bringing delicacies home for lunch in Saint-Cloud and smoking cigars and playing backgammon with Alain Ayache in Le Flandrin after work. Returning to the Palais de Justice he'd been expecting another week-long drama and further duels between his lawyers and the opposition. What shocked him was that from the outset the Appeal Court judges only seemed interested in the PMU's and the prosecution's case, finding wholly and unequivocally in their favour not on the basis of any new evidence submitted but in response to the vehemence of André Lenard's renewed denunciation of his character.

Unlike President Arnaud and his confrères, the Appeal Court judges concluded that there had definitely been a conspiracy surrounding the Prix de Bordeaux and that Monsieur des Moutis was every inch the fraudster and mastermind the PMU had alleged. The judges highlighted what they described as 'a series of coincidences that could not just be fortuitous'.

Firstly, they said it was 'not reasonable' to believe that all eighty-three winning punters had played the Vincennes Tiercé on their own accounts. Some were of too modest means to bet 3,600 francs on an ordinary Sunday morning, and almost certainly had their tickets bought and filled in for them by Monsieur des Moutis and his lieutenants, who had also supplied them with their stake money.

Secondly, the result of the race was by no means easy to predict, and not a single newspaper tipster anywhere in France had given the winning combination.

Thirdly, Des Moutis had told the original trial that he had been given tips that certain runners – Limelight, for example, driven by Roger Vercruysse – could be eliminated. But the

Appeal Court judges suspected that Monsieur des Moutis had in fact paid drivers like Vercruysse to stop their horses. It couldn't be proven on the evidence submitted, but the judges, displaying a low opinion of the trotting-race fraternity, observed that 'it would be naïve in the extreme' not to believe it.

The excesses of Monsieur des Moutis, they concluded, *were* dangerous for the mass of weekend Tiercé players, and the victims of his 'fraud' included punters of modest means who could never possibly bet on his scale. Which was why the maximum 60-franc limit stake multiplied by twenty-five had been brought in, quite correctly, by the Minister of Agriculture in 1962.

Patrice was sentenced to a year's imprisonment – suspended – and also ordered to pay a 3,500-franc fine. His four lieutenants – Jules Carrax, Jacques Guyadet, René Lacoste and Jean Seuret – each received a six-month suspended sentence and a 1,500-franc fine, while Seuret's girlfriend Marie Louise Baumann, who had been the *chauffeuse*, driving the others around PMU bureaux in Lyon and Lille, was given four months suspended. The judges decreed that the other eighty-odd punters, who they described as 'footsoldiers', should face no further action.

As to the blocked gains and stake money of between six and seven million francs – or more like ten million if the Prix Georges de Talhouet-Roy and the Prix d'Amérique were included – the court said that there was 'no precedence in jurisprudence' to determine what should happen to money won on a fraudulent or fixed race. The funds would therefore continue to be held by the Treasury pending further deliberation.

Patrice was devastated. The fine was derisory, and his lawyers were talking publicly of going on to the Conseil d'État, a branch of the French government and effectively the Supreme Court, but privately they believed he had been lucky to escape incarceration. This was not 1968, they warned him. In the summer of 1972 President Pompidou had replaced the progressive Prime Minister Jacques Chaban-Delmas with the more traditional Pierre Messmer, and law and order issues were on the political agenda once again. The Gaullist Pompidou, anxious to reassure his conservative base, had resisted calls to legalise abortion and abolish the death penalty (indeed, two men had been guillotined at the Santé Prison in Paris in November 1972, and another in Marseille in May 1973) and in this climate, warned Patrice's advocates, offenders of any stripe found guilty of conspicuously flouting conservative values could expect to be severely punished.

Des Moutis was advised to forget any thoughts of revenge and to quietly go back to work as an inconspicuous risk assessor. He was particularly urged not to engage in any further betting and racing activities that might incur the wrath of the state. But from Patrice's perspective the PMU and the Police des Courses et Jeux had made it all but impossible for him to resume his former life. It was all there in banner headlines on the front page of Le Figaro: 'Monsieur X condemned.' Patrice said he felt as if he had the plague. Gone was the exotic aura of the gentleman gambler from Saint-Cloud entertaining and enriching family and friends with his Tiercé adventures. He had become a social pariah, a convicted fraudster and traitor to his class, and no self-respecting 16th *arrondissement* hostess would ever want to be associated with him again.

And what of the legal bills, not to mention his ongoing family obligations to Marie-Thérèse and the children? They had all supported him throughout, and the girls and their brother François had been unwavering in their faith in his integrity. How would they cope with this verdict? And what about his unfortunate brother Gilbert and his family? With the insurance business in Neuilly on its knees, where was the money going to come from now? The injustice of it all, as Patrice saw it, enraged and consumed him. What he longed for was one last spectacular and all-embracing coup that would hit the PMU *fonctionnaires* and rock the descendants of Albert Chauvin as never before.

The government and the courts had done everything they could to stop him from profiting from betting on racing legitimately. Might he now be ready to consider profiting from it in other ways? By going back to those friends he'd originally met in the Bar Les Trois Canards in Pigalle when he was doing his illegal bookmaking in the 1950s? The same friends who had helped him get multiple bets down on the Prix de Bordeaux when he was first trying to get around the limit on maximum stakes, and with whom – it was assumed – he'd later helped set up the Prix d'Entressen in Marseille in 1971?

They were hard men, dangerous men, but with no shortage of stake money and no qualms about hurting the PMU . . . and they were always prepared to pay well for a race that went according to plan.

Chapter 26

At the beginning of December 1973 the actor Jean-Paul Belmondo sought to emulate his fellow star Alain Delon by registering his colours with the Société d'Encouragement so that he could become the owner of a couple of Maisons-Laffitte-trained steeplechasers and hurdlers. Belmondo, it seemed, had caught the racing bug and was joining the queue of would-be 'Sunday millionaires' described by Enrico Macias in his still-popular hit song which now accompanied a PMU video of smiling and excited jockeys competing in a Tiercé race at a Paris track.

On Sunday 9 December 1973 the aspiring millionaires were out in force as usual and hurrying to their local PMU *café-tabacs*. The weekend's big Tiercé event was the Prix Bride Abattue, a handicap hurdle at Auteuil to be run over 3,600 metres, or roughly two and a quarter miles, and worth 100,000 francs to the winner.

The principal concern of the tipsters analysing the race in Paris Turf and the other newspapers was that, after heavy rain in the capital, the going was bound to be testing and stamina at a premium. Of the twenty-four runners who were scheduled to face the starter they concentrated on half a dozen who were expected to be able to cope with soft ground and were due to be ridden by some of French jump racing's most experienced jockeys.

The co-favourite Ginger Bread was a progressive, in-form five-year-old with the curly-haired Jean-Paul Ciravegna, partner of the beaten favourite Primo de Solera in the 1969 Prix Georges de Talhouet-Roy, in the saddle.

Georges Pelat's brother René was the trainer of the other co-favourite, Times Square, a course specialist who had run on strongly in a similar race at Auteuil on 18 November. The bay gelding was to be ridden by the 23-year-old Pierre Costes, the brightest star of French jump racing who had recently been crowned champion jumps jockey of 1973 and winner of the coveted *Cravache d'Or*, the Golden Whip. The charismatic Costes, better known as 'Pierrot' to his friends, was a broken-nosed cavalier and laughing boy who had quickly become a hero to the punters.

Cap Horn, also trained by René Pelat and ridden by Christian DaMeda, had run three times at Auteuil that autumn finishing first, second and third. There was some support too for Hasty Love, the mount of the 31-year-old hardman Jean-Pierre Renard, Right Ho, ridden by Michel Chirol (and carrying the prestigious colours of Baron Guy de Rothschild), and Iskander whose jockey Jean-Pierre Philipperon was the brother of the leading flat-racing rider, Maurice.

The general consensus was that any Tiercé combination pairing at least two of Ginger Bread, Times Square and Cap Horn ought to have reasonable prospects of yielding a profit. Nobody seriously fancied the 13-1 shot Toulois, owned and trained by Jean-Marcel Jeuhandeu and ridden by Jacques

Scagliola, and absolutely nobody was tipping the rank outsider Bodensee ridden by Michel Geffroy.

Sunday 9 December was a miserably wet and windy day, and the Auteuil crowd was smaller than usual. By 1973 the PMU had done such a good job at promoting the convenience of off-course betting in the warmth and comfort of a local café that racecourse attendances were falling. Betting shops had been legalised in Britain since 1961 but they were mostly still primitive affairs with an audio-only commentary and basic amenities. They weren't even allowed to sell tea and coffee until 1986. By contrast, punters in Paris had up to 1 p.m. to submit a Tiercé coupon and then, on Sundays, many of them chose to remain in a PMU café or neighbourhood restaurant and enjoy a *poulet du dimanche* before the TV action got underway. There was no need for them to traipse out to the Bois de Boulogne in person. As a result the camaraderie and sense of shared excitement that had characterised a day at the races before and after World War II was ebbing away. It was still present on fête days like Toussaint and Quatorze Juillet – and for the very biggest races, like the Grand Steeplechase de Paris and the Grand Prix de Paris and the Prix de l'Arc de Triomphe on the flat – but it was much diluted for the rest of the time.

Most of those present at Auteuil that December afternoon were part of the regular coterie of owners, trainers and racing managers who were doing extremely well from the funding provided to the sport by the PMU monopoly and had no need to worry about crowd numbers. They ate lunch as usual in the panoramic restaurant, enjoying the selection of hors-d'œuvres and the *filet de boeuf avec sauce béarnaise,* and popped in and out of the weighing room to exchange gossip and news. It was only the hardier souls among them – including a handful of journalists and professional punters – who braved the conditions outside and were able to say afterwards that they had witnessed, first hand, one of the most extraordinary horse races ever run on French soil.

It was, as one reporter noted with masterful understatement, a 'very odd affair'. It later transpired that the Auteuil stewards had been warned by the PMU that morning about 'an abnormal concentration of bets' on nine of the twenty-four runners, and it was precisely those nine, led by Michel Chirol on Right Ho and closely followed by the outsiders Toulois and Bodensee, that set off in the lead with the others all anchored well behind.

After little more than a quarter of a mile there was already a distance of 100 metres between the first and last horse. By halfway two of the leaders had fallen, and it was a group of six – five mud-bespattered no-hopers and Right Ho – that continued to make the running, with the riders of the rest making little or no apparent effort to make ground. The order barely changed as they rounded the Passy turn into the home straight and, with some of the jockeys imitating statues rather than riding flat out, it was the outsider Toulois who loped past the post in first place, with Right Ho second and the unconsidered 'rag' Bodensee in third. Hasty Love came fourth and Ginger Bread, ridden by 'Allez' Ciravegna was fifth. But the other co-favourite Times Square, ridden by the champion Pierre Costes, came nowhere, along with Jean-Pierre Philipperon on Iskander.

Even the Auteuil stewards, not renowned for their vigilance and perspicacity, could hardly have failed to notice that half the field were beaten even before they'd got halfway down the back stretch. This was in a handicap where all the runners were supposedly weighted to bring them closer together not to push them further apart. The officials, who called in some of the jockeys and trainers for an explanation, could see no justifiable reasons why so many of the form horses had run so badly, with only one fancied runner finishing in the first three. Then they received an initial breakdown of the Tiercé betting on the race, and some possible reasons started to suggest themselves.

The Toulois, Right Ho and Bodensee combination – numbers 3, 1 and 14 – paid 13,468.20 francs to a three-franc stake in the correct order, and 2,355 francs to a three-franc stake in any order. And first reports from PMU headquarters in the Rue la Boétie talked of a 'mammoth gamble' on the correct outcome, involving bets totalling over 500,000 francs, placed mainly in the Marseille and Toulon region and concentrating on five of the twenty-four runners to the exclusion of the other nineteen. Early estimates suggested that the winning punters may have won more than ten times their stake money, or approximately £510,000 in UK currency, which would be worth more like £5 million today. But had they won it legitimately?

That night and the following day all kinds of rumours began to spread through the French racing and gambling world. Earlier that month in Marseille thirteen drug traffickers had been sentenced to a combined total of a hundred and seventy-two years in prison for attempting to ship 100 kilograms of heroin across the Atlantic. In a carbon copy of the scenario in the film *The French Connection*, the drugs were hidden inside a Bentley and a Ferrari that belonged to the film producer André Labay and were to be delivered to the Waldorf Astoria hotel in New York. Might there conceivably be a link, some people were asking, between the events in the Midi and what had happened at Auteuil racecourse?

The regular habituees of PMU cafés, poring over the Prix Bride Abattue finishing order in their daily papers, were struck that only one national tipster had correctly predicted the outcome. That was Jean-Claude Briffault in *L'Aurore*, who had backed the Toulois, Right Ho, Bodensee combination himself in the correct order and seemed peeved not to have been given greater credit for his judgement. 'The favourites?' he shrugged. 'Ah well. They were well beaten, each with a different excuse.'

The excuses weren't enough for Monsieur François de Poncins, director of the Société des Steeplechases, who announced on Tuesday 11 December that his organisation had begun a formal inquiry into the Prix Bride Abattue beginning with the 'lack of ardour' displayed by some of the horses and jockeys. At the same time the PMU confirmed that 'suspects had been observed' on the Sunday morning, and an alert sent by them to the Auteuil stewards warning that bureaux in Marseille, Toulon and Nice were all reporting 'a peculiarity' with numerous punters coming in and betting 18 francs multiplied by five, ten and even the maximum twenty-five times on the same combination of horses. Of the nine backed, four – Toulois, Right Ho, Hasty Love and the no-hoper Bodensee – were backed heavily, and all of them were in the leading group soon after the race got underway.

The suspicion was that some of the punters betting identical permutations were in fact straw men or proxy punters betting for unidentified big hitters to help them get around the law on maximum stakes. But wasn't that the favoured tactic of the infamous Monsieur X, people were asking? The same

Patrice des Moutis who had so recently and narrowly escaped imprisonment after appearing in the Court of Appeal at the Palais de Justice? The gambler's alleged methods had been described and expounded on at length, in court and out, over the course of the last two years. Had somebody else decided to copy them? Was there now a Monsieur Y or Monsieur Z complicating matters? Or had the audacious Des Moutis decided to go back in to action himself, despite the threat of incarceration hanging over his head?

The story moved fast, and on Wednesday 12 December the PMU reported that, while 450,000 francs' worth of Tiercé winnings on the Prix Bride Abattue had been paid out, a further 550 million francs won by claimants regarded as suspicious had been temporarily blocked. In all cases, they stressed, payments by cheque were not transferable and would only be made once proof of identification had been supplied.

Off the record the PMU and the Police des Courses et Jeux were briefing certain journalists that they believed some of the suspicious claimants had been paid a premium to bet on behalf of shadowy underworld figures who wished to remain anonymous. As to precisely who those individuals might be, the police said they were concentrating their enquiries on a number of 'big, irregular punters' in the Midi. They also failed to deny a sensational rumour that some top jockeys had been receiving regular 'envelopes' stuffed with cash in return for stopping horses in selected Tiercé races, and that it had been going on for years.

The Jockeys' Association protested their innocence, with their shop steward and spokesman, Michel Geffroy, proclaiming their undying loyalty to their employers, their ignorance of any 'bad faith' in their profession, and their anger at the prejudice now being directed against them by some journalists and members of the public. As far as the events at Auteuil were concerned, one rider said his horse 'just happened to get off to a bad start', while another said he suspected his mount had gone lame. A third, believed to be the Cravache d'Or holder himself, Pierre Costes, said he had 'no idea' exactly what had happened.

Later that morning President and Madame Pompidou hosted a Christmas lunch for orphaned children at the Élysée Palace. It was an awkward occasion. The President was being forced to fend off questions about bugging devices that had been found in the Paris offices of the satirical weekly *Le Canard Enchaîné*. The cameras had been planted by cops disguised as workmen, and the operation had been traced back to a government department. But, regardless of the embarrassment, the head of state was also manifestly unwell, his body bloated and his eyes bulging, his diagnosis with a rare cancer having not yet been revealed. Some of the political correspondents covering the lunch joked that Pompidou looked as if he'd swallowed some of the dope that must have been given to the beaten favourites in the Prix Bride Abattue.

When the story was reported to the Société des Steeplechases their president, François de Poncins, didn't see the funny side, especially as he had to admit that the Auteuil stewards had failed to order post-race urine or saliva tests on the beaten horses, only on the winner, and those had proved negative. But the stewards did have a camera patrol film of the race that they were studying with the police, who were simultaneously examining twenty suspicious winning Tiercé tickets, eight of them placed in Marseille, seven in Toulon, two in Nice and three in Paris.

With the atmosphere becoming more febrile by the moment, the trainer René Pelat, whose brother Georges was a good friend of Patrice des Moutis, then lobbed a stick of dynamite into the mix. 'A racing Mafia exists,' he admitted to a correspondent from *Le Figaro*. 'Nobody can ignore it. Some of them are former racing "faces" in Maisons-Laffitte, well known to trainers and riders who work there. They buy jockeys. Not all of them, but a good number. Some jockeys have been threatened for refusing their advances, and trainers have been compromised.'

More in sadness than anger Pelat described an environment in which temptation was always present and it was all too easy for unscrupulous punters to exploit vulnerable targets. Men like young Jean-Luc Durry, perhaps? Who had allegedly been under pressure not to talk to the police about racecourse corruption before leaving Paris for his mysterious holiday in Cannes in 1971.

Pelat wouldn't discuss specific examples, but the number of jump jockeys who made really big money, he said, could be counted on the fingers of one hand. There were maybe ten others who lived 'a good bourgeois life', but the rest? Well, they made very little, and one fixed race or stopped horse at the behest of big gamblers who wanted something else to win could pay them what they would otherwise take a year to earn. Besides, racing at the top end was an environment dripping with money, from the rich owners like the Rothschilds, the Wertheimers and Daniel Wildenstein to the amounts wagered on the PMU every day. The yearning to join in, to share the good times and the good life and the temptation to take a short cut to attain it was not easy to resist.

Confronted by Pelat's dramatic revelations, the jockeys' spokesman Michel Geffroy was forced to retract the unambiguous rejection of corruption claims he'd made only days before. 'After long consultation' he agreed with Pelat that 'certain members' of his organisation were 'not pure'. What the public wanted to know was how many of them, and just how far did the impurity go?

Plenty far enough believed the Société des Steeplechases, who had compiled their own provisional dossier of events, which they handed to the Seine Prosecutor's Office on Saturday 15 December. Following the same procedures and terminology as after the Prix de Bordeaux in 1962 the deposition lodged a *plainte contre X* – who may or may not have been *the* Monsieur X – for attempted fraud and complicity in fraud. It was the first crucial move in another lengthy investigation that would proceed like a row of dominoes falling one into another until it ended up at the door of Patrice des Moutis.

This time the case was entrusted to the 51-year-old Judge Michaud who, with the Prix de Bordeaux trial still fresh in the memory, cut a strict and business-like figure as he outlined his response. Investigations, said the judge, would be on two fronts. First he would be talking to the jockeys in the Prix Bride Abattue in an attempt to verify the claims of René Pelat regarding a Mafia du Tiercé supposedly fixing races. Secondly he would be instructing the Police des Courses et Jeux to interview the holders of the twenty suspect betting slips blocked by the PMU to determine whether they were indeed 'straw men' betting on the behalf of others and, if that was the case, to identify the mastermind behind it.

To everyone watching the drama unfold, be they small-change punters reading daily reports in *Paris Turf*, or the owners, trainers, jockeys and journalists assembling every race day at Auteuil, Enghien and Vincennes, it was clear that if Des Moutis was involved again the consequences could be severe. Judge Michaud had made it unambiguously clear that the law relating to maximum stakes and proxy punters would be rigorously enforced. If the Prix Bride Abattue had been a last defiant attempt by Monsieur X to flout that law, he faced imprisonment for sure. But if there *was* a Mafia du Tiercé and Patrice was its accomplice or tool, he presumably dare not reveal its secrets to the police for fear of intimidation or even death.

With the departments of Agriculture, Finance and the Interior looking over their shoulders, there was a shake-up within the ranks of the Police des Courses et Jeux. There was no longer a frontline role for Patrice's old foe *Commissaire* Taupin, who had been relegated to a desk job at the department's headquarters in Clichy. Some racing writers had compared Taupin's efforts to entrap Des Moutis with the hapless exploits of a cartoon character called '*Commissaire* Giles' and his 'band of clowns'. But there was nothing comical about his successor.

The Prix Bride Abattue inquiry was to be led by *Commissaire* General Jean Cahen, a slim, wiry pipe-smoker with some of the characteristics, if not the physique, of Georges Simenon's fictional Inspector Maigret. Renowned as a patient, single-minded detective, Cahen had years of experience investigating criminal cases in the Paris Police Judiciaire. The 55-year-old had recently been appointed the new head of the Turf Squad, and in the run-up to Christmas he and his team of investigators fanned out across the country. A special Police des Courses et Jeux office was opened in Maisons-Laffitte, the racing town and northwestern suburb of Paris where the local gossip was that

Cahen already had a hit-list of up to thirty jockeys, trainers and other racing professionals who were all to be grilled in turn.

The story of the Prix Bride Abattue inquiry was big news in Britain too, and covered by the racing lover's bible, the *Sporting Life*, on one side and *The Times* on the other. Neither of them specifically mentioned Patrice at this point (though the English bookies were all talking about him) but the *Life* wanted to know why a group of punters from Marseille and Toulon would wager more than half a million francs on a nondescript Auteuil hurdle race run on heavy ground on what was normally one of the quietest weekends of the French racing year.

The Times, who had sent Patrick Brogan over to cover the Prix de Bordeaux trial at the Palais de Justice and who still employed their own French racing correspondent, Pierre Gillot, continued to focus on the enormous sums of money generated by the PMU: turnover of at least £500 million a year, with £69 million going to the state, of which ten per cent was ploughed back into racing – hence the very generous prize money for French racehorse owners and cheap admission fees for the public. French trainers, reckoned *The Times*, could earn around 500,000 francs a year, and the winning jockeys were on a percentage plus 'a present' from grateful owners. So why would they agree to fix a race?

Well, Rene Pelat had already offered some insights on that subject and, after only a month on the case, *Commissaire* Cahen was convinced that a gambling syndicate was offering some jump jockeys up to four times what they could earn from a winning ride in return for stopping their mounts. Thanks to tip-offs from informants – some of them riders desperate to keep out of trouble themselves – Cahen had his sights on Robert

Laouira, an ex-jockey who claimed he made a living from betting and booking rides for old weighing-room colleagues.

A smooth, good-looking 35-year-old with plump cheeks and long, layered 1970s hair, Laouira had been a friend of Jean-Luc Durry and had accompanied the younger rider to the Villa Lolita in Cannes in 1971. A permanent fixture at race meetings in the Paris region, Laouira seemed to come and go from racecourse weighing rooms with impunity. He was the social secretary always on hand with the drinks and the girls. Cahen suspected he was employed by the race-fixing syndicate to help them look into jockeys' private lives and discover who needed money the most. His job was then to be the 'postman' who handed over thick manila envelopes stuffed with cash in quiet corners and dimly lit car parks out of sight of the stewards.

There was also a suspicion that some racecourse officials had deliberately covered up evidence of fixed races – the 1971 Prix d'Entressen in Marseille, for example. They may have been anxious not to create another scandal that could have hit their Tiercé takings, or they may just have been bribed to look away, as Des Moutis had been expected to do in Rabat in 1949.

But how far back did the trail of corruption go? And if Monsieur X was involved – and Patrice hadn't even been interviewed yet – did the suspicions of jockey collusion cast doubt on the authenticity of his earlier great Tiercé coups? No one was suggesting anything untoward had happened in the Prix Messenia at Saint-Cloud in 1958, or the Prix du Val des Fleurs on Bastille Day in 1961, or Vincennes' Prix du Croisé-Laroche on New Year's Day 1962. They had all been astutely planned and brilliantly executed operations that stayed just the right side of PMU rules as they stood at the time.

But what about that description of the Prix de Bordeaux in *Le Figaro* in December 1962 which described it as a race that 'left a very odd impression' and one that half the runners had no chance of winning after 100 metres? Had some of the drivers, like the rogueish Roger Vercruysse whose mount Normandie never figured despite being one of the favourites, indeed been in on the plot? And had some of the trainers been bribed to withdraw their runners? What about Clown's dismal run in the Prix Georges de Talhouet-Roy? Were his jockey Jean-Jacques Declercq and his trainer Jacques Dubois bribed to stop him that day? Was Start pulled by Jean-Claude 'Bibi' Biard in the same race? And what about the Prix d'Amérique in 1970? Did Snow Speed and Upsalin really collide accidentally at the start? And was Une de Mai's failure to finish in the first three just bad luck in running? Or an aversion to the track? Or were the drivers paid to do the bidding of the syndicate and their mastermind?

In the early years of Patrice's rise to fame, and during the opening rounds of Monsieur X's trial for fraud, the public had generally taken a positive view of him and romanticised his activities. As well as being described as a gambling Robin Hood he was sometimes compared to Arsène Lupin, the fictional gentleman thief and hero of the popular stories by Maurice Leblanc first published in France in 1891. The dashingly attired Lupin, often sporting top hat and tails, may have been a criminal in the strict sense of the word, but he was also the kind of risk-taking adventurer the public could identify with – just like Patrice – and one who often ended up helping the authorities thwart the real villains and cads.

But since the end of the Palais de Justice trial, Patrice's claims to have been a frustrated genius trying to beat a rotten system and merely the 'technical advisor' to a group of friends were wearing thin. Especially as he appeared to have retired behind the walls of his Saint-Cloud villa and was neither taking calls nor doing interviews. Was Robert Laouira also one of his friends? As more details emerged about the 'host of dubious connections' as the *Sporting Life*'s Geoffrey Hamlyn had described them, was Des Moutis keeping silent because he had no choice or because there were certain associations he could no longer truthfully deny? Even his long-time supporters were worried. There was an awful suspicion that perhaps the PMU had been right all along. And that Monsieur X had become so consumed with his feud with the PMU that he had got entangled with the kind of company that no self-respecting gentleman, like Arsène Lupin, should ever keep. Men like Vincent Ascione, for example.

Chapter 27

The city's main paper, *Le Provençal*, was calling it 'the Mystery in Marseille', but to insiders there was nothing mysterious about it. On the afternoon of 15 March 1974 the 62-year-old Vincent Ascione was shot dead outside Le Skating, a bar café in the affluent Prado quarter opposite the entrance to the Parc Borély. It was only a short walk from Le Skating to the racetrack, and the café was a popular stop-off point for punters and 'faces' on their way to and from meetings. There was no fixture at Borély that March Wednesday but the café card schools were almost as popular as the racing, and Ascione was a regular player.

The favourite game was stud poker, and the other players included flash Corsicans in shades and open-necked shirts with gold medallions, off-duty croupiers and dealers from the casinos down the coast, and ex-colonial army paratroopers with bitter memories of Algiers who now hired out as security for nightclubs and bars. The men smoked Gitanes Papier Maïs (yellow-paper cigarettes), and drank cognac and Chivas Regal with ice as they studied their cards.

It was still light on the 15th when Vincent Ascione cashed in his chips and got up to leave but, just as he was about to open the door of his brand-new Matra-Simca sports car which was parked outside, another car drew up with its windows down and a gunman fired a volley of buckshot from an 18-calibre hunting rifle. Ascione was hit in the face and body and flung to the ground. As other café customers took cover, the attackers calmly surveyed the damage and then got back in their car and drove away.

'*Le Plus Pur Borsalino*' ('Pure Borsalino' as in the Belmondo–Delon film) was how *Le Provençal* described it on their following day's front page, and there was an immediate assumption that Ascione had been the victim of a *Milieu* killing. First reports described him as a former taxi driver currently employed as the co-director of the Château de la Malle, a retirement home in the hillside village of Bouc-Bel-Air equidistant from Marseille and Aix-en-Provence. It was said that Vincent ran the home in partnership with his ex-wife and divided his time between the *maison de retraite* and a smart apartment near the beach.

But within twenty-four hours the biography had been updated to disclose that Ascione was, in fact, a low-level boss, or *caid*, in *la pègre*, the Marseille Mafia. He wasn't on the gangsters' A list. He'd never been inside Tany Zampa's opulent villa on the rock overlooking the corniche or invited for post-race drinks with Jacky Imbert. But he had his uses. It was revealed that his former neighbours in Bouc-Bel-Air had been three brothers who ran a garage and auto-repair shop that was a cover for a laboratory manufacturing heroin for export to the US. Two of the brothers had been caught and sentenced to lengthy terms of imprisonment by the Tribunal de Grande Instance in Toulon in 1973. It was assumed that their employers had simply transferred production to another site and that Vincent Ascione had continued to be responsible for overseeing it.

Whatever his association with the French Connection, the evidence suggested that Ascione had been killed because of what he knew about the race-fixing syndicate. At the time of his death he had 3,000 francs on him in cash, but when the police searched his Marseille apartment they found the counterfoils for 160,000 francs' worth of winning tickets on the Prix Bride Abattue Tiercé that had never been cashed. Were they genuine bets placed by Ascione with his own money? Or had he been betting for someone else, who didn't want to be identified, higher up the *Milieu* hierarchy? Someone who was behind the gambling syndicate and wanted to launder money from the drugs trade on fixed races? In which case, were they the organisers of the Prix Bride Abattue scam, and if so had Monsieur X, Patrice des Moutis, assisted them unwittingly or otherwise in the act?

These were all questions that *Commissaire* Jean Cahen had hoped to ask Vincent Ascione personally after being tipped off in Paris that he was an important link man in the organisation. Ascione had been contacted by Cahen in secret, and a meeting had been arranged to take place in Marseille on the morning of 16 March, the day after the ex-cab driver was killed. The obvious conclusion was that the *Milieu* had somehow found out about the rendezvous and taken steps to insure that Vincent would never show up.

Ascione wasn't the first possible witness to the scale and extent of the syndicate's activities to end up dead. To Jean Cahen there were clear similarities with the fate of Jean-Luc Durry, who had been in touch with the police before his mysterious suicide in Cannes three years earlier. If Des Moutis really was involved, might he now be at risk from the *Milieu* too?

If Cahen's investigation was to have any chance of uncovering the truth, he felt he needed to share as little as possible with the Marseille police. He suspected them of being involved in some way in Ascione's murder and, while there were brave crime-fighting figures in the city (like the crusading Judge Pierre Michel, who targeted the French Connection and would be assassinated by the *Milieu* in 1981), there were also elements that were as close to the gangsters as the police force had been to Al Capone's men in Chicago in the 1920s.

To avoid leaks by corrupt officers, Cahen determined to work with a small, close-knit team. One of the key members was *Commissaire* Roger Saunier. A tough laconic *flic* who worked with the anti-gang squad in Paris, Saunier was recommended by his divisional commander Marcel Leclerc when Judge Michaud asked for someone who wasn't easily intimidated to assist Cahen's investigation in both Paris and the Midi. Throughout 1974 the two detectives, supported by a handful of back-up officers, doggedly pursued their enquiries, and Cahen said later that they must have covered thousands of kilometres and that he rarely slept more than two nights running in his own bed.

The investigating team may have been small but they had backing from the highest levels. In April 1974 Georges Pompidou had died in office, succumbing to the rare cancer, Waldenström's Macroglobulinemia, a type of slow-growing lymphoma. The subsequent presidential election was won by the former Finance Minister, the Conservative Centrist Valéry Giscard d'Estaing, who scraped home by half of one per cent against the Socialist candidate, François Mitterrand. Highly intelligent but also haughty and aloof, Giscard tried to project himself as a more contemporary and forward-looking figure than his predecessors. To balance that image he appointed his blunt campaign manager and fixer, Michel Poniatowski as Minister of the Interior. The 53-year-old 'Ponia', who was the descendant of a Polish prince, was keen to establish his law and order credentials as quickly as possible and promised the race-fixing inquiry the same level of support that his Gaullist predecessor Roger Frey had given to the pursuit of the OAS.

Cahen's objective was made clear to him by the Minister: 'To dismantle the Mafia du Tiercé and the syndicate of jockeys, trainers, gamblers and crooks who have made the racecourses their privileged domain.' To that end Cahen and Saunier interviewed hundreds of suspects – from Paris and Maisons-Laffitte to Corsica, Nice and Toulon – but the trail kept coming back to Marseille, and that summer the phlegmatic Saunier flew down to the Midi to check out the principal Marseille suspect in person.

If Paris remained the magnetic centre of French life for everything from politics and administration to high society and finance, the nation's second city was a hot, passionate rough diamond and gateway to the East. Marcel Pagnol may have written lyrically about the blue skies and glassy seas, the scent of basil and thyme and the fishwives loudly selling bream and sardines on the Vieux-Port quay. But to the hard-headed detectives from the north, the port's principal characteristic was its age-old reputation for racketeering and crime. *Commissaire* Saunier's visit began at the bar Le Skating which had been described to him as a popular hangout for *voyous* – mobsters, hoodlums, illegal bookmakers and 'diverse other criminal types'. Saunier discovered that the suspected syndicate 'postman' Robert Laouira was a regular drinker at the bar whenever he was in town visiting 'family and friends'. He also found out that the real owners of Le Skating were Joseph Croce, the leading French Connection drug trafficker who'd been arrested in 1971, and Eugène Matrone, one of the three founder members of the original Bande des Trois Canards in Paris in the 1950s.

Matrone, also known as 'Gegene le Manchot', or One-Armed Gegene, had moved back to Marseille when the Canards broke up in 1965 and had invested his money in an illegal cigarette factory as well as clubs, bars and prostitution. He was still close to his old friends Marius Bertella, now established as an outwardly respectable stud farm owner and breeder in Normandy, and the Canards' former number-one gun, Jacky Imbert, who had become a local hero thanks to his successful second career as a trotting race driver.

On a typical Marseille day of hard bright sunshine and pellucid post-mistral skies, *Commissaire* Saunier watched Jacky le Mat in action at 'Le Borély' racetrack and mingled with the punters and faces who never missed a meeting. The spectators were a reflection of the diverse multicultural make-up of the city: Provençal, Corsican, Italian, Arab, African, Vietnamese. Saunier tried to pump some of them for their views on alleged Tiercé corruption, but no one had a bad word to say about Jacky Imbert and dismissed suggestions that he'd fixed races as the jealous prejudices of the effete sporting establishment up in Paris.

That evening Saunier set out from his hotel near the Vieux Port and walked down a succession of narrow streets still warmed by the sun until he reached a bar in a narrow side street near the foot of the steps leading up to the Basilica of Notre-Dame de la Garde. Washing hung from second- and third-floor balconies, and curious local heads peered down, clocking the *commissaire*'s presence before ducking back into the shadows.

Bar L'Ascenseur was one of Imbert's favourite haunts, and around 10 p.m. the gangster arrived as usual accompanied by two bodyguards. A short, handsome man who'd already worked his way through several wives and mistresses he seemed more amused than alarmed by Saunier's presence. The detective was invited to sit down at a table in the back and over Gitanes and glasses of Pastis, Jacky talked openly about his love of horse and trotting racing and his friendship with Alain Delon.

Le Mat had started out riding horses, he explained. Then one day a friend had let him drive a sulky. It went fast and Imbert, who loved speed and stunt-car driving, was hooked. He drove in his first trotting races in 1969, and in 1971 he finished third in the French amateur trotting-race championship. The following year, aged 43, he was crowned amateur regional champion in the southeast and then national champion, with twenty-nine victories over the course of the season.

As to Delon, well, Jean Pierre 'Bimbo' Roche, a good friend of Tany Zampa, had introduced them when the actor had been filming *Borsalino* and living in a *hôtel particulier*, a beautiful old house, near the Cours Mirabeau, in Aix-en-Provence. One day Jacky mentioned that he had a good chance in a trotting race at Cagnes-sur-Mer the following afternoon. 'I'm going to win,' he said. Delon told him to put a bet on for him. Jacky did and the horse won handsomely and, afterwards, Delon suggested they should start their own trotting stable together.

Jacky approached the famous Vincennes gambler Pierre-Désiré Allaire – 'a trainer of repute', as he described him – and co-owner of the 1970 Prix d'Amérique winner Toscan, who had been one of Des Moutis' recommended Tiercé bets; and in 1973 they founded their own stud and training centre, at Puy-Sainte-Réparade a few kilometres from Aix. Allaire bought and trained the horses there for Delon and his lover of the moment, the actress Mireille Darc, and Jacky, helped by his jockey son, Jean-Louis, drove them. And that, Imbert insisted, was the extent of his involvement in racing.

Le Mat denied all knowledge of what had happened in the Prix Bride Abattue. Yes, he admitted he liked a bet, especially when he'd been given a few tips, and yes, he'd heard of Monsieur des Moutis, or 'the Saint', as they called him at Borély. He was clearly a very bright man and a punter to respect. But who could say there was anything unusual about the Prix d'Entressen in 1971? What did cops and ignorant fucking journalists know about how to drive a sulky?

Yes, Jacky believed he'd met Jean-Luc Durry once or twice years before, and he'd been sorry when he heard about the boy's suicide. But as to Vincent Ascione? Why would anyone be sorry about him? He was worthless – a thief not worth bothering about. Saunier put it to him that there were similarities between Ascione's violent death and the drive-by shooting of Antoine Guérini in Marseille in 1967 and the wounding of Jean-Baptiste Andréani in Paris in 1963 – both crimes which Jacky had been suspected of. And both crimes for which he had never been charged and for which there was no evidence of his involvement, responded Le Mat.

Saunier presumed that Imbert also had no knowledge of the French Connection and the Marseille drug trade either. The gangster agreed, advising the *commissaire* not to believe everything he read in the papers. He himself was content with cigarettes and Pastis, he said. 'That and gambling?' asked Saunier. 'That and the occasional bet,' agreed Jacky, smiling.

Roger Saunier left Marseille tired and frustrated but convinced that the old members of the Trois Canards and the upper crust of the city's underworld were involved up to their necks in running the race-fixing syndicate both in the Midi and in Paris. The five big Prix Bride Abattue winners from Marseille – François Cordeau, Gerard Zarokian, Sauveur Ruggieri, a pimp who posed as a hire car driver, Mathieu Dalmayan and Jean Calliol – were all petty criminals suspected of working for Eugène Matrone and Imbert. It was a similar story with Robert Maitraglis, Pierre Negro and Joseph Auxende, the big three Prix Bride Abattue winners from Toulon, who were in the crew of a young hustler called Jean-Louis Fargette, who had bought two bars in the 'Petit Chicago' district of the city and had managed to ingratiate himself with Matrone, Imbert, Zampa and the other Canards.

Saunier reckoned that the eight Tiercé punters were all straw men used by Imbert, Matrone and Fargette to get round the PMU limit on maximum stakes without revealing their hand. It was the template perfected by Monsieur X, only the *Milieu*'s motive was not just avarice or a yearning to be avenged on the PMU but the need to launder money. They had to find ways to clean the almost embarrassingly large sums of cash coming in each month from the French Connection, so they nominated proxy punters to bet it for them on rigged horse and trotting races. A correct Tiercé result, featuring a number of outsiders and beaten favourites, promised a much bigger pool than a straight-win bet. And so long as the jockeys and drivers did as they were told, the bogus winners received nice clean PMU cheques, which were then cashed and the proceeds paid back to the Canards, with the straw men awarded a premium for their services.

But would the police ever be able to prove any of it in court? The Minister of the Interior, Michel Poniatowski, wanted them to apprehend a mastermind who could be paraded before the public. But Saunier and Jean Cahen knew that getting anyone to testify about the organisers and main beneficiaries of the racket would be extremely difficult as the foot soldiers were all fearful of suffering the same fate as Jean-Luc Durry and Vincent Ascione. The *commissaires* concluded that, for the time being, they should go back to working on the postman, Robert Laouira, and his dealings with the jump jockeys in Paris. They were the weakest link in the pyramid. Subjecting them to the full force of the law might result in some of the most vulnerable cracking under pressure and then, maybe, they would name names and supply evidence linking the syndicate in Marseille with their suspected form expert, the revered professional gambler and tamer of the Tiercé . . . Monsieur X.

Chapter 28

The Tour de France traditionally dominates the sporting headlines in France in high summer, but in 1974 it faced unexpected competition from the Turf. Wednesday 10 July was Stage 12 of the Tour, and the Belgian Jos Spruyt led the riders on the iconic ascent of Mont Ventoux in Provence. The favourite and Yellow Jersey holder Eddy Merckx finished in eleventh place, biding his time before launching another attack in the Pyrenees at the end of the week.

That same mid-week afternoon saw a routine race meeting at Auteuil, the same fixture where Des Moutis had won the Prix Aguado Tiercé in 1961. There was no sign of Patrice in the vicinity in July 1974. The word was that he had gone to ground either at home in Saint-Cloud or at the family château in Finistère. The modestly attended card achieved notoriety all the same. Jump racing's champion jockey Pierre Costes won the last race of the day, a hurdle race over 3,500 metres, on a horse called Red Cross, trained by Patrice's old friend Georges Pelat. It was just another ride and another routine winner for the holder of the Cravache d'Or. Costes weighed in, showered, changed and prepared to leave the racecourse as usual. But on his way out he was confronted by Police des Courses et Jeux officers and representatives of the Société d'Encouragement, a bit like Des Moutis' experience at Longchamp in 1953. The officials told Costes that, on the orders of the Minister of the Interior and pending further investigation, his licence was being withdrawn with immediate effect.

Friends of 'Pierrot' – who had ridden the 7-1 chance and well beaten second favourite Times Square in the Prix Bride Abattue – said that he looked pale and shaken as he was escorted from the track. The news of his exclusion spread rapidly through the racing community and, for every fellow jockey promising him their full support, there were at least three others looking nervously over their shoulders and wondering if they would be next.

The day after Costes lost his licence the Midi newspaper *Nice-Matin* ran an article alleging that Robert Laouira was a prime suspect in the Prix Bride Abattue affair. The former jockey was alleged to have arranged for dozens of *bordereaux* to be filled out bearing the names of the winning combination – Toulois, Right Ho and Bodensee – and the paper claimed that the identical coupons were all for 'friends' of Monsieur Patrice des Moutis. It was the first attempt by the press to publicly associate Patrice with the fixed race.

Laouira was in Marseille at the time and had not yet been formally summoned for an interview with the police. But when he saw the *Nice-Matin* article he went straight back to Paris and began a round of menacing encounters with incriminated jockeys in Maisons-Laffitte. They couldn't be sure if he was acting on his own behalf or whether he was authorised by others but, with a combination of bribes and death threats, Laouira warned the riders to say nothing to anyone about pulling their horses in the Prix Bride Abattue.

Frightened family and friends of the jockeys Michel Chirol and Jean-Jacques Declercq, who had ridden Right Ho and the winner Toulois at Auteuil, contacted the police anonymously anyway, and Jean Cahen decided it was time for him to show his hand.

But even a serious criminal investigation had to pause for the duration of the French summer holidays, and it wasn't until after *la rentrée*, on 18 September, that the Postman, Robert Laouira was arrested by *Commissaires* Cahen and Saunier. He was refused bail by Judge Michaud then confined to the Fresnes Prison on the south side of Paris. When the police came for Laouira at his apartment in Maisons-Laffitte he put up a fight, and an accusation of assaulting an officer was added to the main charge of threatening the lives of the jockeys Michel Chirol and Jean-Jacques Declercq. 'Keep your big fucking mouth shut,' he'd told Chirol – who he suspected of being about to reveal the syndicate's secrets.

The arrests of Laouira and his accomplice Yves Daniel, another former jockey turned postman, were the prelude to a series of dramatic moves by Cahen and Saunier as they attempted to smash the 'Mafia du Tiercé' wide open. Laouira was banned from all French racecourses for life and, once behind bars, protested that, far from corrupting jockeys, the riders had come to him offering their services in return for money. It was exactly the response Jean Cahen had hoped for, further strengthening his hand before striking at the jockeys themselves.

For a brief interlude in October the attention of every Gallic racing lover and punter, not to mention thousands of once-a-year viewers, switched to Daniel Wildenstein's brilliant filly

Allez France who triumphed thrillingly if narrowly in the Prix de l'Arc de Triomphe at Longchamp. Unbeaten throughout the 1974 season, and the first filly to win over a million dollars in prize money, the daughter of the legendary 1965 Arc winner Sea-Bird II was a national heroine. Her profile was helped by the Tiercé's surging popularity and the consequent increase in betting turnover, if not racecourse attendances, in the France of that era.

Allez France had started favourite for the 1973 Arc but had finished second after her jockey Yves Saint-Martin had been outwitted by Lester Piggott on the English challenger Rheingold who went for home early in the straight. Twelve months later Saint-Martin was determined not to make the same mistake, and there was tremendous pressure on him, which only increased when he suffered a leg injury ten days before the race, necessitating a pain-killing injection before he went out to mount up.

It nearly went wrong again as Allez France was travelling so strongly on the approach to the home straight that she swept into the lead with a quarter of a mile still to run, at which point her stamina started to run out. Another French filly Comtesse de Loir, ridden by Jean-Claude Desaint, was running her down at the end but, fortunately for Saint-Martin and the favourite's backers, the winning post came just in time. Photographers raced out onto the track to capture the victorious moment, and horse and rider were the toast of Longchamp as they returned to unsaddle.

The occasion seemed to be the epitome of French racing at its very best. Visiting British and Irish punters, accustomed to competing bookies calling the odds, fumed as usual about the indifferent service provided by the PMU and the lengthy queues to place a bet. But as an aesthetic experience Longchamp was hard to beat – from the autumnal colours on the horse chestnut trees in the paddock to the elegantly dressed men and women who owned and bred the horses, and the rapturous crowds cheering them home. As well as Wildenstein and the Aga Khan and Jacques Wertheimer, Arc day traditionally featured an annual turn-out of the glamorous hostesses, courtesans and socialites who had been among the best patrons and afternoon friends of Des Moutis in his bookmaking days. Women like the Countess Batthyanny, Etti Plesch, María Félix Berger and the gorgeous 62-year-old Madame Suzy Volterra, whose horse Topyo had won the 1967 Arc at odds of 80-1.

Some of the biggest fortunes in Britain, Ireland and the US were represented in the list of *grands propriétaires* too: the Duke of Devonshire; the Texan oilman, Nelson Bunker Hunt; the polo player and former American Ambassador to Dublin, Raymond Guest; and the Hong Kong-based shipping magnate Jim Mullion and his wife, Meg. Their runners were attended by the top professional trainers, jockeys and bloodstock agents, and all of them projected the confident aura of life's winners and swells. This, surely, was what horse racing was all about. This was the Sport of Kings. What could such a spectacle possibly have in common with vulgar touts and postmen handing jockeys envelopes stuffed with cash in far corners of the weighing room? Yet only a couple of months after the Arc, the scandalous underside of the sport was back in the news again, beginning with what seemed like the final chapter in the long saga of the Prix de Bordeaux.

Des Moutis had been an elusive figure since the Prix Bride Abattue, acting out a pale facsimile of his old life as a Paris insurance broker. He still ran most days, cycled and played tennis, and tried to maintain appearances. But he was rarely seen outside Saint-Cloud and Neuilly unless it was the trips to Brignogan with Marie-Thérèse and the family for the *vacances. Commissaire* Cahen had yet to officially question him about the Prix Bride Abattue or summon him to appear before Judge Michaud but he suspected, rightly, that the police were first trying to assemble evidence elsewhere and saving his interrogation until they felt they had built a strong case.

Privately Patrice still held out hopes that the state would refund at least the stake money laid out by his 'friends' and their commandos on the Prix de Bordeaux in 1962. But on 6 December his lawyers informed him that the Supreme Court had rejected their final plea and that President Fougères and the Court of Appeal had ruled that the approximate 6.3 million francs' worth of winnings and stake money from the disputed race should remain unconditionally with the Treasury. The decision came with a further public condemnation, carried by all the newspapers, of the Prix de Bordeaux punters who were described once again as tricksters and frauds.

Des Moutis, enraged by the slur as well as the irretrievable loss of funds, was also informed that he was now under formal investigation by the prosecutor in Marseille regarding the 1971 Prix d'Entressen at Borély. It had long been rumoured that the outcome of the supposedly run-of-the-mill trotting race had been 'arranged' to insure a spectacular Trio payout. The local stewards may have seen nothing untoward at the time but the prosecutor's office took a different view and had Monsieur X in their sights. It was one further depressing fact for Patrice to reflect on, leaving him feeling more threatened and isolated than ever on those long, solitary runs through the wintry Parc de Saint-Cloud. Yet contrary to his fears he was not about to be arrested. Or at least not just yet.

That December police in both France and Britain were on the look-out for Lord Lucan, who had not been seen since allegedly killing the nanny Sandra Rivett, while attempting to murder his wife, in London the previous month. But despite supposed sightings in Paris, Deauville, Cap Ferrat and Monte Carlo, the elusive peer was about to be ousted from the French headlines by a jockey. At dawn on 9 December, a year to the day since the Prix Bride Abattue, the champion Pierre Costes was arrested on the gallops at Maisons-Laffitte. 'Pierrot' – who had been allowed to go on exercising horses for Georges Pelat despite having had his licence taken away – was intercepted by Jean Cahen and Roger Saunier as he dismounted and was driven away in handcuffs still wearing his riding boots and britches.

Costes was brought before Judge Michaud, who'd interviewed him several times before, and warned that he faced serious charges of fraud and attempted fraud. Rejecting a lawyer's application for bail the judge ordered the jockey to be removed to the Santé Prison in central Paris, though within a few days he was transferred – for his own safety, said the police – to the massive new Fleury-Mérogis jail in the suburbs.

Georges and René Pelat and Pierrot's wife Annie, mother of their two-year-old son Stephane, vowed to stand by him no matter what, while the trainer Patrick Bidoux claimed that the arrest was 'a scandal' and an outrage. 'I have known him for fifteen years,' he added, as if that alone should be proof enough of the rider's innocence. But no sooner had French racing begun to digest the sensational news of Pierrot's downfall than it was hit by a cascade of new indictments as Jean Cahen and Saunier played more of their cards.

Early on the morning of Wednesday 11 December – as Normandy fishermen blockaded the mouth of the Seine in the nation's latest industrial dispute – the police arrested the jockeys Jean-Pierre Renard, Jean-Paul Ciravegna and Jean-Pierre Philipperon, along with the trainer Jacques Beaume and his son Jean-Jacques junior. The jockeys, who were all in their late twenties or early thirties, were high-profile names at the peak of their careers. Renard, 'the Fox', renowned for his short temper, had ridden the unplaced Hasty Love in the Prix Bride Abattue. But earlier that year he'd been on board the victorious Chic Type, trained by Jean-Jacques Beaume, in the 1974 Grand Steeplechase de Paris, the French equivalent of the Cheltenham Gold Cup. Renard, who was retained by the respected trainer Dominique Sartini, had also won the 1972 running of the classic handicap the Prix du Président de la République for Daniel Wildenstein.

Jean-Paul Ciravegna rode the beaten favourite Ginger Bread in the Prix Bride Abattue and had won the 1972 Grand Steeplechase de Paris while Jean-Pierre Philipperon – brother of the leading flat-racing jockey Maurice Philipperon – rode the well-beaten Iskander in the Prix Bride Abattue. He'd started out in racing working for the respected Chantilly trainer Jacky Cunnington junior and had been employed at one point to ride for the Deauville *femme fatale* María Félix Berger. Despite being tipped for the top by Cunnington, he was described by *Commissaire* Cahen as 'a bad character'.

The trainer Jacques Beaume was a portly, smug, self-satisfied type who shared Des Moutis' enthusiasm for champagne and Cuban cigars, and hosted extravagant card parties for jockeys, owners and trainers at his luxurious Maisons-Laffitte villa.

Beaume's son, Jean-Jacques, trainer of Renard's 1974 Grand Steeplechase de Paris winner, was a noted gambler suspected of ordering the flat-racing jockey Claude Cimmino to stop one of his horses at Saint-Cloud in 1971 prior to a tilt at a big Tiercé race at Longchamp a few weeks later.

As the jockeys were driven away in separate police cars, Renard looked tough and taciturn, Philipperon sick and *Allez* Ciravegna distraught. *Commissaire* General Cahen, addressing the press afterwards, described the operation as 'sad but necessary'. In the initial stages of their investigation, he said, the police had been met by 'a wall of silence' in the racing world. But as his men had kept digging away at their task they had found 'a catastrophic gangrene', and he warned that when 'everyone knows what we have discovered in that world they will be astonished'.

As rumours multiplied that Des Moutis and other gamblers might be the next to be rounded up, the police maintained their focus on the jockeys. On Thursday 12 December, the 25-year-old Christian DaMeda, who began working as an apprentice at the age of 15 and who partnered the unplaced Cap Horn in the Prix Bride Abattue, became the fifth one to be arrested.

That same morning *Le Figaro* ran a cartoon of a horse refusing at a fence which was actually a prison wall, and propelling the jockey over the top into the arms of a waiting guard who was grinning unpleasantly. 'The world of racing has been decapitated,' declared the paper's correspondent Michele Morrice invoking comparisons with the guillotine.

On 13 December ten more suspects felt the blade on their necks, beginning with the jockey Jean-Pierre Creveuil, who had won the 1973 Grand Steeplecase de Paris riding Giquin for

María Félix Berger. The unhappy rider was taken into custody by Jean Cahen and interrogated late into the night on the orders of Judge Michaud.

Meanwhile, Roger Saunier began a forty-eight-hour return trip to the Midi, rounding up the five Marseillais punters – Frankie Cordeau, Gerard Zarokian, the pimp Sauveur Ruggieri, Mathieu Dalmayan and Jean Calliol – and their three Toulon counterparts, Robert Maitraglis, Pierre Negro and Joseph Auxende. On 14 December another Marseille gambler, Jean Henrisey, was added to the bag, joining the others in the city's fearsome Baumettes Prison.

Nobody arrested Jacky Imbert or Eugène Matrone or Jean-Louis Fargette, although *Le Provençal* did return to the story of the 160,000 francs' worth of Prix Bride Abattue winnings found in the apartment of Vincent Ascione, and wondered again about the death of Jean-Luc Durry in 1971.

In the bar cafés around La Canebière in Marseille and the Toulonnaise '*rade*', or port, there was much talk about vulnerable young jockeys fascinated by money, and among the faces at Borély racetrack there was some sympathy for the arrested punters too. But those sentiments were not shared by *Commissaire* Cahen, who painted a vivid picture of 'a well organised and powerful gang with a clear hierarchy operating on all the racecourses of France'.

The gates of a handful of the top prisons in France may have clanged shut on some of the top jockeys and other gang members, but for the public there was a continued sense of shock that the former 'demigods of Sunday', as Enrico Macias had described them – men who were winning and living the good life – could be mixed up with organised crime. With no awareness of the irony that would one day surround their remarks, commentators compared the downfall of Costes, Renard, Ciravegna and Philipperon to being told that their cycling heroes Eddy Merckx, Raymond Poulidor and Bernard Thévenet had been exposed for cheating and race-fixing during the Tour de France. People were asking how they could possibly do such a thing – how could it have happened?

On 21 December the magazine *Paris Match* ran a three-page feature on the 'Mafia du Tiercé unmasked', accompanied by vivid colour and black and white photographs of the alleged conspirators. One picture, taken in 1973 in the jockeys' changing room at Auteuil, featured a victorious Pierre Costes, still in his riding silks, surrounded by his *copains*, or friends. Some of them wore plain clothes with long 1970s hair and sideburns; some were expensively groomed and coiffeured. Others wore a mixture of black and brown leather jackets and houndstooth check with their red and black polo-neck jerseys. It was still several months before the fall, and the photograph oozed confident, cocky camaraderie. You half-expected Robert de Niro, Ray Liotta and Joe Pesci to be in the background there somewhere too, applauding the French Goodfellas for playing the game with style.

'Are they victims of an organisation manipulating them?' asked the magazine. A question it felt unable to fully answer, detailing instead the supposedly 'massive gambling debts' afflicting all the riders, and the fatal attractions in the shape of girls, cars, clubs, dinners and champagne that lay in wait for all young prodigies fêted by Paris life. One of them had recently built a beautiful house he couldn't afford. Another was earning 100,000 francs a year but living off 200,000.

Jean-Pierre Philipperon, his face weak but sly, was reputed to have been a regular player in the clandestine high-stakes card games – hosted originally by the Trois Canards – in Montmartre and Pigalle. But the biggest gambling parties were said to have taken place at the Maisons-Laffitte home of the trainer Jacques Beaume where Pierre Costes, in particular, had run up ruinous losses totalling eight million old francs. An unnamed colleague described the champion at the poker table with his cards in his left hand, his face sweating, his breathing light but quick. Costes, he said, was 'a great jockey' with an 'ice-cool nerve' but added that he was also 'quite mad' and 'the most fragile of the accused'. He had won 430,000 francs in 1973 and been top of the racing hit parade, but he had paid no tax that year and then lost a fortune at cards. So when Robert Laouira came along with his syndicate friends and asked Costes to do them 'a service', taunting him with comments like, 'You're not afraid, are you?' he was in no fit state to turn them away.

The trainer Georges Pelat had tried to offer Costes and his wife Annie a stable home life, inviting them to family meals at his house where, he admitted, Patrice des Moutis was sometimes present too. But Pelat couldn't lock the jockey up at night, and the following morning Costes would often appear on the gallops sweating, red-eyed and hoarse from all the cigarettes he'd smoked while playing poker through the night.

Paris Match had found a black and white photo of the plump trainer Jacques Beaume, perched on a rail in a racecourse paddock, cigarette holder in hand and looking down patronisingly at a young jockey. Beaume was allegedly the Mephistophelian figure who introduced the riders to the men with the meridional accents and elegant tailoring who would in turn send Robert Laouira back to the weighing rooms with those precious envelopes stuffed with cash.

In his 11 December press conference *Commissaire* Cahen had compared the structure of the race-fixing syndicate to a pyramid. The jockeys were on the lowest rung, he said. Then there were the middlemen like Jacques Beaume, Robert Laouira and the late, unlamented Vincent Ascione. Then there were the financiers, presumed to be drug traffickers of the Marseille and Corsican *Milieu*, and then at the top there was a mastermind who had not yet been identified.

The infantry were under arrest but, according to Cahen, it was only when the mastermind was in prison that the racing world would be able to breathe freely once again. Some investigative journalists thought Cahen should really have been talking about a brains trust with several different figures all playing complementary roles. Off-the-record briefings indicated that the *commissaires* believed that Des Moutis, the by now embittered Monsieur X, was the syndicate's technical advisor and form expert, recommending which races to 'arrange' and which horses to bet on to be sure of the maximum profit, just as he had done in the Prix de Bordeaux twelve years earlier. But it was also inferred from further comments from the Quai des Orfèvres that the police did *not* believe that Patrice was the sole Godfather and kingpin linking it all together.

In January 1975 Cahen gave the press an almost exact description of the mastermind he was targeting, but without supplying a name. The suspect was said to be a racehorse owner and breeder who possessed a stud farm in Normandy, bought for 2.5 million francs in 1964, and who had built his fortune in Marseille and Paris in the 1950s. In recent times he had allegedly been implicated in the drugs trade as well as a series of robberies. But the suspect had friends in high political places and had been awarded a prestigious Mérite Agricole award in 1969 for the innovative management of his stud. Crime writers and regular *habitués* of the racecourse had no doubts. They recognised this man at once. It was a description of the former leader of the Bande des Trois Canards, Marius Bertella.

A reporter for *Weekend* magazine attempted to doorstep Bertella at his home in Normandy. The 48-year-old jockey's son was the owner of the half-timbered Haras Des Chartreux near Branville in the department of Calvados. The beach resorts of Deauville and Trouville were only ten kilometres away, and Paris in easy reach within a couple of hours, while the lush agricultural Norman countryside was at the epicentre of the French thoroughbred breeding industry.

The distinguished historian and Francophile Richard Cobb used to say that *faux manoir* country life in Normandy held a particular sentimental attraction for French gangsters and *enfants de Paris* once they made it to the big time. Cobb always preferred stories of crooks and café dwellers to the lives of great men, and in his 1986 collection *People and Places* he wrote about the notorious outlaw Jacques Mesrine, who was Public Enemy Number One in France in the 1970s. The gangster, who robbed the Deauville casino in 1978, returned to Normandy continually, even while he was on the run, and something about the wagon wheels, red- and white-check tablecloths, brass lamps and half-timbering – not to mention all that *Poulet Vallée d'Auge* with cider, cream and Calvados – seemed to tickle every self-made racketeer's fancy.

Marius Bertella was no exception and, although he didn't much care for publicity, he agreed to answer a few of *Weekend*'s questions nonetheless. 'Yes,' he said. 'I own one of the most beautiful stud farms in France.' He had bought it for three million francs in 1964 and 'yes,' he added, 'I received the Mérite Agricole medal. And you know why?' The award – bestowed by the Fifth Republic for outstanding services to agriculture and once only second in prestige to the Légion d'Honneur – had been for his imaginative stewardship of the Haras Des Chartreux. As well as building barns with a much greater emphasis on light and clean air than in some traditional stud farms, he had fitted the boxes with close-circuit television so as to be able to continually monitor the well-being of the mares and their foals.

Quizzed as to his past and the origins of his wealth, Bertella said that he first left Marseille for Paris in 1949, and that since then all his activities had been legitimately accounted for. But how exactly had he made his fortune? 'I won it,' he said, 'thanks to some friends who introduced me to a consortium of banks financing various casinos.' Clubs like the Aviation Club de France and the Grand Cercle, formerly owned by the Guérini family but now under the control of their Corsican nemesis – and Marius Bertella's business partner – Marcel Francisci. There was no mention of the unfortunate circumstances in which Jean-Baptiste Andréani had been forced to give up running the Grand Cercle after being shot and crippled by Marius Bertella's other business partner Jacky Imbert in 1963. Neither was there any reference to the drive-by shooting of Antoine Guérini in Marseille in 1967.

Bertella claimed to be 'outraged' that his name had been mentioned in connection with drugs. He was 'a father and family man', he said, and had seen the damage that drugs can do. Yes, of course, he was a racing enthusiast. He bred horses and he went to Deauville every year and to Longchamp and Chantilly and, yes, he'd read about Patrice des Moutis. But as to the Prix Bride Abattue and the race-fixing scandal, well, he was as much in the dark as everyone else. He admitted that he'd had some dealings with the police in the past and had first been interviewed by them back in 1956, but they had found nothing then and they would find nothing now. He was a proud Gaullist and patriot and public-spirited to boot, and he would be happy to meet *Commissaire* Cahen at any time if people thought there was something he could do to help.

An exhausted Cahen, who was apparently not amused when he read the *Weekend* interview, declined to say where or when he would be talking to Marius Bertella. But he told Saunier that completing their inquiry satisfactorily and obtaining the outcome demanded by the Interior Minister Poniatowski was becoming like trying to pick the winners of a Tiercé race where the jockeys might not be trying, the favourites might not be 'off' and the winning post kept moving.

The hyperactive 'Ponia' kept inserting himself into proceedings, still acting like a campaign manager determined to burnish the image of the presidency. The attempts by Giscard to present himself as a man of the people had been greeted with derision, especially when he put on a v-necked pullover and invited the dustmen for breakfast at the Élysée Palace and took a ride on the Metro with a cameraman in tow. His government's accomplishments would eventually include legalising abortion, lowering the voting age to 18, raising the minimum wage and investing in the new high-speed TGV train network. But to most citizens their president remained a snooty type who preferred shooting partridge with Prince Juan Carlos of Spain in the royal forest at Chambord and flew to St Moritz for lunch with the Shah of Iran. It was left to Poniatowski to demonstrate that the administration was in touch with popular sentiment, and few things were more popular in France in 1975 than the Tiercé.

At the end of January, lawyers for the imprisoned jockeys Costes, Renard, Philipperon, Ciravegna, DaMeda and Creveuil managed to get them released on bail. But in the same week, and without waiting for the niceties of a trial, Poniatowski announced that all six jockeys were banned for life from riding or holding any other positions in the racing industry.

The ban was intended to show that the government was on the side of aggrieved punters who had lost money on fixed races, and was in keeping with Ponia's assertion that, where serious crimes were concerned, justice should be 'swift and brutal'. The minister was still longing for the police to identify a race-fixing mastermind. The 700-page dossier which Cahen submitted to Judge Michaud in February – merely an intermediate account of his inquiry – lent heavily in favour of Marius Bertella as the prime mover. It documented his career from his purchase of the Bar Cabaret Les Trois Canards from Baro Ferret in 1951 to his leadership of the Three Ducks Gang with Eugène Matrone, co-owner of the bar Le Skating, and the sudden enrichment that had enabled him to move to Normandy and buy a stud farm in the 1960s.

Bertella was laundering drug money, of that Cahen was sure. He also had no doubt that the real winners of the Prix Bride Abattue Tiercé were not the Midi punters under arrest, although they were guilty of trying to defraud the PMU, but Jacky Imbert, Jean-Louis Fargette and their crew. He also believed Jacky le Mat was responsible for ordering the killings of Jean-Luc Durry and Vincent Ascione.

Cahen was being briefed by investigators in Paris targeting the French Connection but it was not the *commissaire*'s job to take down the drug smugglers. His mission was to smash the race-fixing syndicate and arrest the gamblers and jockeys enabling it to function. Making a case against the syndicate's *Milieu* ringleaders that would stand up in court would be extremely difficult. Bertella had friends in parliament and the Ministry of Agriculture, which had awarded him his medal, while nobody dared to testify against Fargette and Imbert. But there was one big name who could be successfully prosecuted. Cahen's report also linked the PMU's long-standing foe Patrice des Moutis to the Prix Bride Abattue. After hours of interrogation some of the jockeys and their middlemen had claimed that the gentleman from Saint-Cloud had met with them in Le Flandrin on Monday 3 December 1973. Des Moutis, Robert Laouira and other *turfistes* they described as 'a bit special' had explained that they were preparing to defraud the Tiercé in the most audacious way the following Sunday at Auteuil. According to Pierre Costes it was then that he was offered money to pull his horse in the Tiercé race and not to finish in the first three. It was agreed that Des Moutis and the other punters would receive a telephone signal on the Sunday morning confirming that the jockeys were going to go ahead with the plan. As a result of those 'phone tips', as Patrice innocently described them, he had backed the winning Tiercé combination himself, using proxy punters to place 70,000 francs' worth of bets winning a total of 1.5 million.

Bertella and Imbert may have been out of reach but Judge Michaud agreed with *Commissaires* Cahen and Saunier. It was time to bring in Monsieur X.

Chapter 29

It was a Monday evening, 17 February 1975, when Jean Cahen and his men turned up at the Des Moutis house on the Rue de Béarn. They had timed their arrival to coincide with Patrice and Marie-Thérèse's return from a week's skiing in Val-d'Isère. The family coffers were not quite empty yet, it seemed, and despite the pressures and the mounting strain of trying to live normally under the shadow of suspicion, the couple had been trying to maintain the habits and customs of their old, charmed life.

Commissaire Cahen noted that Patrice and Marie-Thérèse looked bronzed and well from the Alpine sun. He hoped that they'd enjoyed their holiday but, unfortunately, his was not a social visit. Patrice, who was smartly dressed as always in a dark suit and tie, was told that he was formally under arrest on suspicion of fraud and conspiracy to commit fraud. Accompanied by Cahen and two uniformed officers, he was led out of the house in handcuffs and driven first to the local Police des Courses et Jeux headquarters in Clichy and then to Judge Michaud's chambers.

His interrogation went on for the best part of three days and at the end of each day he was taken back to Clichy and locked up in a police cell overnight. It was said afterwards that Patrice 'found it hard to contain his fury' at his treatment, and that his language had more in common with a pimp or street crook than a member of the Breton–Norman nobility.

Cahen and Michaud put it to Des Moutis that, enraged by what he regarded as his unjust treatment at the hands of the courts and the PMU, he had allowed himself to become a pawn of the *Milieu*. They had lent him their help, for a bit of fun, when he needed proxy punters to help him get his money down on the Prix de Bordeaux in 1962, and they had never really gone away.

Cahen said that some of the arrested jockeys had claimed that Patrice had been paid to identify Tiercé races with the biggest potential payout should certain outsiders get lucky and the favourites run below par. The *Milieu* needed a form expert to help them pick out which horses to stop and which jockeys to bribe, and to advise them on the number of permutations they should bet and to what stake. That, suggested the *Commissaire*, had become Patrice's role – in the Prix Bride Abattue, in the Prix d'Entressen at Marseille in 1971, and maybe as far back as the Prix d'Amérique and the Prix Georges de Talhouet-Roy and other fixed races they had yet to uncover.

Des Moutis angrily denied the accusations and insisted he had done nothing wrong, but Cahen persisted. Some of the jockeys, he said, referred to Patrice as '*Mon Oncle*' and were saying that they had met up with him and Laouira to plan the Prix Bride Abattue finishing order in Le Flandrin. There was photographic evidence too, claimed Cahen: pictures of Patrice talking to Costes, Renard and Philipperon.

Again Patrice indignantly denied committing any crime. Of course there might be pictures, he said. He was a racing lover and good friend of the trainer Georges Pelat. The disgraced Pierre Costes had ridden for Georges and René Pelat all the time, and sometimes Patrice had met him and other riders at Pelat's house.

Cahen reminded Patrice of his comment in his Radio Monte Carlo interview in 1970 when he'd said he preferred jump racing to the flat. It was the jump jockeys that were now under arrest, and Cahen said he believed that Patrice, like the riders, had become entangled in the underworld's net, maybe initially imagining that he could walk away when he'd had enough. Only the gangsters wouldn't let him walk away. The *Milieu* had eyes bigger than their stomachs. They demanded first one fixed race and then another and then another. They not only wanted to win the Tiercé and clean their dirty drug money, they wanted to fleece the mug punters who patronised their illegal bookmaking rackets in the Midi. But they ended up bribing and threatening so many jockeys that the evidence of corruption became too blatant to ignore. Cahen said he sympathised with a man of Patrice's background and education and the position he found himself in. 'Tell us about Marius Bertella,' he said. 'Tell us about Jacky Imbert and Eugène Matrone and Jean-Louis Fargette. If you co-operate . . . we can help you.'

Des Moutis looked at the detective as if he were an idiot, a madman, and Cahen concluded that Patrice wouldn't – or couldn't – say anything about Bertella or Jacky le Mat or how he'd come by those Prix Bride Abattue telephone 'tips' on the morning of Sunday 9 December 1973. In which case there was nothing more that the *Commissaire* could do.

On the afternoon of Thursday 20 February Patrice was taken back to Michaud's chambers where the judge informed him that, due to the severity of the charges, he was activating the year's suspended prison sentence imposed by the Court of Appeal at the Palais de Justice in June 1973.

Patrice was handcuffed once again and put in the back of a black unmarked Citroën DS. Then, in the waning afternoon light and with Jean Cahen sitting beside him on the back seat, he was driven back to the Police des Courses et Jeux headquarters and from there to the Fresnes Prison on the southern side of Paris.

The route took them from Clichy down to Porte Maillot, not far from Patrice's office in Neuilly-sur-Seine. The warmth of the lighting in the cafés and shop windows was in sharp contrast to the slate grey February sky. Along the way they passed office workers, shoppers and children on their way home from school. The sight of families and couples meeting happily and without a care was a painful reminder to Des Moutis of everything he was about to lose.

At the Porte Maillot roundabout they joined the southbound section of the Paris ringroad, the Boulevard Périphérique. With rush hour approaching, the traffic was heavy and progress slow, and for Des Moutis it was the longest and most depressing journey of his life. He was like the doomed *Nouvelle Vague* lover in *Ascenseur pour l'Échafaud* riding his fate to the end of the line, and it was as if the Wheel of Fortune had deposited him on its very lowest rung.

They passed the Bois de Boulogne, Auteuil racecourse hidden from view somewhere up there behind the trees. They passed Roland Garros and the Parc des Princes, where Patrice had spent many a happy hour watching tennis and rugby, swung left at the Porte de Saint-Cloud and carried on past Issy-les-Moulineaux towards Orly airport and the Périphérique exit at Montrouge. The last part of the drive was due south through the *banlieues*, suburban neighbourhoods looking poorer by the minute, and an hour after leaving Clichy they finally arrived at their destination.

The Citroën came to a halt outside the front entrance to the Fresnes, and the driver rolled down his window and exchanged a few words with the guards in the checkpoint. The big green double doors opened. The car, bearing the *Commissaire* and his prisoner, drove through under the arch of the main gate and then the doors shut firmly behind them.

The Fifth Republic had finally got their man.

'Monsieur X in prison,' proclaimed the TV bulletins and newspaper headlines the following day. Patrice's admission that he had won one and a half million francs on the Prix Bride Abattue Tiercé after he'd been 'given some telephone tips' on the Sunday morning was greeted with ridicule in some quarters and confusion in others. Who exactly were these well-informed tipsters? Jockeys? Trainers? Other speculators? And where were they now? In prison too, or still at large?

Des Moutis had also admitted using three friends, or asscociates, to place his bets for him, defending them against allegations of conspiracy to defraud and maintaining that he'd no choice as the PMU now simply blocked his wagers as a matter of course. His arguments didn't sway Judge Michaud or *Commissaire* Cahen, and the three proxy punters – Pierre Nicolas, who was a professional bridge player, Michel Bes, described as an entrepreneur, and Francis Arpin, a physiotherapist – were also taken into custody and charged with being in breach of PMU rules. As middle-class professionals rather than jockeys or obvious low-life characters, they were quickly released on bail, but their detentions further incensed Des Moutis when he heard about it in his cell in the Fresnes.

Alessandri and Sarfati, the same firm of lawyers that had unsuccessfully defended Patrice in the Prix de Bordeaux trial, were working again on his behalf. But they warned him that, with more of the arrested jockeys desperate to save their skins, the evidence against him was mounting. Not just regarding the Prix Bride Abattue either, but in connection with the Prix d'Entressen at Parc Borély in 1971 too. Indeed, the Marseille prosecutor was also looking into the suspicious outcomes of the same race in 1972 and 1973, with the *Milieu* again suspected of taking a hand. The lawyers' view was that, whatever chances they may have of rebuffing the Auteuil charges, the Marseille scenario was looking bad.

Marie-Thérèse and the family and friends of Patrice may have been distraught at his incarceration but the word from PMU headquarters at the Rue la Boétie was that the secretary general, Pierre Crespin, had been seen rubbing his hands with glee over the downfall of his old enemy. The arrogant bad-tempered punter who had raged against Crespin, Maurice Alexandre and André Carrus after the disappointing Grand Prix d'Amiens Tiercé return in July 1961 had had his comeuppance.

With Monsieur X now locked away and unable to respond, it was easier for the PMU and the government to attribute the role of race-fixing mastermind to Patrice while drawing a discreet veil over the involvement of the Mérite Agricole winner and Gaullist sympathiser Marius Bertella and his friends. The stud owner's contacts seemed to insulate him from the law whereas there was no comparable protection for Des Moutis who had been virtually abandoned by Paris society, while his alter ego

Monsieur X was no longer depicted as a romantic hero but as a deranged gambler and villain.

All the publicity surrounding Patrice and talk of the Mafia du Tiercé and the race fixing gang appeared to have had little or no affect on the Tiercé's popularity. On Sunday 16 February there had been a pool of ten million francs at Auteuil, with thousands of those sentimentalised 'little' punters still picking numbers not on the basis of form but because they corresponded to their wives' or children's birthdays or their *carte grise* (ID number). It was confirmation, if any was still needed, of just how good a job André Carrus and his sons and heirs had done in addicting the French public to gambling.

Betting turnover was up again in the following weeks too despite the lurid revelations at the trial of Robert Laouira, who was brought before President Arnaud and the 13th Correctional Court at the Palais de Justice on 26 February. The proceedings, described at first as a mere *aperitif* to the trial of Costes, Renard, Philipperon and the other Prix Bride Abattue jockeys (for which there was, as yet, no fixed date) turned out to be spicy enough in their own right.

The 32-year-old Laouira was described by the Prosecutor, Maître de Cayle, as 'more of a hood than a jockey' and as a man with 'an easy manner and mocking smile sometimes punctuated by flashes of anger' that betrayed the malice beneath the surface. He was accused of extorting six million old francs from the rider Jean-Jacques Declercq, claiming it was a long-standing debt he'd forgotten about, and of threatening to blow up the jockey Michel Chirol's house and family with dynamite. Declercq and Chirol's crime, in his eyes, had been their possible willingness to reveal the secrets of the Prix Bride Abattue to *Commissaire*

Cahen. In fact, the jockeys had wavered and had not wanted to appeal directly to the police, but an anonymous phone call from someone close to them had alerted the Brigade Criminelle to the danger the pair were in and the menace represented by Laouira, his sidekick Yves Daniel and their methods of persuasion.

'The Postman' who accused Chirol and Declercq of 'lying through their teeth' was sentenced to two years imprisonment by President Arnaud, who had been the senior judge at the Prix de Bordeaux trial in 1971. In his summing-up Arnaud declared that 'in this dark affair' he had no doubt that Laouira was 'the instrument of other more dangerous and powerful men as yet unknown'. Some members of the public may have imagined that the judge was referring to Des Moutis, and the PMU did nothing to discourage that notion. But only a couple of days after Laouira's conviction, they were given a vivid glimpse of what really dangerous and powerful men were capable of in Paris in broad daylight – men who were not so much accomplices of Monsieur X as part of the underworld culture that, Cahen believed, had taken him prisoner.

On the afternoon of Friday 28 February eighteen plain-clothes members of the anti-gang squad led by *Commissaire* Marcel Leclerc – who had first questioned Patrice after the Prix Georges de Talhouet-Roy in 1969 – had assembled under a wintry sun outside the Bar Café Thélème at number 12 Boulevard Saint-Germain, not far from the Pantheon and the Sorbonne. *Les flics*, who were all armed, were in a fleet of vans and unmarked cars, some of them parked around the corner on Rue du Cardinal Lemoine. The police had been tipped off that the Thélème was to be the venue for what was described as 'a Yalta of crime' – a reference to the 1945 Yalta Conference in the

Crimea at which Churchill, Roosevelt and Stalin met to discuss the future shape of Europe after World War II.

The leading protagonists at the Thélème were expected to be the Zemour family, a Jewish *pied noir* clan who had taken over the mantle and businesses of the Perrets and the Trois Canards in Pigalle and Montmartre after the Three Ducks left for Normandy and Marseille. As well as running the prostitution and *hôtels de passe* rackets, along with extorting money from the Paris wine and spirits trade, the Zemours had hoped to be offered a share of the casino gambling businesses run by Marcel Francisci. The Corsican, who had presided over the demise of the Guérini empire, spurned the Zemours as too volatile to be trustworthy partners. But the police still suspected the Zemours of being involved in the Tiercé and general race-fixing syndicates and of lending muscle to the bribery of the jockeys.

The supplicants seeking a partnership with the Zemours that last day of February were a group variously termed the Sicilian Gang and the Bande Lyonnais, led by Jean-Claude Vella and a character called Louis the Pimp from Auteuil. They were allies of the former Zemour gangster Roger Bacri, who had a stake in the French Connection drugs trade and wanted Zemour approval to expand his markets from the Paris suburbs into the capital.

The Jewish *pieds noirs* were not that enthusiastic about drug dealing so a summit had been set up at the Thélème, which was a regular Sicilian meeting place, to enable Bacri to discuss his proposals. But Marcel Leclerc and his fellow commanders reckoned that, far from negotiating, the two bands were more likely to engage in a Wild West-style gunfight, which offered the police, who were always struggling to get evidence against any of the gangs, an opportunity to catch them in the act and, if nothing else, arrest them for the possession of illegal weapons.

At 3.30 p.m. the 71-year-old Edmond Zemour, the family's senior citizen, had arrived outside the café in a black BMW and was met by his 45-year-old nephew William, also known as Zaoui, who had a .38 revolver in his belt. The two men and William's younger brother Edgar and their henchmen went in to the café where there were half a dozen customers drinking coffee and *chocolat chaud*, including two Algerian lawyers discussing a case at the nearby Palais de Justice.

Shortly after 4 o'clock a detective hiding on Rue du Cardinal Lemoine near the back entrance to the Tour d'Argent restaurant, saw what he thought were some of the Sicilians arrive and go in through a side door of the café. A few minutes later a mêlée, as the detective described it, began inside the Thélème, and Leclerc – assuming the Sicilians were going to open fire – sounded the alarm and the *flics* went in with guns drawn. In the ensuing shootout the café owner and his wife and their customers hit the floor in panic as bullets flew, glass and china were smashed and gangsters and cops took cover behind chairs and tables and threw themselves over the counter.

William Zemour was shot four times, including once in the head, and his bodyguard Jo Elbaz was killed. William's brother Edgar was hit five times in the back, and his Uncle Edmond damaged a knee. Eight men were injured in total, including two police officers and one of the Algerian lawyers, who was wrongfully arrested on suspicion of being a gang member and bundled into a police van where he suffered a broken jaw and a fractured skull. William Zemour subsequently died of his wounds, and his funeral at Bagneux Cemetery on 10 March drew thousands of mourners. William's coffin was borne to the traditional Jewish resting place in southwestern Paris in a Rolls Royce Silver Cloud, and the extravagant floral displays were a match for the *Boardwalk Empire* heyday of Capone and Bugs Moran.

The gun battle that killed William Zemour and Jo Elbaz was being held up as further evidence of the way Paris was becoming 'a second Chicago', repeating *Weekend*'s accusation about the Tiercé in 1969 – and there was criticism of the police for opening fire on the main thoroughfare of the Left Bank in daylight hours. Especially when it was revealed that there had been no Sicilian Gang members in the café. Roger Bacri had apparently set the whole thing up as a trap for the Zemours, hoping they would open fire first on the police, which they did, and that their power would be undermined as a result.

Marcel Leclerc was unrepentant. 'I prefer to have them out of circulation,' he said, referring to the dead and arrested racketeers. 'The public say they want action but then they are outraged if we overstep the mark. Well, let the finer spirits manage by themselves the next time there is a dangerous arrest to be made.'

The shootout had occurred only a day after the sentencing of Robert Laouira and within a week of the arrest and imprisonment of Monsieur X, and the three events seemed to morph together in the popular imagination, to the detriment of Des Moutis, who had also been taken 'out of circulation' and was finding his first experience of prison life devastating.

Chapter 30

The Fresnes, which was built in the closing years of the nine-teenth century, had three long cell blocks four storeys high, with cells on each floor and netting across the upper landings to prevent suicides. The cells were small and claustrophobic, measuring approximately four metres long, two and a half metres wide and three metres high. Each cell had a high window, a thin, hard bed and a lavatory bowl attached to the wall, but throughout the prison the standards of basic hygiene had not greatly improved since some of the mutinous OAS Generals had protested about it during their incarceration after the failed Algiers Putsch fourteen years earlier.

The Generals, like Edmond Jouhaud, were not the only political prisoners to have been housed at the Fresnes during the jail's history. In World War II the Germans had interned Resistance members and captured British SOE agents in the prison, and many of them were tortured there horribly before being shipped to concentration camps in the east as the Allies closed in on Paris in August 1944. After the Liberation General de Gaulle's provisional government held leading collaborators at the Fresnes, including the head of the Vichy government

Pierre Laval who was shot in the prison courtyard in 1945 after trying to delay his execution by swallowing poison.

Capital punishment was still on the statute books in France in 1975 despite Giscard d'Estaing's promise to create a modern, progressive state. Executions in Paris generally took place at the Santé in Montparnasse but there was a death row at the Fresnes too – Roger Degueldre and Jean-Marie Bastien-Thiry were both confined there before being shot at Fort d'Ivry – and the guillotine was stored in the basement. Condemned men shared morbid jokes about heads popping out like corks from a champagne bottle when the blade fell.

Adjusting and surviving in this environment was a formidable challenge for Des Moutis. Whereas the ex-jockey Laouira, who was also in the Fresnes, enjoyed a measure of protection and comfort, even with other inmates deputed by the *Milieu* to look out for him Patrice had to fend for himself. His health was the first thing to suffer. There was little useful work in the prison, and opportunities for exercise – normally a regular part of his routine – were minimal. He had scant appetite for the food, which was far removed from the elegant fare he'd enjoyed on a daily basis in Neuilly and Saint-Cloud, and access to the contraband stashes of alcohol and tobacco depended on money and influence. Patrice still had some of the former but he also had to work out how to juggle the competing demands of other prisoners offering protection, at a price, or threatening him with violence unless he cut them in on the proceeds of his Tiercé coups.

Whenever Marie-Thérèse came to visit she took off her jewellery and dressed down in an attempt to deflect attention from her husband, while making comparable efforts to be positive and lift his spirits with talk of lawyers and further appeals. The worst moments for Patrice came after his wife had gone and he was taken back to his cell and forced to listen to jangling keys, clanking bars and the sounds of his fellow convicts – cries of pain, threats and propositions – echoing through the long prison night.

Monsieur X may have been locked away but there was no diminution of interest in his story by the tabloid newspapers and their readers. A popular photograph of Des Moutis at the time, taken during the uproar over the PMU's refusal to pay the Prix Georges de Talhouet-Roy winnings in 1969, showed him posed outside an empty Auteuil racecourse and looking over the perimeter fence. In his customary suit and tie and with a cigarette in hand, the handsome six-foot Centralien with the Roman nose and dark hair cut a suitably brooding and existential figure.

Some of Patrice's supporters wrote letters to the press, expressing the hope that he would not be in prison long and that, when his freedom was eventually restored, he'd confound the PMU and prove his innocence of all the charges that had been laid at his door. Others feared he was now an irredeemably fallen hero who, thanks to the bets he'd admitted placing on the blatantly fixed Prix Bride Abattue, had forfeited any further claim to public sympathy. But one big question remained: was he really the patron of a gang or, as Cahen perceived it, a prisoner in hock to the *Milieu*?

It seemed that a resolution of these competing views would have to wait until the completion of *Commissaire* Cahen's inquiry, which was still in full cry. The big box-office hit film in France in the spring of 1975 was *Peur Sur La Ville*, or *Fear Over the City*, a thriller starring Jean-Paul Belmondo playing a cop – for the first time in his career – pursuing both a serial killer and a cunning professional criminal, at one point chasing him over the rooftops of Paris. The equally hard-boiled real-life duo, Cahen and Saunier, were continuing to spread fear through the French racing fraternity as they continued their hunt for the crooked jockeys and their paymasters. In classic police style, and with Interior Minister Michel Poniatowski still breathing down their necks, they had been repeatedly interrogating Costes, Philipperon, Ciravegna and the other banned riders one by one, then using their conflicting stories to persuade them to turn on each other.

Lawyers were not always present at these interrogations – as was often the way back then– and, with the aid of the new information they'd obtained, the police were able to bring in more jockeys in April and May, all of whom had ridden beaten horses in the Prix Bride Abattue. On 9 April they arrested the gin rummy fan Michel Jathan, another one of Auteuil's biggest stars and the rider of the Prix Georges de Talhouet-Roy winner Maestro II. Jathan's telephone had been tapped, revealing that he had been in regular contact with Laouira to negotiate his fees for stopping horses. It also revealed that a week before the Prix Bride Abattue he had accompanied Laouira to a meeting with another rider, Henri Mathelin, in Le Flandrin – Patrice's favourite café on Avenue Henri-Martin – successfully persuading his fellow jockey to accept 20,000 francs for co-operating with the fix.

The week after Jathan it was the turn of Henri Mathelin himself – who protested that Laouira had corrupted him and that he'd been powerless to resist – and Jean-Claude Biard, who had ridden the unplaced Start in the Prix Georges de

Talhouet-Roy. And the week after that Roland Kléparski, who had been aboard Mano Capon in the Prix Bride Abattue, and Robert Lautier and Robert Jayhan who had ridden Next Time and Kotkiait, were also brought before Judge Michaud and charged with conspiracy and attempted fraud. Just like their more famous colleagues who'd been arrested the previous December, they were all banned from race riding until further notice and spent several uncomfortable days and nights in custody until their representatives were able to arrange bail.

At this rate there would soon be no qualified jump jockeys left in Paris. Their profession was being wiped out. 'Yes, it's sad,' wrote Pierre Jotreau in the 19 April edition of *Weekend*. 'But if the honesty of the Tiercé is the prize, we must endure it.' In some quarters the riders' plight inspired mockery as well as sadness and condemnation. The situation was summed up by a cartoon in *Nouvel Observateur* in which two racing and gambling 'types' in trenchcoats and fedoras were seen playing a game of poker dice. Only when they shook the cup it wasn't the dice that fell out . . . it was a jockey.

With so many big names on the sidelines, some of them never to return, the 1975 Grand Steeplechase de Paris, run at Auteuil on 22 June, had an unavoidably anti-climactic feel. The winner Air Landais, owned by Madame Marie-Claire Frolich, an associate of Daniel Wildenstein, was trained by her husband Georges Pelat who had been interviewed as part of the race fixing inquiry but never charged. The winning ride went to the apprentice Patrick Beyer but should have gone to Pierre Costes who had yet to win the Grand Prix and who might now never get the chance. The former champion had been released on bail that January along with the 1973 and 1974 Grand Prix winning riders Ciravegna and Renard. But their non-attendance at Auteuil and the charges hanging over them were as sobering for lovers of French jump racing as it would be if Ruby Walsh, Barry Geraghty, Richard Johnson and other stars of the English and Irish weighing room were suspected of corruption and banned from riding in the Grand National or the Cheltenham Gold Cup.

At least the jockeys had their freedom again – for the moment anyway – and on Thursday 10 July, a year to the day since Pierre Costes had lost his licence, Des Moutis' lawyers managed to prise open the doors of the French justice system just long enough to get Patrice released from the Fresnes Prison, albeit under the strictest conditions.

After enduring one hundred and forty-two days of confinement, Patrice was beginning to feel that luck had permanently deserted him. But at the beginning of the month Maîtres Alessandri and Sarfati had gone back to the Court of Appeal, pleading that Des Moutis was not a threat to public safety and not likely to abscond and that, as there had still been no date or timetable set for the Prix Bride Abattue proceedings to begin, there was no justification for keeping him locked up any longer.

The court agreed, but reluctantly and in the teeth of Judge Michaud's objections, stipulating that he must first pay bail up front of 400,000 francs and that, once set free, he must be largely confined to his house and could not go beyond Paris and the three adjacent departments of the Hauts-de-Seine, which included Neuilly and Saint-Cloud, Seine-Saint-Denis and the Val-de-Marne. There were to be no trips to the Var or Bouches-du-Rhône or Corsica, the presumed homes of his race-fixing and money-laundering confederates and, cruelly, no summer holidays in Brittany or Normandy either. But worst of all for Patrice he was forbidden to have any involvement whatsoever with horse racing and was not allowed to publish any articles in *Spécial Dernière* or any other magazine – or give any tips in print under his own name or a pseudonym. Failure to comply with these terms would see him returned to the Fresnes immediately.

Des Moutis accepted the conditions – anything was better than one more hour in jail – but with bitterness in his heart. He said to friends that the Fifth Republic seemed determined to deprive him of his freedom and his living. What did they want to do? Destroy him utterly?

Worryingly, that did appear to be on Judge Michaud's agenda. Cahen's dossier now ran to a thousand pages and as of 1 July he had arrested a total of 104 suspects. Michaud confirmed that, thanks to the *Commissaire*'s investigation, he was now formally linking the Prix Georges de Talhouet-Roy result to the outcome of the Prix Bride Abattue in the belief that the beaten favourites in both Auteuil races had been pulled by their jockeys, partly at Monsieur X's bidding. Patrice was also served with formal documents summoning him to appear before the 'Tribunal de Grande Instance de Marseille' on 24 October 1975 to answer charges of fraud over the two-million-franc Tiercé won by him and others for a 100,000-franc stake on the Prix d'Entressen at Borély in February 1971. Everywhere he looked it seemed the net was closing.

Patrice's family and friends worried that he was in no fit state to defend himself. Marie-Thérèse and the children were shocked by the extent to which his strength and vitality had been eroded by those five months in the Fresnes. He went inside 'an athlete six feet tall' – who all his life had been 'extremely mindful of his fitness, running, cycling and going regularly to the gym' – but he had lost two stone in prison, and almost as bad as his physical deterioration was the severe depression that had overtaken him and the feeling that his whole professional and social life had turned irrevocably against him.

Looking grey and suddenly much older, Patrice was in pain and suffering from an abnormal heart rate or 'paroxysmal tachycardia'. Marie-Thérèse managed to get him to see a cardiologist, who diagnosed him with Bouveret-Hoffmann syndrome and said that his heart was sometimes jumping from seventy beats a minute to a hundred or even two hundred. The acceleration lasted anything between a few minutes and several hours, and the cardiologist could only speculate on what intolerable pressures or threats were the cause of such anxiety. But he had no doubt that the condition had been aggravated by the combination of physical and mental stress Des Moutis had experienced in prison.

Marie-Thérèse was incensed by the doctor's report. Three times between March and May their lawyers had implored the Interior Ministry to release Patrice from the Fresnes on health reasons. Each time the request had been denied, confirming Marie-Thérèse's belief that her husband's destruction had been ordained by a vindictive state.

The eternally loyal Alain Ayache was equally shocked by the 'terrible toll' prison had taken on his old friend. Monsieur X, he said, was 'a broken man'. The once energetic, super-charged gambler who 'used to smoke five Havana cigars a day and eat and drink like an English milord' now just lay prone on the sofa all day, chain-smoking and watching TV. The insurance companies were ignoring him and he had 'no more taste for life'.

A similarly distressing image greeted Victor Chandler when he went to see Patrice in an attempt to lift his spirits while he was over in Paris for the 1975 Prix de l'Arc de Triomphe. The 24-year-old Chandler had taken over running the family business after Victor senior died of liver cancer, aged 50, in April 1974. The once prodigal 'Young Victor' discovered that, other than his father's good name and contacts, the firm was nearly bankrupt and, with a mother and two sisters to take care of, he was being forced to grow up fast.

Chandler's trips to the Arc were as much about trying to persuade old French account holders to settle their debts as to watch the racing but, with so many big punters present, he also hoped to do a little illegal bookmaking at Longchamp, à la Des Moutis, out of sight of the Police des Courses et Jeux. It was something that his father used to get up to at the Arc every year, getting himself arrested in 1969 when Des Moutis, though not able to be present on course, had helped to facilitate his release.

Victor looked up to Patrice and had always regarded him as the perfect example of how a proper racing and gambling man ought to live. But when he got to the house in Saint-Cloud on the morning of Sunday 5 October he was dismayed to find his hero curled up on the couch just as Ayache had described. His eyes were listless, his face pale and he was still wearing his dressing-gown and pyjamas. They talked for about an hour about nothing much and Patrice seemed to have little interest in the big race. He had always been a man with a lot to say, but when it came to the Prix Bride Abattue and the Prix de Bordeaux, Victor sensed a certain obstinate refusal to discuss them. He just lay there on the sofa, smoking cigarette after cigarette.

The Englishman could tell that Des Moutis felt he had been blackballed by the worlds of work and fun, but he also got the impression that he was fearful, not only of the police and the continuing judicial inquiry, but of whoever else might come calling, uninvited. A former chauffeur was hanging around in the background, possibly now doubling as a bodyguard, and Chandler thought that he might have had a gun.

Victor left Patrice about midday and went on to the races at Longchamp. He never saw the Frenchman again.

The 1975 Prix de l'Arc de Triomphe was won by a German owned and trained outsider Star Appeal, who romped home unexpectedly by three lengths and was returned at 118-1 on the PMU. The favourite and defending champion Allez France was unlucky in running and finished fifth. Reactions afterwards ranged from the jubilation of Star Appeal's connections, who received the trophy from President Giscard d'Estaing, to the gloom and disbelief of the local *turfistes* who couldn't believe their heroine Allez France had been beaten.

The subdued spirits at the racecourse mirrored the mood throughout France that autumn. Michel Poniatowski wanted the nation to celebrate the first five hundred days of Giscard's reign, but there was little public enthusiasm. At the end of May the last Americans had been driven out of Vietnam, warming the hearts of old Gaullists who remembered the French army's humiliation at Dien Bien Phu in 1954. With the US in disarray Giscard thought there was now a vacancy for France to bridge the gap between east and west, but he got it badly wrong on a trip to Russia in October. The Soviet leader Leonid Brezhnev was so offended by a speech Giscard made calling for ideological détente that he cancelled a second meeting they were meant to have had the next day. The French President and his entourage were forced to limp back to Paris, cartoons depicting them as the modern-day equivalent of Napoleon's Grande Armée during the disastrous retreat from Moscow in 1812.

At home the economy was stagnating – partly due to the fuel shortages caused by the oil price crisis in 1973 – and the French Communist party were considering an alliance with François Mitterrand's Socialists, sending nervous tremors through the stock market. The left were running neck and neck with Giscard in the opinion polls and the prospect of a future Fifth Republic government including Communist ministers so alarmed the racehorse owner Daniel Wildenstein that he was already thinking of sending some of his best horses to be trained in England.

Away from red scares and racing upsets it was the autumn when Parisians were talking about a collection of stunning new photographs of Brigitte Bardot by Ghislain Dussart with a text by Françoise Sagan, and applauding François Truffaut's film *The Story of Adele H* which was about Victor Hugo's daughter and made a star of the 20-year-old Isabelle Adjani.

It was the autumn of the bestselling books *The Ducks of Ca Mao*, *L'Indésirable* and *Villa Triste* by the journalist and biographer Olivier Todd, the philosopher Régis Debray and the future Nobel Prize winning novelist Patrick Modiano. It was the autumn of new nationwide advertising campaigns for Rémy Martin, Byrrh and Gauloise . . . And it was the autumn when Patrice Jean-Henry des Moutis – Monsieur X – was found dead in the garden of his house in Saint-Cloud.

Chapter 31

It was the postman who made the discovery. Paul Avril's daily round, which he had been doing for three years, was normally a gentle progress, partly on foot and partly by van, delivering the mail to a mix of commercial and residential addresses.

On the morning of Friday 17 October 1975, Avril's route was the same as usual. The florist. The *traiteur* (delicatessen). A chemist's shop. An art gallery. A couple of banks. Some newly completed apartment buildings on the way down to the station, and the town's signature large, late-nineteenth century houses and stockbroker villas. The weather was colder than the previous week, and across Paris there was the first scent of winter in the air from the bonfires of fallen leaves in the parks and gardens.

It was 9.45 a.m. when Avril turned into the calm, tranquil quarter leading down the hillside towards the Seine. He often used to see Monsieur X in the Rue de Béarn in the days before he went to prison. Sometimes he'd be on his way out to his office in Neuilly. Sometimes he'd be returning from a run in the Parc de Saint-Cloud. The postman liked the tall, handsome, easygoing gentleman who was always friendly and would call out, '*Salut*,' or '*Bonjour*.' They would joke about when Patrice was going to give the postman some tips for the Tiercé. Maybe this weekend, he would say. Or maybe the next. You never know.

Avril had a letter to deliver to the Des Moutis house that Friday morning, but when he pushed open the gate and walked up to the front door, he noticed something lying on the ground in the garden away to his left. He called out but there was no reply, so he went over to take a look. What he found was the body of Monsieur des Moutis, barefoot and clad only in his dressing gown and pyjamas, and with a 12-gauge shotgun lying on the ground by his side.

Patrice had met his 'rendezvous with death' in the manner of Ernest Hemingway. All of the back of his skull and the lower left side of his face had been blown away, and there was blood, bone and brain tissue all over the ground.

The shocked postman could hardly imagine what could have been the cause of such a terrible event. It looked like suicide ... but surely a man as strong and confident as Monsieur des Moutis used to be would never have taken his own life?

Visibly distressed, Avril hurried over to the house to raise the alarm. The only other person present was the Guinean cleaner, who collapsed in tears when she heard the news. Marie-Thérèse was out. She had left before nine to drive her youngest daughter Olivia to school and then had gone on to do some shopping. It wasn't until half-past ten that she returned to discover the gruesome scene in the garden. Her reaction was a mixture of shock, disbelief and tears hardening to anger directed at what she believed were the malign forces that had brought this day about.

When she went upstairs to their bedroom Marie-Thérèse found a note on her husband's bedside table. It was addressed not to her but to Judge Michaud. 'Your honour,' it began. 'At the time of our first interview, I told you that my incarceration, which you had ordered, was not a good measure for me, my family or my professional activities. I did not realise just how catastrophic the consequences of those 142 days in prison would be. My family life is broken. I can no longer exercise my profession as an expert. These were the only two reasons that pushed me to end my days, for I did not commit any offence in the affair of the Prix Bride Abattue nor in the Prix Georges de Talhouet-Roy. Please accept, sir, my respects and my regrets.'

Given the desperate circumstances in which the note was written, it was extraordinarily composed and polite. But what distress it hinted at beneath the surface. The shame of Patrice's imprisonment had placed yet more pressure on the Neuilly insurance business, his brother Gilbert's livelihood, which was continuing to lose money. Then there were domestic and marital tensions probably not fully appreciated by those outside the family. Their social life was destroyed. There were the shrinking horizons for Marie-Thérèse and the children, living with the stigma and embarrassment of having a notorious convicted criminal as a husband and father. Maybe Patrice had decided they would be better off without him?

But was it definitely suicide? The local police seemed happy to think so. They came to the house and examined the body and the shotgun – a beautiful old family heirloom, they noted approvingly – and read the note. A pathologist told Marie-Thérèse that, in the circumstances, there would have to be an inquest and post-mortem. But they imagined it would all be very straightforward.

The cleaner, who had been present since 8 a.m. that morning, said that Monsieur des Moutis hadn't seemed interested in getting up or getting dressed that day. But around 9 a.m. she had passed Monsieur carrying his shotgun, which was normally kept under lock and key in the gun room in the corridor. The cleaner had seen Monsieur go out in to the garden but she never heard the shot.

Marie-Thérèse had to ring her son François, who was at university, and her daughters Patricia and Nicole and tell them of their father's death, and then break the news to Olivia when she'd been fetched home from school. Understandably all of the children were devastated. At twelve-thirty Marie-Thérèse's mother and father arrived at the house to support her.

Violent death was not an everyday occurrence in Saint-Cloud but word had got around and a crowd of people gathered in the street to watch Patrice's body being wheeled out on a stretcher and placed in an ambulance to be driven to the mortuary in Nanterre. By lunchtime the death was being reported on the radio and TV news as reporters hurried out to Saint-Cloud in search of details. Other than the note to Judge Michaud, did Patrice leave any other letters that might have implicated potential assassins? Or did he take his secrets to the grave? And why hadn't he left some kind of note for his wife? Had a rift opened up between them? Or had his death been so sudden and unplanned that there had been no time for him to write a farewell?

The press went to Longchamp too, where there was racing on the afternoon of the 17th – the big race was the Prix de Newmarket – and again on Saturday 18 October. The racecourse management were entertaining guests in the top-floor panoramic restaurant but, both there and down below, the mood was bittersweet, and in between races all the talk around the bars, the weighing room and the unsaddling enclosure was of Patrice's death. Everyone who had been a one-time friend, defender, ally and admirer of Monsieur X was feeling diminished by a loss that touched them all.

Professional punters and faces like Jules Carrax, Jacques Guyadet, René Lacoste and Jean Seuret, who had been Patrice's lieutenants on the Prix de Bordeaux coup, proudly recalled his greatest moments, and raged at the PMU. Friends like Alain Ayache and the trainers Georges and René Pelat remembered the many happy winning days and bacchanalian hours they had spent in Patrice's company, while some of the glamorous female owners and hostesses and cinq à sept companions shed a silent tear and blew a kiss to Patrice for all eternity, even as their unsmiling Société d'Encouragement husbands looked away.

The local police may have reckoned it was an open-and-shut case but not everyone was so easily convinced. When the newspapers hit the streets the next day they reflected the sadness many people felt at the violent end to an adventure story that had thrilled and captivated the nation for more than a decade and a half.

'I regret this tragic outcome,' said André Carrus in *Le Figaro*. 'But I do not understand the reason.'

Others were in the dark too, fuelling intense speculation about 'the strange death of Monsieur X', as *L'Aurore* described it, and the many unanswered questions that had been left behind. Was it really suicide, and was Des Moutis the sole agent of his demise? Or were the PMU in some way responsible? Or the government? Or the *Milieu*? Or a combination of all three?

A distraught Marie-Thérèse blamed the effects of prison life and the state's hounding of her husband going back more than a decade. Talking to radio and TV interviewers, she said Patrice had not been the same man since his release from the Fresnes and that he'd had two cardiac arrests between July and October and frequent bouts of depression. Yet only eight months before he'd been skiing happily in Val-d'Isère, and despite a sea of troubles, she said, he had never talked to her of giving up hope.

Close friends, like Alain Ayache, found it equally inconceivable that he would commit suicide. His love of life and family was so strong and his temperament so positive – at least before he went to jail – and he'd once been the epitome of health and vigour. Like his old friend and bookmaking client the Aly Khan, whose fatal car crash in 1960 had taken place less than a mile from Saint-Cloud, they said of Des Moutis that he was 'too alive to die'.

The punters Jules Carrax and Jacques Guyadet and Patrice's old bridge-playing companion Philippe Loic felt there were suspicious circumstances surrounding the 'suicide' that must be looked into. Was it not the third violent death in the racing and gambling world in four years? Maybe all three of them were connected and the work of the Mafia du Tiercé? Jean-Luc Durry had supposedly shot himself in the head with a .22 rifle in 1971. Vincent Ascione had been gunned down with buckshot in 1974, and now Des Moutis had died from a shotgun blast to the head and, like Durry before him, there were no witnesses. On top of that, Jean-Baptiste Andréani had been crippled by a shotgun volley outside Le Grand Cercle in Paris in 1963. Were the similarities merely coincidental?

It was Stavisky all over again, said veteran journalists. Maybe Patrice did die by his own hand, but might he not have been confronted with certain options – early that morning or the previous night – and left in no doubt that if he didn't pull the trigger someone else would?

It was a theory that appeared to hold little interest for the authorities charged with tidying up the details of Patrice's death. Despite Judge Michaud's ongoing investigations, his office was not consulted, and neither was contact made with *Commissaires* Cahen and Saunier. The Police Judiciaire in Hauts-de-Seine compiled a dossier inside a week and handed it over to Madame Richier, the investigating magistrate in the Parquet de Nanterre, the local prosecutor's office. In turn she was quick to affirm that it was all just 'normal procedure' and that, as far as she could see, there were 'no surprises' and that Patrice's suicide was already practically 'an established fact'.

But family, friends and a gamut of French opinion from left to right continued to press for more information, while also reflecting on the contrasts and conflicting versions of the maverick overreacher Monsieur X.

'What made an authentic nobleman,' as *France-Soir* liked to call him, 'who loved his family and was a winner in life as well as on the racecourse, grab his hunting rifle on a Friday morning, go out into the garden and point it at his head?' On the surface he'd always appeared to be a 'Breton thoroughbred' who had carried himself with distinction into his fifth decade. But was he really a mathematical genius . . . or a crook with no scruples? Was he just a man of the world who loved the company of fellow gamblers close to the edge . . . or was he a member of the *Milieu*? Were the claims made on his behalf, portraying him as a Don Quixote or Robin Hood defending the interests of the little punter, justified? Or was he, in fact, a wolf with sharp teeth determined to strip every available bit of meat off the bone, leaving only scraps for the little men?

Some observers found a salutary aspect to Patrice's fate that appeared to give satisfaction to moralists and voyeurs alike. Here was a man from a privileged background with its cast of distinguished soldiers and sailors, who had seemed to enjoy an enviable marriage and a most fortunate situation in life. What's more, he had been a pupil at one of the country's most prestigious educational institutes, the École Centrale – and yet look how he'd ended up. His downfall had the kind of titillating allure that, in Britain, would be associated with tales of old Etonians winding up at the Old Bailey charged with treason or fraud.

Des Moutis had always attributed his success as a punter to his mathematical skills, honed at the École Centrale in the 1940s, and to his love of racing and knowledge of form, and André Carrus was always generous about Patrice's talents and refused to simply categorise him as a villain. But after his death other figures from the past re-emerged to assert that 'justice was sceptical' about the gambler's claims to have acted scientifically and with objectivity. The courts, they said, were still inclined to believe that not just the Prix de Bordeaux and the Prix Bride Abattue but the Prix Georges de Talhouet-Roy and the Prix d'Amérique as well as the Prix d'Entressen were all fixed by Monsieur X on behalf of the Mafia du Tiercé.

The most graceless comment came from Roger Taupin, Patrice's old scourge in the Police des Courses et Jeux, who was contemptuous to a degree. 'He was no saint or Robin Hood,' pronounced the *Commissaire* with grim satisfaction. 'He was just a vulgar crook.' But that wasn't how the Brigade Criminelle detective Marcel Leclerc would remember him. 'He may have been a crook,' he said, with a smile, 'but he was never vulgar.'

Leclerc had a sneaking fondness for Patrice going back to the first time they met in the Café Sainte-Foy in Neuilly after the Prix Georges de Talhouet-Roy. He liked talking to him about horses and racing and – along with *Commissaires* Cahen and Saunier, who rarely displayed much sympathy towards the criminals they arrested – he had his doubts about the popular idea that Monsieur X had been the main architect and beneficiary of the race-fixing syndicate. Leclerc, like Cahen and Saunier, believed the racket dated back to the late sixties and the rise of the *Nouvelle Vague* gangsters Tany Zampa and Jacky Imbert, who had gone into the drug-trafficking and money-laundering business with Marius Bertella, Eugène Matrone and the old Trois Canards.

After further investigation in Marseille Saunier had discovered that one of the Godfathers, probably Bertella, had flown into a rage at not receiving 'a bigger piece of the pie' from the Prix d'Entressen fix and had demanded that Des Moutis should make amends by arranging another fixed race, which turned out to be the Prix Bride Abattue.

By mid-October Patrice's court date in Marseille, where he would have had to account for his role in the Prix d'Entressen, was fast approaching. If he told the judges what he knew about Bertella, Imbert, Matrone and Fargette, the consequences for himself – or, even worse, for his wife and family – could have been fatal. But if he offered no meaningful evidence in his defence and was convicted again as the diabolical race-fixer Monsieur X, he'd go back to prison for a long time. Not to the Fresnes this time either, but to Baumettes in Marseille – a prospect he found insupportable. Turning his dilemma over and over in his mind those last days in Saint-Cloud, he realised by 17 October, a week before the trial was due to begin, that he had finally run out of road.

Patrice's Marseille advocate Maître Lambert, talking of his 'infinite shock and sadness' at his client's death, said that the gambler had telephoned him the night before he died, and had sounded deeply depressed. Lambert claimed that Des Moutis told him that he had been 'sequestered' in the house for a week or more and that every day members of the Milieu had been threatening him with violence and even death if he didn't agree to set up another race for their benefit.

That the situation was desperate was also confirmed by a journalist from Le Figaro who came forward to say that earlier in the week he'd spoken for two hours with Patrice, who'd had 'tears in his eyes' and had ended the conversation with the words 'when you put yourself in the hands of these people . . . you are lost'. It was not a description that impressed Ayache, who retorted that 'Pat was not a man who ever had tears in his eyes'.

The death of the famous gambler was reported around the world, including in newspapers in the US and Australia as well as Britain, with The Times and the Sporting Life once again to the fore. 'Des Moutis left many friends in the racing world which is nothing if not broad minded,' wrote Geoffrey Hamlyn in the Life, and again in his 1994 autobiography. 'But it's a major tragedy that so gifted a man should have lent himself to these appalling frauds which inevitably ended in his ruin.'

The tragedy was felt keenly among London's high-rolling gambling community, many of whom knew Patrice well – but nobody was really that surprised by his fate. The bookie-gamblers who followed the big money had all had dealings with the underworld at one time or another – some of them cordial, some menacing, some just the usual bookmaker's struggle to get paid. As Victor Chandler always said, in his profession you got the opportunity to walk on both sides of the street – in the light and in the shadows and, despite Victor's personal affection for Patrice, he'd sensed for some time that the Frenchman was in deep in a dangerous situation from which there was no way back.

Ben Miller, a lifelong friend of Victor Chandler and of his father and grandfather before him, was one of the London commission agents who placed bets on behalf of wealthy gamblers who didn't want to deal with a bookmaker in person. 'Benno', as he was known, had an office just off Bond Street, and in the 1950s, through to the 1970s he sometimes relayed bets to and from Paris for Des Moutis, Peter O'Sullevan and their well-connected French friends. Miller liked Patrice too, but he was characteristically blunt when asked about what the bookies in London believed had happened to him. 'He had his head blown off by the Corsican Mafia,' he said, barely pausing to reflect. 'It was the same with the young jockey, Durry. He was supposed to have shot himself in the back of the head with a .22 rifle from five feet away. That takes some doing.' Benno reckoned the French government were happy to go along with the official version of Patrice's death 'because they wanted to be rid of him and the Mafia helped them to do it'.

If Sir Peter O'Sullevan, who died in 2015, or his famed BBC and *Daily Express* colleague and fellow punter Clive Graham were alive today, they may well have backed up Miller's view. But, at the time of her husband's death in the 1970s, that conclusion was one that Marie-Thérèse des Moutis categorically rejected.

'Stupid,' was how she described the *Milieu* hypothesis when the Nanterre inquest opened. 'It's pure invention,' she said to Madame Judge Richier. 'It was the law with its harassment and hounding that killed my husband, and prison that prevented him from being able to work and caused his illness.' She insisted that Patrice was not a fixer or a criminal but just a shrewd punter who won more often than he lost and was persecuted by the PMU because of it. 'He was not responsible for everything that's wrong with the world of racing,' she said, dismissing talk of menaces against the family. Would Patrice have left their 14-year-old daughter Olivia, the adored youngest child, to go alone to school in Neuilly if he'd thought she might be at risk? Of course he wouldn't.

Marie-Thérèse's defence of her husband was moving and heartfelt. But in the course of the same testimony she went on to say that Patrice had 'never, not even for one moment, suggested taking the suicide route' as a way out of his depression, raising again the possibility that – despite her denials of underworld involvement – it wasn't a straightforward death. Or that by the 1970s theirs was a marriage in which Patrice didn't tell her everything and kept certain people and things secret from her partly out of guilt and partly for fear of her own safety. Or maybe she did know what went on but understood that the *Milieu* should always be absolved from involvement publicly, again to protect her and the children from their attentions and to avoid any further punitive actions by the state.

Tragically for Marie-Thérèse des Moutis and her children and grandchildren, the drama had not yet run its course and there was still more heartbreak to come. On the night of 11 November 1976 Marie-Thérèse and her daughters were away at Brignogan, the family house in Finistère. But François Henry des Moutis, Patrice and Marie-Thérèse's son, was alone in the big house in Saint-Cloud. The not quite 22-year-old with blonde hair and the slightly earnest good looks of a young Robert Redford was a graduate student in Paris. But for the last twelve months François had been haunted by the horror of his father's death and convinced that there were buried secrets and guilty men that might help to explain it. He had been doing his best to ask questions of the police, of Judge Michaud, of the PMU and the Société d'Encouragement, and maybe also to contact gamblers with links to the *Milieu* in central Paris after dark. Yet despite his dogged persistence and his good faith, it seemed his every enquiry was brushed away and every door closed in his face. Overwhelmed by the feeling that Patrice had been the sacrificial victim of a plot that would never be exposed, François sunk into a depression similar to the one that had gripped his father.

In the early hours of 12 November François went into the garden in Saint-Cloud and shot himself with the same gun that had killed Patrice. He left behind what was described as 'a love letter to his family' in which he said that, in the name of his father, he could 'go on no more'. The Mafia du Tiercé had claimed its fourth life.

Chapter 32

The family and friends of François des Moutis might have reasonably expected that some of the trails of enquiry he had pursued and some of the names and answers he was looking for would have been aired in the big trial of the Prix Bride Abattue jockeys which finally began on 16 October 1978. The first official race-fixing trial in French history, it was a marathon affair which went on until the end of November, and once again journalists from all around the world came to Paris to report on it.

Thirteen jockeys, one former jockey and no fewer than forty punters – including the nine arrested in Marseille and Toulon in December 1974 by *Commissaire* Roger Saunier – were arrayed before President l'Homme and his fellow judges in the 13th Correctional Court in the Palais de Justice. It was exactly the same high-ceilinged court room with the four chandeliers where Patrice des Moutis and his lieutenants had been tried over the Prix de Bordeaux six years earlier. But despite the lengthy investigation and all the police time and man hours that had been put in and all the money that had been spent, *Commissaire* Saunier admitted under cross-examination that 'the real commanders' of the operation were missing. There was no Marius Bertella or Jacky Imbert, no Jean-Louis Fargette or Eugène Matrone, and there was no Patrice des Moutis either. In their absence it was the jockeys who took the fall for stopping their mounts for money for 'others unknown', as the prosecutor put it.

One of the riders, Jean-Pierre Creveuil, had agreed to testify against the others, and in return he was allowed to go free along with Michel le Fait and François Bony. But the other ten all received heavy fines and suspended prison sentences of between six months and three years. The lack of custodial punishment was little comfort given their lifetime bans from racing and riding, penalties that Interior Minister Poniatowski insisted would be rigorously upheld.

It was goodbye to all that, and for some of the jockeys there were hard times ahead. One of them became a waiter in a café, another a *pompier*, or fireman. A couple just drifted into obscurity. The judges had been tempted to make an example of Pierre Costes, but the golden boy and Cravache d'Or winner managed to escape prison with a convincing display of contrition and atonement. Pleading an addiction to alcohol and gambling, Pierrot agreed to further medical and psychological examination prior to a course of treatment that would have to be satisfactorily completed if he was to avoid jail. He stuck to the programme and, in 1985, was allowed to begin a second career as a trainer in Maisons-Laffitte where he remained until his death in 2014.

There was said to be 'not much love' between Costes and some of the other accused – especially the hardman Jean-Pierre Renard, who had a previous conviction for assaulting a policeman and kept his own counsel throughout. Robert Laouira, who had been paroled from prison for threatening the lives of Michel Chirol and Jean-Jacques Declercq, was back in the dock like the ghost of the undead and responding to questioning with the same facile smile. He was the defendant with the closest links to the *Milieu* and, in the absence of the lead actors, the judges sent him back to the Fresnes for a second time. When he came out he wrote a book about his riding and weighing-room days, hinting at the existence of a conspiracy to frame Des Moutis as the race-fixing mastermind. But with his former *Milieu* bosses still very much alive, and remembering the fate of Jean-Luc Durry and Vincent Ascione, he – perhaps wisely – declined to be too specific.

The name of Patrice des Moutis came up repeatedly in the courtroom. As President l'Homme remarked, Monsieur X was 'unavoidably absent', but his life and mysterious death hovered over the proceedings like a spectre. It was as if he were the favourite character in a long-running soap opera that had been killed off by the scriptwriters contrary to popular acclaim.

With no Monsieur X to cross-examine, and defendants like Renard refusing to talk, the trial failed to prove beyond reasonable doubt that there had been a genuine conspiracy between Patrice and the jockeys to assist his various Tiercé bets. The trainer Jean-Jacques Beaume said that his horse Porticcio finished unplaced in a small race at Saint-Cloud because he was not fully fit and he had not wanted the jockey Claude Cimmino to 'assasinate him'. Cimmino contradicted him saying he'd been ordered to finish no nearer than fourth because Porticcio was being saved for a Mafia du Tiercé coup in a few weeks' time. It was the trainer's word against his rider's but, with no master gambler or gangster in court to admit planning the coup, both men were acquitted.

Beaume's father Jacques, *Milieu* facilitator and host of the lavish poker parties in Maisons-Laffitte, received a fine and a suspended sentence and handed in his licence.

The ambitions of the Tribunal de Grande Instance in Marseille had been curtailed too, with Patrice's death depriving them of the opportunity to apportion blame to him as the author of the Prix d'Entressen scam in 1971. But judges in Nice did convict the gambling trainer Pierre-Désiré Allaire – who had helped to set up Alain Delon's equestrian centre at Le Puy-Sainte-Réparade, near Aix-en-Provence – of conspiracy to defraud, along with the controversial trotting driver Roger 'Green Thighs' Vercruysse and another trotting driver, Paul Nivol. The three men all received fines and suspended sentences.

The Nice trial was another court appearance that Jacky Imbert managed to sidestep. But *Commissaires* Cahen and Saunier had more than convinced the racing authorities that Jacky had been one of the biggest winners of the Prix Bride Abattue, thanks to the five straw men who had placed bets on his behalf. None of the Marseillais punters – Frankie Cordeau, Gerard Zarokian, Sauveur Ruggieri, Mathieu Dalmayan and Jean Calliol – had been prepared to testify against Le Mat at the Palais de Justice, but they were all convicted with the jockeys nonetheless.

More than three years before, Imbert had been banned from all French horse and trotting race tracks for life, along with his son Jean-Louis, though, at the time, being excluded from the likes of Borély and Cagnes-sur-Mer was the least of Imbert's worries. At the beginning of 1977 a feud had broken out in

Marseille between Le Mat and his former partner Gaëtan 'Tany' Zampa, who objected to Jacky running his own gang in the city and creaming off a share of the profits from illegal gambling, prostitution and drugs.

On 1 February 1977 three gunmen, one of them believed to be Zampa, ambushed Le Mat as he returned to his apartment in the Résidence Trois Caravelles at Cassis, 20 miles outside Marseille. The unsuspecting Imbert had just got out of his Alfa Romeo and was still in the garage when the attackers opened fire. Hit by a total of seven bullets and fifteen pieces of buckshot, he was left for dead with the words, 'Let him die like a dog,' allegedly ringing in his ears. But to the joy and astonishment of his wives, lovers, family and friends – and to the horror of Gaëtan Zampa – he survived. His right arm was paralysed but, as a report in Le Monde drolly observed, 'He'll just have to learn to shoot with his left.' In the course of the next year eleven of Zampa's men were killed in retaliation for the attack, although Imbert was never charged with any of their murders.

Zampa's gang collapsed and, like Al Capone, he was arrested for tax evasion and fraud. He died in his cell in Baumettes prison in 1984. The official verdict – yet again where the Milieu were concerned – was suicide, although the circumstances surrounding his death were highly suspicious.

Now hailed as 'L'Immortel' by the Marseillais, and played by Jean Reno in the 2010 French film of that name (entitled 22 Bullets in the UK) the indestructible Imbert is still alive and living in Marseille with his fourth wife Christine, who owns a hairdressing salon and boutique, Starlet's le Matou. Despite his ban from all French racecourses, Imbert returned to Borély one night in the late seventies, a couple of years after surviving the assassination attempt in Cassis, and was given a standing ovation by the punters. Also known as 'the Last Godfather' in Marseille, he was acquitted of setting up an illegal cigarette factory in 2005 but received a two-year sentence for extortion in 2008. He insists his days as a gangster ended long ago.

Imbert's other *Milieu* confederates experienced contrasting fates. Marcel Francisci, the Corsican businessman and friend of Alain Delon who commissioned Le Mat to shoot Jean-Baptiste Andréani in 1963 and Antoine Guérini four years later, became an elected Gaullist party politician as well as the leading casino owner on the Mediterranean and in Paris. But in January 1982 he was shot dead in the underground car park of his apartment building on the Rue de la Faisanderie in the capital. At the time he was rumoured to be in possession of a tape-recorded conversation between two high-ranking lawyers with connections to the new Socialist administration of President François Mitterrand. No one was ever charged with his murder.

Imbert's one-time ally, fellow member of the Bande des Trois Canards and co-Prix Bride Abattue Tiercé winner, Jean-Louis Fargette, also successfully avoided prosecution for race fixing and related charges. The three Toulonnais straw men who put on his Auteuil bets – Robert Maitraglis, Pierre Negro and Joseph Auxende – went down with the others at the Palais de Justice, but Fargette was protected by his alliance with Maurice Arreckx, the senator and right-wing Mayor of Toulon from 1959 to 1985.

In 1980 there was a police operation to break up a new illegal bookmaking racket on the Côte d'Azur. Fourteen men and five women were arrested in Marseille and Toulon after a seven-month investigation into a *nouveau gang de PMU* that was said to have laundered between 30 and 40 million francs on fixed races. Memories of Monsieur X and the Mafia du Tiercé came flooding back as Jean-Louis Fargette, who was suspected of running the racket, diplomatically moved across the frontier to Italy. His great ambition was to buy the old ocean liner the *France*, once the longest passenger ship ever built, and turn her into a floating casino in Toulon harbour. But in March 1993 the 44-year-old was caught up in another underworld feud and shot dead in Vallecrosia midway between Bordighera and Ventimiglia. His funeral took place at Valette-du-Var outside Toulon and was attended by two thousand mourners.

Fargette's political ally Maurice Arreckx was finally brought down in 1994 and sentenced to four years' imprisonment for accepting a million-franc bribe to award a *Milieu*-related construction company the contract to build a Maison du Technologie in Toulon.

The old Trois Canards founder member and Le Skating bar owner Eugène Matrone kept a much lower profile than Fargette and Imbert, and that no doubt helped him to survive into old age, dying peacefully in Marseille in February 2013. He was buried in Mazargues cemetery, situated roughly halfway between Borély racecourse and Baumettes.

Marius Bertella, the original leader of the Bande des Trois Canards and the man suspected of being the real race-fixing mastermind – and the one who put the finger on Des Moutis – also successfully avoided the limelight for forty years. But then in the winter of 2013, the same month that Eugène Matrone died, he turned up as one of the defendants in a high-profile corruption case in Belgium. The elderly stud farm owner was charged, along with his son Vincent, of being one of a group of *Milieu* investors who, over a twenty-year period, had systematically defrauded the Namur casino of between 49 and 75 million Euros.

The handsome *belle époque* gaming house on the left bank of the Meuse had been a social highpoint in Namur in the days when the town on the edge of the Ardennes had a military garrison. The last Belgian army units left in 1977, and three years later the casino was acquired by a Franco-Belgian syndicate headed – in a twist Des Moutis would have loved – by one Michel Gonzalez, a former *commissaire* with the Police des Courses et Jeux in France. But *Commissaire* Gonzalez was just a front man for the real buyers, who included Gilbert Zemour (younger brother of William who was fatally wounded in the Bar Thélème shootout in Paris in 1975), Jean-Dominique Fratoni, who ran the Ruhl casino in Nice, and the *Milieu*'s favourite film star Alain Delon, who was 'invited' to buy a stake worth 20 million Belgian francs.

A few years after the purchase, part of the casino was 'ravaged by fire' – almost certainly started deliberately to claim the insurance money – and rebuilt with the leisure and tourist trades in mind. Then in 1991 Delon sold his shares, which according to the Belgian prosecutor had always been entirely fictitious, to his 'old friend' Bertella, who joined the casino's board of directors.

Where once Bertella and his other old friends had stood accused of looting the worlds of horse and trotting racing and fixing the Tiercé, now they used the Namur casino as their cash cow, with everyone from croupiers to the restaurant staff assisting them in swindling the customers and skimming and laundering money year after year.

It was an investigation into the affairs of the former casino manager Armand Khaïda, who lived in luxury in Chantilly and gambled millions on French horse racing, that led to the unravelling of the scandal and prosecution of the directors. Bertella, who shuffled into court each day pleading old age, infirmity and ignorance of all wrong-doing, was fined 75,000 Euros and sentenced to three years' imprisonment suspended on appeal.

It was almost forty years since Patrice des Moutis had gone into his garden in Saint-Cloud one fine October morning and blown his brains out, and thirty-five since a generation of French jump jockeys had been effectively wiped off the map. More than a dozen of the riders were temporarily jailed at the time of their arrests but, to this day, out of the 104 Mafia du Tiercé suspects identified by *Commissaire* Jean Cahen, Patrice and Robert Laouira are the only two to have served actual terms of imprisonment. The suspicion remains that politicians and other men of influence in both Paris and on the Côte d'Azur were happy to keep it that way and continually intervened to shield others from the consequences of their actions.

The eternally loyal Marie-Thérèse des Moutis, who died in 1999, never stopped campaigning on her husband's behalf, using television and radio appearances to harass and hound the Carrus family and other senior PMU executives just as they had once hounded Patrice. But throughout that time the organisation founded by first Joseph Oller and then Albert Chauvin continued to grow into an all-powerful corporate behemoth. When André Carrus died in 1980, his sons Jacques and Pierre took the helm alongside Pierre Crespin and

Maurice Alexandre. The brothers shared their father's kindly moustachioed appearance, along with his almost complete disinterest in betting and horse racing but, like André, they held to the central belief, enshrined by the state, that in France vice must be organised.

Jacques and Pierre had begun the move away from the manual recording of Tiercé bets in 1965, and within twenty years all PMU bets were being registered electronically thanks to twenty-two thousand terminals manned by agents, or *controleurs*, and seven thousand eight hundred sales points. By 2016 the total had grown to seventy thousand terminals and twenty-five thousand outlets, and the company was the monopoly provider of on-course betting at three hundred racetracks in France, elsewhere in Europe and in Africa.

The Tiercé is still available on certain races, though since 1989 it's been eclipsed in popularity by the Quinté which operates on the same basis, extending the principle to predicting the first five in the correct order or any order on the day's specified event. The biggest pay-out on a single Quinté race to date was €10,552,310, won by a punter in Brittany in 2011 and the wager now accounts for 20 per cent of daily turnover.

In keeping with it's corporate status the PMU's Paris headquarters are no longer in the old Haussman building on Rue la Boétie, but in a concrete and glass bastion at 2 Rue du Professeur Florian Delbarre, overlooking the Seine near Boulogne-Billancourt and the Parc André Citroën. High flyers from the Grande Écoles continue to be employed there including the sons and daughters of wealthy 16th *arrondissement* families.

Jacques Carrus died in 2010, and his brother Pierre seven years later, but their family link to the PMU lives on in the

Groupe Carrus, which is run by Jacques' sons, Jerome and Pierre Antoine. Their company continues to supply the bet management system and related technology that underpins Pari-Mutuel betting in France and seventeen other countries, from Russia, Germany, Switzerland and Spain to Morocco, Tunisia, the Lebanon, Congo Brazzaville, Guinea and Mali.

In the realm of online sports betting in France on events like football, cycling, rugby and tennis, European competition laws have finally forced the PMU to accept ten licensed competitors. But it retains its monopoly on all terrestrial betting on French horse and trotting racing, and is one of seven operators – and much the biggest – permitted to offer online wagering. All seven online firms are only allowed to provide a Pari-Mutuel betting service not British-style fixed-odds bookmaking.

The total spend in France on sports betting and online casino games fell by nearly a billion Euros between 2011 and 2015, with a lot of small-change punters apparently preferring to play the French national lottery scratch cards. But in the financial year 2014–15 the PMU was still able to generate turnover of 9.9 billion Euros and a gross profit of 2.48 billion Euros.

One of the most persistent chroniclers and critics of the PMU in France has been the respected author and journalist Christophe Donner, whose 2012 book, *À quoi jouent les hommes* (*What Games Men Play*), is partly a history of the Pari-Mutuel from the nineteenth century to the present day. Donner acknowledges that the PMU monopoly, which for years operated a narrow inflexible system, does now have some outside competition. And yes, the Tiercé has been a boon to French racehorse owners, breeders and trainers – just as Marcel Boussac intended it to be – and provided French racing with a guaranteed income much higher than the funding British racing gets from bookmaking. Yet Donner deplores the way successive Fifth Republic governments – from De Gaulle to Pompidou, Giscard and their successors – have, as he sees it, strangled their own creation with their exorbitant tax take on the one hand and inflated salaries and pensions for high-ranking PMU *fonctionnaires* on the other. He despairs of a system which employs people with no knowledge of betting or racing who, in his words, rationalise things on paper but destroy them on the ground. He blames them for addicting people of 'modest means' to gambling, and holds the PMU in general and the Tiercé in particular responsible for destroying the atmosphere and character of French racing and, outside of the biggest days, for emptying the racetracks.

It's a lament that anyone who makes regular trips to French race meetings will be familiar with. The Prix de l'Arc de Triomphe in October remains one of the most exciting, atmospheric and star-studded racing occasions anywhere in the world. But that's because almost half the fifty thousand strong crowd are from Britain and Ireland, along with other racing-mad countries like Japan, Hong Kong and Australia, and they bring their knowledge and love of the sport and their gambling fervour with them. There are other well-attended days – like the Grand Steeplechase de Paris at Auteuil and the Prix de Diane at Chantilly in June, and the best August holiday meetings at Deauville – but on most other Sundays throughout the year the average attendance at the Paris metropolitan tracks is no more than a few thousand at best, and on midweek afternoons it's virtually non-existent.

France Galop, the organisation that currently administers French racing, is aware of the problem and has made various populist attempts to redress it. But Christophe Donner would say France Galop is saddled with an inheritance left by the PMU's relentless promotion of the Tiercé, turning the racing and betting experience into the equivalent of the national lottery and encouraging most potential punters to follow the action in their local PMU café or stay at home and watch and bet online and on TV.

On a visit to Chantilly on a September Thursday ten days before the Arc in 2016, there were more wasps in the wine glasses than paying spectators. But one constituency always remains the same, and up around the unsaddling enclosure and weighing room was the usual cast of well-dressed, well-fed and contented-looking French owners, trainers and racing managers who – thanks to prize money levels and breeders' premiums mostly unimaginable in Britain – continue to live comfortably while no doubt toasting the memory of André Carrus every night and thanking him for their good fortune.

There are some clouds on the horizon. The five years of falling returns have forced France Galop to consider cutting up to 25 million Euros from their prize money fund and making further cuts of 10 million Euros in-house. In October 2017 a group of irate stakeholders responded in the best French tradition by staging a strike at Saint-Cloud racecourse. A prestigious day's sport, including international challengers, was brought to a halt after just one race. But the strikers weren't the biggest or most famous French trainers and the France Galop President, Édouard de Rothschild, was quick to infer that any spending cuts could be reversed within a few years.

In the final chapter of *What Games Men Play* Christophe Donner noted that French racing remembers its own and that all the courses in France have a race named after André Carrus – from Maisons-Laffitte near Paris, where Jacques Carrus used to attend to present the trophy to the winning owner, to small country tracks like Villedieu-les-Poêles and Graignes in Normandy. The old PMU director general's patron Marcel Boussac, the *grand seigneur* of French racing and breeding, has races named after him too, along with the Rothschild family and French racing's English founder Lord Henry Seymour.

There are no races named after Patrice des Moutis but, while the Prix Bride Abattue has been discontinued, some of the other Tiercé events he won still exist, like the Prix Georges de Talhouet-Roy at Auteuil and the Prix d'Amerique and the Prix du Croisé-Laroche at Vincennes. More surprisingly, there are very few races in the French calendar named after the Pari-Mutuel's creator Joseph Oller, and Christophe Donner has a theory about that. His view is that Oller definitely had his creation – and the profits that would have accrued to him from it – stolen by the Frenchman Albert Chauvin and his relations, including his son-in-law André Carrus and Carrus' sons.

But did Oller gain his belated revenge through the exploits of Monsieur X? Donner reckons that André Carrus had enemies inside the PMU who were either descendants of or disaffected supporters of Joseph Oller and secret allies of Des Moutis. He believes they colluded with Monsieur X in 1961, encouraging him to place large bets in outlying towns like Granville where they calculated there was the greatest possible potential to inflict maximum losses and embarrassment on the PMU and undermine the company's position. He thinks they may also have been party to Patrice's ingenious 1962 New Year's Day tour of more than ninety Paris PMU offices by foot, betting the legal maximum in each one. In each case the full extent of Patrice's wagering only became clear to the senior *fonctionnaires* at the Rue la Boétie after the races had been run. Perhaps this was because other of the company's executives sympathetic to Joseph Oller were in on the plan and did their best to provide a smokescreen of disinformation until after Monsieur X had struck? Perhaps too by the time of the Prix de Bordeaux coup in December 1962 those same Oller sympathisers had been rooted out and moved on by Pierre Crespin and Maurice Alexandre, which might be why the Paris senior management became aware of the Vincennes raid almost as soon as it got under way?

Before his death in 2010, Jacques Carrus agreed to be interviewed by Christophe Donner and rebuked him, like all journalists, for not understanding 'one very simple thing'. The Pari-Mutuel, he said, was not a company in the conventional business sense. It was a public service a bit like the Paris department store Bon Marché and no more belonged to the descendants of Oller than it did to the family of André Carrus.

Maybe not, replied Donner. But what about his point? Did the spirit of Joseph Oller reach out from beyond the grave to help Des Moutis undermine the PMU? The 86-year-old Jacques Carrus lowered his eyes. 'If you put that in a novel,' he said, 'no one would believe it.' But what about you, Monsieur? Donner persisted. What do you believe? 'I have nothing to say about it,' said Carrus. 'But I do know that the whole affair ruined my father's life.' 'Yes,' replied Donner quietly, 'and it cost Des Moutis his life.'

As a rebellious young Frenchman in the 1960s and 1970s Donner admits he completely idolised Monsieur X, thrilling not to his mathematical skill or form-book expertise but to the fearlessness and sang-froid he displayed when embarking on such a high-risk game. What a contrast Patrice's tale of adventure and bold individualism presented to the overpowering corporate success story of the PMU. Yet one thing continued to bother Christophe Donner: why had such a clever, smart, charming character as Des Moutis lent himself, as Geoffrey Hamlyn put it, to such a blatantly obvious fraud as the Prix Bride Abattue? Why did he ever get mixed up with the *Milieu* in the first place?

The answer may be that there is no simple answer other than that Des Moutis was a classic example of what the French call *un homme avec deux visages*. He was an aristocratic Breton, intelligent and seductive; a man who loved his wife and children with the utmost tenderness; a man who enjoyed running, cycling, playing tennis and rugby, going hunting in winter and messing about on boats in summer. Yet he was also a ruthless professional gambler who had played for the house in Morocco and was prepared to work through countless white nights filling in hundreds of *bordereaux* and was absolutely determined to take as much Tiercé money as he possibly could, and to hell with the little man.

He was a gentleman renowned for his conversation in the best *salons*, his elegant turn of phrase, his distinguished tone and air, and his many adoring female companions. Yet he was also a gangster's accomplice with a fierce temper capable of the strongest language, as André Carrus and Maurice Alexandre discovered in their office in 1961, and as *Commissaire* Jean Cahen discovered when he came to arrest him at his house in Saint-Cloud fourteen years later.

He was the acclaimed Centralien and scion of generals and admirals of the fleet. Yet, like Alain Delon, he also was a friend of the *mauvais garçons* and shadowy enigmatic characters who inhabited the racetracks each afternoon and the clubs and casinos by night.

He was Patrice Jean Henry des Moutis. And he was also his alter ego, Monsieur X. His alias still adopted as a username today by enthralled punters posting on internet chatrooms in France and beyond. '*Je suis Monsieur X,*' they begin, like Spartacus. '*Je suis Monsieur X . . . Je suis Monsieur X . . .*' In their mind's eye they too are forever walking out of a bank in Paris fifty years ago, holding a black valise containing half a billion francs in cash, getting into their Mercedes and driving away to lunch on the Boulevard Saint-Germain, and on towards their destiny.

Acknowledgements

I am especially grateful to my editor, Charlotte Atyeo, who was a passionate supporter of the project from the outset and a constant source of energy, enthusiasm and insightful comment. I should also like to thank her colleagues Holly Jarrald and Sarah Connelly for all their help and hard work, Charlotte Croft, the Publisher, James Watson, the jacket designer, and Cordelia Unger-Hamilton who kindly translated correspondence with French sources.

I count myself fortunate to have had the wonderful Ian Preece – who edited *Doped* and *Blown* – as my copy editor. As always he brought a calm, thoughtful perspective to the story and picked up on details that others might have missed.

I remember reading about Patrice des Moutis at the time of his trial in Paris in the 1970s but my first proper conversation about him was with Geoffrey Hamlyn in 1985. The charming, diminutive Geoff worked for more than fifty years as a betting correspondent for the old Sporting Life and knew all the big bookmakers and gamblers. Geoff's recollections kindled my interest but I might never have embarked on this book had it not been for the assistance of the bookmaker Victor Chandler beginning some fifteen years later. Victor knew Patrice well, as did his father Victor senior before him, and supplied me with fascinating descriptions of the man and his house in Saint-Cloud as well as indicating the direction I should look in.

After VC it was logical to move on to talk to the former commission agent Benno Miller who placed bets for all the leading English and French gamblers in the 1950s, '60s and '70s. That in turn led to my foremost racing hero, the broadcaster and journalist Sir Peter O'Sullevan who died in 2015. Peter was both a fluent French speaker and a consummate punter with unrivalled contacts in French racing. His early season forays to Chantilly to glean intelligence of likely prospects for the big races to come were the stuff of legend. Peter was a friend of Patrice des Moutis for over twenty years and, like Victor and Geoffrey Hamlyn, was greatly saddened by his death.

Desmond Stoneham, the doyen of English racing correspondents in France, kindly put me in touch with his old colleagues Michel Bouchet and Jean-François Pre and Janie André, daughter of the 1950s and '60s Deauville hotel owner François André, shared memories of her father.

As well as many hours spent poring over old French newspapers in the British Library I was lucky to stumble on the French journalist Richard de Lesparda's short book *La Maffia du Tiercé* (Éditions J'ai lu, Flammairion, 1970). Written while Monsieur X was still at large, it was packed with interesting details including recorded conversations between Patrice and André Carrus as well as Patrice's 1969 interview with Radio Monte Carlo.

Thierry Colombié's book *Stars et Truands* (Fayard, 2013) educated me about the hierarchy of the French underworld and the connections between show business and the Milieu while the historian Richard Cobb's collection *People and Places*

(Oxford University Press, 1985) is replete with atmospheric essays on French low life and crime. *Paris In The Fifties*, a memoir by the former Time Correspondent Stanley Karnow (Three Rivers Press, 1997) is a loving portrait of the city and the era and Alastair Horne's *A Savage War Of Peace* (New York Review Of Books, 1977) and Frederick Forsyth's brilliant debut novel *The Day Of The Jackal* (first published by Hutchinson in 1971) are masterful accounts of the Algerian War and the founding of the Fifth Republic and the battle between De Gaulle and the OAS.

Of all the French sources I discovered, the most intriguing was Christophe Donner's book *À quoi jouent les hommes* or *What Games Men Play* (Grasset, 2012). Donner chronicled the rise of the PMU and interviewed Jacques Carrus before his death, confronting him with the suggestion that while the Tiercé, his father's brainchild, had enriched French racing it had also diminished it as a national pastime.

Finally I couldn't possibly have completed Monsieur X without the tireless support and encouragement of my agent Clare Conville and the tolerance, fortitude and kindness of my wife Sara. Her understanding of a writer's moods and methods is without equal.

Index